ASPECTS OF CHURCH HISTORY

ASPECTS
OF
CHURCH HISTORY

VOLUME FOUR
in the Collected Works
of

GEORGES FLOROVSKY

Emeritus Professor of Eastern Church History
Harvard University

NORDLAND PUBLISHING COMPANY
BELMONT, MASSACHUSETTS 02178

MAJOR WORKS BY GEORGES FLOROVSKY

The Eastern Fathers of the Fourth Century (in Russian)
The Byzantine Fathers from the Fifth to the Eighth Century (in Russian)
The Ways of Russian Theology (in Russian)
Bible, Church, Tradition: An Eastern Orthodox View (Vol. I in *The Collected Works*)
Christianity and Culture (Vol. II in *The Collected Works*)
Creation and Redemption (Vol. III in *The Collected Works*)

Library of Congress Catalog Card Number 74-22862
ISBN 0-913124-10-9

PRINTED IN THE UNITED STATES OF AMERICA

About the Author

Born in Odessa in 1893, Father Georges Florovsky was Assistant Professor at the University of Odessa in 1919. Having left Russia, Fr. Florovsky taught philosophy in Prague from 1922 until 1926. He was then invited to the chair of Patrology at St. Sergius' Orthodox Theological Institute in Paris.

In 1948 Fr. Florovsky came to the United States. He was Professor and Dean of St. Vladimir's Theological School until 1955, while also teaching as Adjunct Professor at Columbia University and Union Theological Seminary.

From 1956 until 1964 Fr. Florovsky held the chair of Eastern Church History at Harvard University. Since 1964 he has taught Slavic studies and history at Princeton University.

Fr. Georges Florovsky, *Emeritus Professor of Eastern Church History* at Harvard University and recipient of numerous honorary degrees, is a member of the American Academy of Arts and Sciences.

About *The Collected Works of Fr. Florovsky*

The *Collected Works* of Fr. Georges Florovsky will be published in English and will contain his articles in Slavic studies as well as in Church History and Theology which have previously appeared in Russian, German, French, Bulgarian, Czech, Serbian, Swedish and English. Each volume will be arranged thematically. Included in the *Collected Works* will be his two major works on the Church Fathers (*The Eastern Fathers of the Fourth Century* and *The Byzantine Fathers from the Fifth to the Eighth Century*). The last volume of *The Collected Works* will contain an *Index* to the entire corpus.

Table of Contents

I
ASPECTS OF PATRISTIC THOUGHT AND HISTORY

Patristic Theology and The Ethos of the Orthodox Church

I

IN 1872 WILHELM GASS published his *Symbolik der Griechischen Kirche.* Gass was an expert scholar, especially competent in the field of Byzantine studies. His monographs, *Gennadius und Pletho* (Breslau 1844) and *Die Mystik des Nikolaus Kabasilas* (Greifswald 1849), were notable contributions to the study of late Byzantine theology, little known at that time. His *Symbolik* also was an able book, well written and well documented. Yet, a problem of method was involved in his exposition. It was at this methodological point that Gass was strongly challenged by another distinguished German scholar, Ferdinand Kattenbusch.[1]

In fact, Gass based his exposition of Greek doctrine, mainly and deliberately, on the alleged "symbolic books" of the Eastern Church, in particular on Peter Mogila's *Orthodox Confession* (in its revised Greek version) and the Decrees of the Jerusalem Council of 1672. Now, Kattenbusch contested the adequacy of such an approach. In his opinion, the

This article originally appeared as "The Ethos of the Orthodox Church" in *The Ecumenical Review,* Vol. XII, No. 2 (Geneva, 1960), pp. 183-198. It was a paper presented to the Faith and Order Orthodox Consultation in Kifissia, Greece, August 16-18, 1959. Reprinted by permission of the author.

so-called "symbolic books" of the Eastern Church could not be regarded as an authentic source. They were not spontaneous expressions of the Orthodox faith. They were occasional polemical writings addressed primarily to the problems of Western controversy, between Rome and the Reformation, in which the Christian East was not intrinsically involved. The XVIIth century was not, Kattenbusch contended, a creative epoch in the history of the Eastern Church. In order to grasp the genuine spirit of the Orthodox Church one had, according to Kattenbusch, to go back to that crucial epoch—*die Gründungsepoche,* when the distinctive Greek tradition in theology and worship had been formed; that is, to the period of great *Christological* controversies in the Ancient Church. In order to understand the Orthodox Church, at her very heart, one had to turn to the fathers, to St. Athanasius, the Cappadocians, and indeed to Pseudo-Dionysius, rather than to Mogila or Dositheos. Moreover, one could properly understand the Orthodox tradition only out of its own central vision. Kattenbusch rightly stressed the centrality of the Christological vision in the total structure of the Greek theological system: *der Inbegriff aller Themata.* It was this synthetic or comprehensive method that Kattenbusch used in his own exposition of Eastern Orthodoxy, some years later.[2]

Kattenbusch was right. The alleged "symbolic books" of the Orthodox Church have no binding authority, as much as they might have been used by particular theologians and at particular times. Their authority is subordinate and derived. In any case, they have no authority by themselves, but only in so far as they are in agreement with the continuous tradition of the Church. And at certain points they betray an obvious Western influence. This influence was characteristic of certain stages in the history of modern Orthodox *theology,* but in no sense is it characteristic of the Orthodox *Church herself.* We may quote at this point an apt statement by the late Professor Nicholas Glubokovsky. "As a matter of fact, Orthodoxy has no 'symbolic books' in the technical sense of the word. All the talk about them is extremely conditional and conformable only to the Western Confessional schemes, in opposition to the nature and history of Orthodoxy. It considers itself the right or authentic teaching of Christ in all its primitiveness and incorruptibility; but then—what particular distinguishing doctrine can it have except that of the Gospel of Christ? The Orthodox Church herself down to the present time does not make use of any special 'symbolical books', being satisfied with the general traditional documents which have the character of defining the faith."[8]

Gass was not impressed by the arguments of Kattenbusch. His reply was firm and sharp. There was no "Greek Church" in Ancient times: *damals noch gar keine Griechische Kirche gab, d.h., keine Griechische Separatkirche.* The Fathers of the Church, in Gass's opinion, were quite *irrelevant* for the understanding of contemporary Orthodoxy. For Gass, the modern Greek Church was not identical with the Ancient Church: she has widely departed or deviated from the early foundations. Gass made this point quite emphatically in his *Symbolik.* Indeed, Kattenbusch also spoke of the *Griechische Partikularkirche.* But with him it was rather a statement of fact. In his opinion, all the distinctive marks of this *Partikularkirche* were established already in the age of Chalcedon and Justinian. Certain distinctive, but not necessarily divisive, features had developed in the East and in the West already in the early centuries of Christian history, and one speaks legitimately of "particular" traditions: Eastern and Western, Carthaginian and Roman, Alexandrinian and Antiochene. In any case, since the final break with Rome, the "Greek Church" actually existed as a *Partikularkirche,* just as did the "Roman Church." But Gass went much further. In his view, the modern Eastern Church, and probably already the Byzantine, was actually a "new church," a new "denominational" formation, separated from the ancient Church by a long and complex process of decay and deviation. In other words, she was just a particular "denomination," among others, and had to be characterized as such. For this task only the modern "symbolic books" were relevant.[4]

The *Auseinandersetzung* between Gass and Kattenbusch was much more than just an episode in the history of modern scholarship.[5] Nor was their disagreement simply methodological. Again, Gass was not alone in his approach. It is still typical of Western scholarship, both Roman and Protestant, to characterize Orthodoxy on the basis of modern and contemporary documents, without clear discrimination between authoritative statements and writings of individual authors, and without any proper historical perspective. It is enough to mention the various studies of such authors as M. Jugie and Th. Spacil. It is logical from the Roman point of view: the Orthodox Church, as a "schism," must have her distinctive, schismatic features, and cannot be "identical" with the Catholic Church of old, even in her Eastern version. The ultimate question is, therefore, theological. Is the contemporary Orthodox Church *the same church,* as in the age of the Fathers, as has been always claimed and contended by the Orthodox themselves? Is she a legitimate continuation of that ancient Church? Or is she no more than a new *Separatkirche?* This dilemma is of decisive relevance for the contemporary ecumenical conversation, especially between the Protestants and the Orthodox. Indeed, the Orthodox are bound to claim that the only "specific" or "distinctive" feature about their own position in "divided Christendom" is the fact that the Orthodox Church is essentially identical with the Church of all ages, and indeed with the "Early Church," *die Urkirche.* In other words, she is not *a* Church, but *the* Church. It is a formidable, but fair and just claim. There is here more than just an unbroken *historic continuity,* which is indeed quite obvious. There is above all an ultimate *spiritual and ontological identity,* the same faith, the same spirit, the same ethos. And this constitutes the distinctive mark of Orthodoxy. "This is the Apostolic faith, this is the

faith of the Fathers, this is the Orthodox faith, this faith has
established the universe."

II

Following the Holy Fathers... It was usual in the Ancient
Church to introduce doctrinal statements by phrases like this.
The great *Decree* of Chalcedon begins precisely with these
very words. The Seventh Ecumenical Council introduces its
decision concerning the Holy Icons even in a more explicit
and elaborate way: *following the Divinely inspired teaching
of our Holy Fathers and the tradition of the Catholic Church*
(Denzinger 302). Obviously, it was more than just an appeal
to "antiquity." Indeed, the Church always stresses the identity
of her faith throughout the ages. This identity and permanence, from Apostolic times, is indeed the most conspicuous
token and sign of right faith. In the famous phrase of Vincent
of Lérins, *in ipsa item catholica ecclesia magnopere curandum
est ut id teneamus quod ubique, quod semper, quod ab
omnibus creditum est* (*Commonitorium* c. 2.3). However,
"antiquity" by itself is not yet an adequate proof of the true
faith. Archaic formulas can be utterly misleading. Vincent
himself was well aware of that. Old customs as such do not
guarantee the truth. As St. Cyprian put it, *antiquitas sine
veritate vetustas erroris est* (*Epist.* 74). And again: *Dominus,
Ego sum, inquit, veritas. Non dixit, Ego sum consuetudo*
(*Sententiae episcoporum numero* 87, c. 30). The true tradition is only the tradition of truth, *traditio veritatis*. And this
"true tradition," according to St. Irenaeus, is grounded in, and
guaranteed by, that *charisma veritatis certum,* which has been
deposited from the very beginning in the Church and preserved
in the uninterrupted succession of Apostolic ministry: *qui
cum episcopatus successione charisma veritatis certum ac-
ceperunt* (*Adv. haereses* IV. 40. 2). Thus, "tradition" in the
Church is not merely the continuity of human memory, or

the permanence of rites and habits. Ultimately, "tradition" is the continuity of divine assistance, the abiding presence of the Holy Spirit. The Church is not bound by "the letter." She is constantly moved forth by "the spirit." The same Spirit, the Spirit of Truth, which "spake through the Prophets," which guided the Apostles, which illumined the Evangelists, is still abiding in the Church, and guides her into the fuller understanding of the divine truth, from glory to glory.

Following the Holy Fathers... It is not a reference to abstract tradition, to formulas and propositions. It is primarily an appeal to persons, *to holy witnesses.* The witness of the Fathers belongs, integrally and intrinsically, to the very structure of the Orthodox faith. The Church is equally committed to the *kerygma* of the Apostles and to the *dogmata* of the Fathers. Both belong together inseparably. The Church is indeed *"Apostolic."* But the Church is also *"Patristic."* And only by being *"Patristic"* is the Church continuously *"Apostolic."* The Fathers testify to the Apostolicity of the tradition. There are two basic stages in the proclamation of the Christian faith. *Our simple faith had to acquire composition.* There was an inner urge, an inner logic, an internal necessity, in this transition—from *kerygma* to *dogma.* Indeed, the *dogmata* of the Fathers are essentially the same "simple" *kerygma,* which had been once delivered and *deposited* by the Apostles, once, for ever. But now it is— this very *kerygma*—properly articulated and developed into a consistent body of correlated testimonies. The apostolic preaching is not only kept in the Church: it *lives* in the Church, as a *depositum juvenescens,* in the phrase of St. Irenaeus. In this sense, the teaching of the Fathers is a permanent category of Christian faith, a constant and ultimate measure or criterion of right belief. In this sense, again, Fathers are not merely witnesses of the old faith, *testes antiquitatis,* but, above all and primarily, witnesses of the true faith, *testes veritatis.* Accordingly, our contemporary appeal to the Fathers is much more than a historical reference—to the past. "The *mind* of the Fathers" is an intrinsic term of reference in Orthodox theology, no less than the word of the Holy Writ, and indeed never separated from it. The Fathers themselves were always servants of the Word, and their theology was intrinsically exegetical. Thus, as has been well said recently, "the Catholic Church of all ages is not merely a child of the Church of the Fathers, *but she is and remains* the Church of the Fathers."[6]

The main distinctive mark of Patristic theology was its "existential" character. The Fathers theologized, as St. Gregory of Nazianzus put it, "in the manner of the Apostles, and not in that of Aristotle," ἁλιευτικῶς οὐκ ἀριστοτελικῶς (*Hom.* XXIII. 12). Their teaching was still a "message," a *kerygma.* Their theology was still a "kerygmatic theology," even when it was logically arranged and corroborated by intellectual arguments. The ultimate reference was still to faith, to spiritual comprehension. It is enough to mention in this connection the names of St. Athanasius, St. Gregory of Nazianzus, St. Maximus the Confessor. Their theology was a witness. Apart from the life in Christ theology carries no conviction, and, if separated from the life of faith, theology may easily degenerate into empty dialectics, a vain *polylogia,* without any spiritual consequence. Patristic theology was rooted in the decisive commitment of faith. It was not just a self-explanatory "discipline," which could be presented argumentatively, i.e., ἀριστοτελικῶς, without a prior spiritual engagement. This theology could only be "preached," or "proclaimed," and not be simply "taught" in a school-manner; "preached" from the pulpit, proclaimed also in the word of prayer and in sacred rites, and indeed manifested in the total structure of Christian life. Theology of this kind can never be separated from the life of prayer and from the practice of virtue. "The climax of purity is the beginning of theology," in the phrase of St. John Klimakos (*Scala Paradisi,* grade 30). On the other hand, theology is always, as it were, no more than *"propaideutic,"* since its ultimate aim and purpose are to bear witness to the Mystery of the Living God, in word and in deed. "Theology" is not an aim in itself. It is always but a way. Theology presents no more than an "intellectual contour" of the revealed truth, a "noetic" testimony to it. Only in an act of faith is this contour filled with living content. Yet, the "contour" is also indispensable. Christological formulas are actually meaningful only for the faithful, for those who have encountered the Living Christ, and have acknowledged Him as God and Saviour, for those who are dwelling by faith in Him, in His Body, the Church. In this sense, theology is never a self-explanatory discipline. It appeals constantly to the vision of faith. "What we have seen and have heard, we announce to you." Apart from this "announcement" theological formularies are of no consequence. For the same reason these formulas should never be taken out of their spiritual context. It is utterly misleading to single out certain propositions, dogmatic or doctrinal, and to abstract them from the total perspective in which only they are meaningful and valid. It is a dangerous habit just to handle "quotations," from the Fathers and even from the Scripture, outside of the total structure of faith, in which only they are truly alive. "To follow the Fathers" does not mean simply to quote their sentences. It means *to acquire their mind,* their φρόνημα. The Orthodox Church claims to have preserved this *mind* [φρόνημα] and to have theologized *ad mentem Patrum.*

At this very point a major doubt may be raised. The name of "Church Fathers" is normally restricted to the teachers *of the Ancient Church.* And it is currently assumed that their authority, if recognized at all, depended upon their "antiquity," i.e., upon their comparative chronological nearness to the "Primitive Church," to the initial or Apostolic "Age" of Christian history. Now, already St. Jerome felt himself constrained to contest this contention: the Spirit breathes indeed in all ages. Indeed, there was no decrease in "authority," and no decrease in the immediacy of spiritual knowledge, in the course of Church History—of course, always under the control of the primary witness and revelation. Unfortunately, the scheme of "decrease," if not of a flagrant "decay," has become one of the habitual schemes of historical thinking. It is widely assumed, consciously or subconsciously, that the early Church was, as it were, closer to the spring of truth. In the order of time, of course, it is obvious and true. But does it mean that the Early Church actually *knew and understood* the mystery of the Revelation, as it were, "better" and "fuller" than all subsequent ages, so that nothing but "repetition" has been left to the "ages to come"? Indeed, as an admission of our own inadequacy and failure, as an act of humble self-criticism, an exaltation of the past may be sound and healthy. But it is dangerous to make of it the starting point of our theology of Church History, or even of our theology of the Church. It is widely assumed that the "age of the Fathers" had ended, and accordingly should be regarded simply as an "ancient formation," archaic and obsolete. The limit of the "patristic age" is variously defined. It is usual to regard St. John of Damascus as "the last Father" in the East, and St. Gregory the Great or Isidor of Seville as the last in the West. This habit has been challenged more than once. For instance, should not St. Theodore of Studium be counted among the Fathers? In the West, already Mabillon suggested that Bernard of Clairvaux, the *Doctor Mellifluus,* was actually "the last of the Fathers, and surely not unequal to the earlier ones."[7] On the other hand, it can be contended that "the Age of the Fathers" has actually come to its end much earlier than even St. John of Damascus. It is enough simply to recall the famous formula of the *Consensus quinquesaecularis* which restricted the "authoritative" period of Church History actually to the period up to Chalcedon. Indeed, it was a Protestant formula. But the usual Eastern formula of "Seven Ecumenical Councils" is actually not very much better, when it tends, as it currently does, to *restrict* the Church's spiritual authority to the eight centuries, as if the "Golden Age" of the Church had already passed and we are now dwelling probably in an Iron Age, much lower on the scale of spiritual vigor and authority. Psychologically, this attitude is quite comprehensible, but it cannot be theologically justified. Indeed, the Fathers of the Fourth and Fifth centuries are much more impressive than the later ones, and their unique greatness cannot be questioned. Yet, the Church remained fully alive also after Chalcedon. And, in fact, an overemphasis on the "first five centuries" dangerously distorts theological vision and prevents the right understanding of the Chalcedonian dogma itself. The decree of the Sixth Ecumenical Council then is regarded just as a kind of "appendix" to Chalcedon, and the decisive theological contribution of St. Maximus the Confessor is usually completely overlooked. An overemphasis on the "eight centuries" inevitably obscures the legacy of Byzantium. There is still a strong tendency to treat "Byzantinism" as an inferior sequel, or even as a decadent epilogue, to the patristic age. Probably, we are prepared, now more than before, to admit the authority of the Fathers. But "Byzantine theologians" are not yet counted among the Fathers. In fact, however, Byzantine theology was much more than a servile "repetition" of Patristics. It was an organic continuation of the patristic endeavor. It suffices to mention St. Symeon the New Theologian, in the Eleventh century, and St. Gregory Palamas, in the Fourteenth. A *restrictive* commitment of the *Seven* Ecumenical Councils actually contradicts the basic principle of the *Living Tradition* in the Church. Indeed, *all Seven*. But *not only* the Seven.

The Seventeenth century was a critical age in the history of Eastern theology. The teaching of theology had deviated at that time from the traditional patristic pattern and had undergone influence from the West. Theological habits and schemes were borrowed from the West, rather eclectically, both from the late Roman Scholasticism of Post-Tridentine times and from the various theologies of the Reformation.

These borrowings affected heavily the theology of the alleged "Symbolic books" of the Eastern Church, which cannot be regarded as an authentic voice of the Christian East. The *style of theology* has been changed. Yet, this did not imply any change in doctrine. It was, indeed, a sore and ambiguous *Pseudomorphosis* of Eastern theology, which is not yet overcome even in our own time. This *Pseudomorphosis* actually meant a certain *split in the soul* of the East, to borrow one of the favorite phrases of Arnold Toynbee. Indeed, in the life of the Church the tradition of the Fathers has never been interrupted. The whole structure of Eastern Liturgy, in an inclusive sense of the word, is still thoroughly patristic. The life of prayer and meditation still follows the old pattern. The *Philokalia,* that famous encyclopaedia of Eastern piety and asceticism, which includes writings of many centuries, from St. Anthony of Egypt up to the Hesychasts of the Fourteenth century, is increasingly becoming the manual of guidance for all those who are eager *to practice Orthodoxy* in our own time. The authority of its compiler St. Nicodemus of the Holy Mount, has been recently re-emphasized and reinforced by his formal canonization in the Greek Church. In this sense, it can be contended, "the age of the Fathers" still continues alive in the "Worshiping Church." Should it not continue also *in the schools,* in the field of theological research and instruction? Should we not recover "the mind of the Fathers" also in our theological thinking and confession? "Recover," indeed, not as an archaic pose and habit, and not just as a venerable relic, but as an existential attitude, as a spiritual orientation. Actually, we are already living in an age of revival and restoration. Yet it is not enough to keep a "Byzantine Liturgy," to restore a "Byzantine style" in Iconography and Church architecture, to practice Byzantine modes of prayer and self-discipline. One has to go back to the very roots of this traditional "piety" which has been always cherished as a holy inheritance. One has to recover the patristic mind. Otherwise one will be still in danger

of being internally split—between the "traditional" pattern
of "piety" and the un-traditional pattern of mind. As "worshipers," the Orthodox have always stayed in the "tradition
of the Fathers." They must stand in the same tradition also
as "theologians." In no other way can the integrity of Orthodox existence be retained and secured.

It is enough, in this connection, to refer to the discussions at the Congress of Orthodox theologians, held in Athens
at the end of the year 1936. It was a representative gathering:
eight theological faculties, in six different countries, were
represented. Two major problems were conspicuous on the
agenda: first, the "External influences on Orthodox Theology
since the Fall of Constantinople"; secondly, the Authority of
the Fathers. The fact of Western accretions has been frankly
acknowledged and thoroughly analyzed. On the other hand,
the authority of the Fathers has been re-emphasized and a
"return to the Fathers" advocated and approved. Indeed, it
must be a *creative return.* An element of self-criticism must
be therein implied. This brings us to the concept of a
Neopatristic synthesis, as the task and aim of Orthodox
theology today. The *Legacy of the Fathers* is a challenge for
our generation, in the Orthodox Church and outside of it.
Its recreative power has been increasingly recognized and
acknowledged in these recent decades, in various corners of
divided Christendom. The growing appeal of patristic tradition is one of the most distinctive marks of our time. For
the Orthodox this appeal is of special urgency and importance,
because the total tradition of Orthodoxy has always been
patristic. One has to reassess both the problems and the
answers of the Fathers. In this study the vitality of patristic
thought, and its perennial timeliness, will come to the fore.
Inexhaustum est penu Patrum, has well said Louis Thomassin,
a French Oratorian of the Seventeenth century and one of
the distinguished patristic scholars of his time.[8]

III

The synthesis must begin with the central vision of the Christian faith: Christ Jesus, as God and Redeemer, Humiliated and Glorified, the Victim and the Victor on the Cross.

"Christians apprehend first the Person of Christ the Lord, the Son of God Incarnate, and behind the veil of His flesh they behold the Triune God." This phrase of Bishop Theophanes, the great master of spiritual life in Russia in the last century, may serve appropriately as an epigraph to the new section of our present survey.

Indeed, Orthodox Spirituality is, essentially and basically, Christocentric and Christological. The Christocentric emphasis is conspicuous in the whole structure of Orthodox devotional life: sacramental, corporate, and private. The Christological pattern of Baptism, Eucharist, Penance, and also Marriage, is obvious. All sacraments are, indeed, sacraments of the believer's life *in Christo*. Although the Eucharistic Prayer, the *Anaphora,* is addressed and offered to the Father and has, especially in the rite of St. Basil, an obvious Trinitarian structure, the climax of the Sacrament is in the Presence of Christ, including also His ministerial Presence ("for Thou Thyself both offerest and art offered"), and in the personal encounter of the faithful with their Living Lord, as participants at His "Mystical Supper." The utter reality of this encounter is vigorously stressed in the office of preparation for Communion, as also in the prayers of thanksgiving after Communion. The preparation is precisely for one's meeting with Christ in the Sacrament, personal and intimate. Indeed, one meets Christ only in the fellowship of the Church. Yet, personal emphasis in all these prayers is dominant and prevailing. This personal encounter of believers with Christ is the very core of Orthodox devotional life. It suffices to mention here the practice of the *Jesus Prayer*—it is an intimate intercourse of penitent sinners with the Redeemer. The Akathistos Hymn to the "Sweetest Jesus" should also be mentioned in this connection. On the other hand, the whole of the Eucharistic rite is a comprehensive image of Christ's redemptive *oikonomia,* as it was persistently emphasized in the Byzantine liturgical commentaries, up to the magnificent *Exposition of the Holy Liturgy* by Nicholas Kabasilas. In his other treatise, *The Life in Christ,* Kabasilas interpreted the whole devotional life from the Christological point of view. It was an epitome of Byzantine spirituality.[9]

Christ's Mystery is the center of Orthodox faith, as it is also its starting point and its aim and climax. The mystery of God's Being, the Holy Trinity, has been revealed and disclosed by Him, who is "One of the Holy Trinity." This Mystery can be comprehended only through Christ, in meditation on His Person. Only those who "know" Him can "know" the Father, and the Holy Spirit, the "Spirit of adoption"—to the Father, through the Incarnate Son. This was the traditional way, both of Patristic theology, and of Patristic devotion. The *lex credendi* and the *lex orandi* are reciprocally interrelated. The basic pattern is surely the same in both. The aim of man's existence is in the *"Vision of God,"* in the adoration of the Triune God. But this aim can be achieved only through Christ, and in Him, who is at once "perfect God" and "perfect Man," to use the phraseology of Chalcedon. The main theme of Patristic theology was always the Mystery of Christ's Person. Athanasian theology, as well as Cappadocian theology, was basically Christological. And this Christological concern permeated the whole theological thinking of the Ancient Church. It is still the guiding principle of Orthodox theology today. Indeed, there is actually nothing specifically "Eastern" in this. It is simply the *common ethos* of the Ancient Church. But, probably, it has been more faithfully preserved in the Eastern Tradition. One can evolve the whole body of Orthodox belief out of the Dogma of Chalcedon.

In Patristic theology the Mystery of Christ has been always presented and interpreted *in the perspective of Salva-*

tion. It was not just a speculative problem. It was rather an existential problem. Christ came to solve the problem of man's destiny. This soteriological perspective is conspicuous in the thought of St. Irenaeus, St. Athanasius, the Cappadocians, St. Cyril of Alexandria, St. Maximus, St. Symeon the New Theologian, up to St. Gregory Palamas. Yet, "Soteriology" itself culminates in the concept of "New Creation." It was both the Pauline and the Johannine theme. And the whole dimension of Christology is disclosed only in the doctrine of *the Whole Christ—totus Christus, caput et corpus,* as St. Augustine loved to say. The doctrine of the Church is not an "appendix" to Christology, and not just an extrapolation of the "Christological principle," as it has been often assumed. There is much more than an "analogy." Ecclesiology, in the Orthodox view is an integral part of Christology. There is no elaborate "ecclesiology" in the Greek Fathers. There are but scattered hints and occasional remarks. The ultimate reason for that was in the total integration of the Church into the Mystery of Christ. "The Body of Christ" is not an "appendix." Indeed, the final purpose of the Incarnation was that the Incarnate should have "a body," which is the Church, the New Humanity, redeemed and reborn in the Head. This emphasis was especially strong in St. John Chrysostom, in his popular preaching, addressed to all and to everybody. In this interpretation Christology is given its full existential significance, is related to man's ultimate destiny. Christ is never alone. He is always the Head of His Body. In Orthodox theology and devotion alike, Christ is never separated from His Mother, the *Theotokos,* and His "friends," the saints. The Redeemer and the redeemed belong together inseparably. In the daring phrase of St. John Chrysostom, inspired by Ephes. 1. 23, Christ will be *complete* only when His Body *has been completed.*

It is commonly assumed that, in counterdistinction from the West, Eastern theology is mainly concerned with Incarnation and Resurrection and that the "theology of the Cross," *theologia crucis,* has been under-developed in the East. Indeed, Orthodox theology is emphatically a "theology of glory," *theologia gloriae,* but only because it is primarily a "theology of the Cross." The Cross itself is the sign of glory. The Cross itself is regarded not so much as a climax of Christ's humiliation, but rather as a disclosure of Divine might and glory. "Now is the Son of man glorified, and God is glorified in him." Or, in the words of a Sunday hymn, "it is by the Cross that great joy has come into the world." On the one hand, the whole *oikonomia* of Redemption is summed up in one comprehensive vision: *the victory of Life.* On the other, this *oikonomia* is related to the basic predicament of fallen man, to his existential situation, culminating in his actualized "mortality," and the "last enemy" is identified, accordingly, as "death." It was this "last enemy" that had been defeated and abrogated on the tree of the Cross, *in ara crucis.* The Lord of Life did enter the dark abyss of death, and "death" was destroyed by the flashes of His glory. This is the main motive of the divine office on Easter Day in the Orthodox Church: "trampling down death by death." The phrase itself is significant: Christ's death is itself a victory, Christ's death dismisses man's mortality. According to the Fathers, Christ's Resurrection was not just a glorious sequel to the sad catastrophe of crucifixion, by which "humiliation" had been, by divine intervention, transmuted and transvaluated into "victory." Christ was victorious precisely on the Cross. *The Death on the Cross itself was a manifestation of Life.* Good Friday in the Eastern Church is not a day of mourning. Indeed, it is a day of reverent silence, and the Church abstains from celebrating the Holy Eucharist on that day. Christ is resting in His tomb. But it is the Blessed Sabbath, *requies Sabbati Magni,* in the phrase of St. Ambrose. Or, in the words of an Eastern hymn, "this is the blessed Sabbath, this is the day of rest, whereon the Only Begotten Son of God has rested from all His deeds." The Cross itself is regarded as an act of God. The act of Creation has been completed on the Cross.

According to the Fathers, the death on the Cross was effective not as a death of an Innocent One, not just as a sign of surrender and endurance, not just as a display of human obedience, but primarily as the *death of the Incarnate God,* as a disclosure of Christ's Lordship. St. John Chrysostom put it admirably: "I call Him King, *because I see Him crucified,* for it is appropriate for a King to die for His subjects" (*in crucem et latronem,* hom. I). Or, in the daring phrase of St. Gregory of Nazianzus, "we needed a God Incarnate, we needed God put to death, that we might live" (*Hom.* 45. 28). Two dangers must be cautiously avoided in the interpretation of the mystery of the Cross: *docetic* and *kenotic.* In both cases the paradoxical balance of the Chalcedonian definition is broken and distorted. Indeed, Christ's death was a *true death.* The Incarnate did truly languish and suffer at Gethsemane and on Calvary: "by His stripes we are healed." The utter reality of suffering must be duly acknowledged and emphasized, lest the Cross is dissolved into fiction: *ut non evacuetur crux Christi.* Yet, it was the Lord of Creation that died, the Son of God Incarnate, "One of the Holy Trinity." The Hypostatic Union has not been broken, or even reduced, by Christ's death. It may be properly said that God died on the Cross, but in His own humanity. "He who dwelleth in the highest is reckoned among the dead, and in the little grave findeth lodging" (Office of Good Saturday, Canon, Ode IX). Christ's death is a human death indeed, yet it is death within the hypostasis of the Word, the Incarnate Word. And therefore it is a resurrecting death, a disclosure of Life. Only in this connection can we understand adequately the whole sacramental fabric of the Church, beginning with Baptism: one rises with Christ from the baptismal font precisely because this font represents the grave of Christ, His "life-bearing grave," as it is usually described by the Orthodox. The mystery of the Cross can be understood only in the context of the total Christological vision. The mystery of Salvation can be adequately apprehended only in the contest

of an accurate conception of Christ's Person: *One Person in
two natures.* *One* Person, and therefore one has to follow
strictly the pattern of the Creed: it is the Son of God who
came down, became man, suffered and died, and rose
again. There was but One Divine Person acting in the story
of salvation—yet Incarnate. Only out of this Chalcedonian
vision can we understand the faith and devotion of the
Eastern Orthodox Church.

IV

Let us turn, in conclusion, to the immediate purpose of our
present gathering together. We are meeting now in an ecumenical setting. What is actually our meeting ground? Christian charity? Or deep conviction that all Christians somehow
belong together, and the hope that ultimately the "divided
Christians" may be re-united? Or do we assume that certain
"unity" is already given, or rather has never been lost? And
then—what kind of "unity"? In any case, we are meeting
now as we are, i.e., precisely *as divided,* conscious of the
division and mutual separation. And yet, the "meeting" itself
constitutes already some kind of "unity."

It has been recently suggested that basic division in the
Christian Word was not so much between "Catholics" and
"Protestants," as precisely between East and West. "This
opposition is not of a dogmatic nature: neither the West nor
the East can be summed up in one set of dogmas applying to
it as a whole... The difference between East and West lies
in the very nature and method of their theological thinking,
in the very soil out of which their dogmatic, liturgical and
canonical developments arise, in the very style of their religious life."[10] There is some element of truth in this descriptive
statement. We should not, however, overlook the fact that
these different "blocs" of insights and convictions did actually
grow out of a *common* ground and were, in fact, products

of a *disintegration of mind.* Accordingly, the very problem of Christian reconciliation is not that of a *correlation* of parallel traditions, but precisely that of the *reintegration* of a distorted tradition. The two traditions may seem quite irreconcilable, when they are compared and confronted as they are at the present. Yet their differences themselves are, to a great extent, simply the results of disintegration: they are, as it were, *distinctions* stiffened into *contradictions.* The East and the West can meet and find each other only if they remember their original kinship in the *common past.* The first step to make is to realize that, inspite of all peculiarities, East and West belong organically together in the Unity of Christendom.

Now, Arnold Toynbee, in his *Study of History,* contended that "Western Europe," or, as he put it himself, "the Western Christian Society," was an "intelligible," i.e., "self-explanatory" field of study. It was just "self-contained." Obviously, there were also several other fields of study, i.e., certain other "societies," but all of them were also "self-contained" and "self-explanatory." One of them was the Christian East—the Eastern Christian Society, as Toynbee labelled it. Indeed, all these "societies" actually "co-exist," in the same historic space. Yet they are "self-explanatory." This contention of Toynbee is highly relevant for our task. Do we really belong to the two different and "self-explanatory" worlds, as he suggests? Are these worlds really "self-explanatory"? Indeed, Christendom is sorely divided. But are the divided parts really "self-explanatory"? And here lies the crux of the problem.

The basic flaw of Toynbee's conception is that he simply ignores *the tragedy* of Christian disruption. In fact, East and West are not independent units, and therefore are not "intelligible in themselves." They are *fragments* of one world, of one Christendom, which, in God's design, ought not to have been disrupted. The tragedy of division is the major and crucial problem of Christian history. An attempt to view Christian history as one comprehensive whole is already, in a certain sense, a step in advance toward the restoration of the broken unity. It was an important ecumenical achievement when the "divided Christians" realized that they did belong together and therefore had to "stay together." The next step is to realize that all Christians have "common history," that they have had a common history, a common ancestry. This is what I have ventured to describe as "ecumenism in time." In the accomplishment of this task the Orthodox Church has a special function. She is a living embodiment of an uninterrupted tradition, in thought and devotion. She stands not for a certain "particular" tradition, but for the Tradition of ages, for the Tradition of the Undivided Church.

Every scribe which is instructed unto the Kingdom of Heaven is like unto a man that is an householder, which bringeth forth out of his treasure things new and old (Matt. 13. 52).

The Fathers of the Church and The Old Testament

THE FAMOUS PHRASE of St. Augustine can be taken as typical of the whole Patristic attitude towards the Old Dispensation. *Novum Testamentum in Vetere latet. Vetus Testamentum in Novo patet.* The New Testament is an accomplishment or a consummation of the Old. Christ Jesus is the Messiah spoken of by the prophets. In Him all promises and expectations are fulfilled. The Law and the Gospel belong together. And nobody can claim to be a true follower of Moses unless he believes that Jesus is the Lord. Any one who does not recognize in Jesus the Messiah, the Anointed of the Lord, does thereby betray the Old Dispensation itself. Only the Church of Christ keeps now the right key to the Scriptures, the true key to the prophecies of old. Because all these prophecies are fulfilled in Christ.

St. Justin rejects the suggestion that the Old Testament is a link holding together the Church and the Synagogue. For him quite the opposite is true. All Jewish claims must

"The Old Testament and the Fathers of the Church" originally appeared in *The Student World,* XXXII No. 4 (1939), 281-288. Reprinted by permission of the author.

be formally rejected. The Old Testament no longer belongs
to the Jews. It belongs to the Church alone. And the Church
of Christ is therefore the only true Israel of God. The Israel
of old was but an undeveloped Church. The word "Scriptures"
itself in early Christian use meant first of all just the Old
Testament and in this sense obviously this word is used in
the Creed: "according to the Scriptures," i.e. according to
the prophecies and promises of the Old Dispensation.

The Unity of the Bible

The Old Testament is copiously quoted by all early
writers. And even to the Gentiles the message of salvation
was always presented in the context of the Old Testament.
This was an argument from antiquity. The Old Covenant
was not destroyed by Christ, but renewed and accomplished.
In this sense Christianity was not a new religion, but rather
the oldest. The new Christian "Scriptures" were simply
incorporated into the inherited Hebrew Bible, as its organic
completion. And only the whole Bible, both Testaments
together, was regarded as an adequate record of Christian
Revelation. There was no break between the two Testaments,
but a unity of Divine economy. And the first task of Christian theology was to show and to explain in what way the
Old Dispensation was the preparation and the anticipation
of this final Revelation of God in Jesus Christ. The Christian
message was not merely a proclamation of some doctrines,
but first of all a record of mighty acts and deeds of God
through the ages. It was a history of Divine guidance,
culminating in the person of Christ Jesus whom God has
sent to redeem His people. God has chosen Israel for His
inheritance, to be His people, to be the keeper of His truth,
and to this Chosen People alone the Divine Word was
entrusted. And now the Church receives this sacred heritage.
The Old Testament as a whole was regarded as a Chris-

tian prophecy, as an "evangelical preparation." Very early some special selections of the Old Testament texts were compiled for the use of Christian missionaries. The *Testimonia* of St. Cyprian is one of the best specimens of the kind. And St. Justin in his *Dialogue with Trypho* made an attempt to prove the truth of Christianity from the Old Testament alone. The Marcionite attempt to break the New Testament away from its Old Testament roots was vigorously resisted and condemned by the Great Church. The unity of both Testaments was strongly emphasized, the inner agreement of both was stressed. There was always some danger of reading too much of Christian doctrine into the writings of the Old Testament. And historical perspective was sometimes dangerously obscured. But still there was a great truth in all these exegetical endeavors. It was a strong feeling of the Divine guidance through the ages.

The Old Testament as Allegory

The history of Old Testament interpretation in the Early Church is one of the most thrilling but embarrassing chapters in the history of Christian doctrine. With the Greek Old Testament the Church inherited also some exegetical traditions. Philo, this Hellenized Jew from Alexandria, was the best exponent of this pre-Christian endeavor to commend the Old Testament to the Gentile world. He adopted for this task a very peculiar method, a method of allegory. Philo himself had no understanding of history whatever. Messianic motives were completely overlooked or ignored in his philosophy of the Bible. For him the Bible was just a system of the Divine Philosophy, not so much a sacred history. Historical events as such were of no interest and of no importance for him. The Bible was for him just a single book, in which he failed to discern any historical perspective or progress. It was treated by him rather as a collection of glorious parables and didactic stories intended to convey and to illustrate certain philosophical and ethical ideas.

In such an extreme form this allegorical method was never accepted by the Church. One has however to recognize a strong influence of Philo on all exegetical essays of the first centuries. St. Justin made a large use of Philo. Pseudo-Barnabas (early 2nd century) once went so far as to deny the historical character of the Old Testament altogether. Philonic traditions were taken up by the Christian school of Alexandria. And even later St. Ambrose was closely following Philo in his commentaries and could be justly described as *Philo latinus*. This allegorical exegesis was ambiguous and misleading.

It took a long time before the balance was established or restored. And still one must not overlook the positive contribution of this method. The best exponent of allegorical exegesis in the Church was Origen and his influence was enormous. One may be shocked sometimes by his exegetical daring and licence. He used indeed to read too much of his own into the sacred text. But it would be a grave mistake to describe him as a philosopher. He was first of all and throughout a Biblical scholar, certainly in the style of his own age. He spent days and nights over the Bible. His main purpose was just to base all doctrine and all theology on a Biblical ground. He was responsible to a great extent for the strength of the Biblical spirit in the entire patristic theology. He did much more for an average believer; he made the Bible accessible to him. He steadily introduced the Old Testament into his preaching. He helped the average Christian to read and to use the Old Testament for their edification. He always stressed the unity of the Bible, bringing both Testaments into a closer relation. And he made a new attempt to build the whole doctrine of God on a Biblical basis.

Origen's limitations are obvious. But his positive contribution was much greater. And it was he who by his example taught Christian theologians to go back always for their inspiration to the sacred text of Scriptures. His line was followed by most of the Fathers. But he met strong opposition at once. There is no room to dwell at length on the controversy between the two exegetical schools in the Early Church. The main features are commonly known. The Antiochene school stood for "history," Alexandrinians rather for "contemplation." And surely both elements had to be brought together in a balanced synthesis.

History or Preaching

The main Alexandrinian presumption was that, as being Divinely inspired, the Scriptures must carry in them some *universal* message, for all nations and ages. Their purpose was just to exhibit this message, to discover and to preach all these riches of Divine wisdom which have been providentially stored in the Bible. Beneath the letter of the Holy Writ there are some other lessons to be learned only by the advanced. Behind all human records of manifold revelations of God one can discern the Revelation, to apprehend the very Word of God in all its eternal splendor.

It was assumed that even when God was speaking under some special circumstances there was always something in His word that passes all historical limitations. One has to distinguish very carefully between a direct prophecy and what one might describe as an application. Many of the Old Testament narratives can be most instructive for a believer even when no deliberate "prefiguration" of Christian truth has been intended by the sacred writers themselves. The main presupposition was that God meant the Holy Writ to be the eternal guide for the whole of mankind. And therefore an application or a standing re-interpretation of the Old Testament was authorized.

The Antiochene exegesis had a special concern for the direct meaning of the old prophecies and stories. The chief

exponent of this "historical" exegisis was Theodore of
Mopsuestia, known in the East simply as "the Interpreter."
And although his authority was gravely compromised by his
condemnation for his erroneous doctrines, his influence on
the Christian exegesis of the Old Testament was still very
considerable. This "historical" exegesis was often in danger
of missing the universal meaning of Divine Revelation by
overemphasis of the local and national aspects of the Old
Testament. And even more, to lose the sacred perspective,
to deal with the Old Testament history as if it were merely
the history of one single people among the nations of the
earth and not a history of the only true Covenant of God.

St. John Chrysostom has combined the best elements of
both schools in his exegetical endeavor. He was an Antiochene scholar himself, but he was in many respects a follower
of Origen as well. Allegories may be misleading. But one
has not to overlook the "typical" meaning of events themselves. Old Testament institutions and personalities were
also the "types" or "figures" of the things to come. History
was prophetic itself. Events themselves do prophesy, they
did and do point out to something else, beyond themselves.
The Early Fathers can hardly be described as "fundamen-
talists." They were always after the Divine truth, after the
Divine message itself, which is often rather concealed under
the cover of the letter. The belief in Inspiration could rather
discourage the fundamentalist tendency. The Divine truth
cannot be reduced to the letter even of Holy Writ. One
of the best specimens of Patristic exegesis was the *Hexa-
emeron* of St. Basil, who has succeeded in bringing forward
the religious truth of the Biblical narrative of the creation
with real balance and sound moderation.

The Old Testament and Christian Worship

The Patristic attitude towards the Old Testament was

reflected in the history of Christian worship. The Jewish roots of Christian Liturgy are obvious. But the whole system of Christian public worship was linked closely to the practice of the Synagogue as well. The Psalms were inherited from the Jews, and they became a pattern of the whole Christian hymnography in the early Church. The Psalms form the skeleton of Christian offices until now. They were the basis of all devotional literature in old days.

The student of public worship in the Eastern Orthodox Church would be impressed by the amount of Old Testament references, hints and images, in all offices and hymns. The unity of the two Testaments is stressed throughout. Biblical motives are superabundant. Many hymns are but variations on the pattern of the Old Testament songs, from the song of Moses at the crossing of the Red Sea up to the song of Zechariah, the father of John the Baptist. On great festivals numerous lessons from the Old Testament are appointed and actually read to stress that Christian perfection was but a consummation of what was pre-figured and foreshadowed, or even directly predicted of old. And specially in the offices of Holy Week this Old Testament preparation is particularly emphasized. The whole worship is based upon this conviction that the true Covenant was always one, that there was a complete agreement between the Prophets and the Apostles. And all this system was established just in the later Patristic age.

One of the most striking examples of this devotional Biblicism is the glorious *Great Canon* of St. Andreas of Crete, read at the Great Compline in Lent. It is a strong exhortation, an appeal for repentance, composed with a real poetical inspiration and based upon the Bible. The whole series of Old Testament sinners, both penitent and impenitent, is remembered. One can be almost lost in this continuous stream of names and examples. One is emphatically reminded that all this Old Testament story belongs to one as a Christian. One is invited to think over again and again this

wonderful story of Divine guidance and human obstinacy
and failures. The Old Testament is kept as a great treasure.
One has to mention as well the influence which the *Song of
Songs* had on the development of Christian mysticism.
Origen's commentary on this book was in St. Jerome's opinion
his best composition, in which he surpassed himself. And
St. Gregory of Nyssa's mystical commentary on the *Song of
Songs* is a rich mine of a genuine Christian inspiration.

The Old Testament as the Word of God

It has been more than once suggested that in the Greek
Fathers the primitive Christian message was hellenized too
much. One has to be very cautious with all such utterances.
In any case it is the Fathers who have kept all the treasures
of the Old Testament and made them the indispensable
heritage of the Church, both in worship and in theology. The
only thing they never did is this: they never kept fast to
the Jewish limitations. The Holy Writ for them was an
eternal and universal Revelation. It is addressed to all mankind now simply because it was addressed to all nations by
God Himself even when the Divine Word was delivered
by the prophets to the Chosen People alone. It means that
one cannot measure the depth of Divine Revelation
with the measure of some past time only, however sacred
those times may be. It is not enough to be sure that the
ancient Hebrews understood and interpreted the Scriptures
in a certain way. This interpretation can never be final. New
light has been thrown on the old revelations by Him Who
came just to accomplish and to fulfil the Law and the
Prophets. The Scriptures are not merely historical documents.
They are really the Word of God, the Divine message to
all generations. And Christ Jesus is the Alpha and Omega
of the Scriptures, both the climax and the knot of the Bible.
This is the standing message of the Fathers to the Church
Universal about the Old Dispensation.

St. Athanasius' Concept of
Creation

I

THE IDEA of Creation was a striking Christian innovation
in philosophy. The problem itself was alien and even
unintelligible to the Greek mind: *de rerum originatione
radicali.* The Greek mind was firmly addicted to the conception of an Eternal Cosmos, permanent and immutable in
its essential structure and composition. This Cosmos simply
existed. Its existence was "necessary," it was an ultimate or
first *datum,* beyond which neither thought nor imagination
could penetrate. There was, indeed, much movement within
the world—"the wheel of origin and decay." But the Cosmos
as a whole was unchangeable, and its permanent structure
was repeatedly and unfailingly exhibited in its rotation and
self-iteration. It was not a static world, there was in it an
intense dynamism: but it was a dynamism of inescapable
circulation. The Cosmos was a periodical, and yet a "neces-

This article originally appeared in *Studia Patristica,* Vol. VI, ed. F. L.
Cross (Berlin: Akademie Verlag; Texte und Untersuchungen zur Geschichte
der altchristlichen Literatur, Band 81, 1962), 36-57. Reprinted by permission
of the author.

sary" and "immortal" being. The "shape" of the world might be exposed to changes, it was actually in a constant flux, but its very existence was perennial. One simply could not ask intelligently about the "origin" or "beginning" of the Cosmic fabric in the order of existence.[1]

It was precisely at this point that the Greek mind was radically challenged by Biblical Revelation. This was a hard message for the Greeks. Indeed, it is still a hard message for philosophers.

The Bible opens with the story of Creation. "In the beginning God created the heaven and the earth." This has become a credal statement in the Christian Church. The Cosmos was no more regarded as a "self-explanatory" being. Its ultimate and intrinsic dependence upon God's will and action has been vigorously asserted. But much more than just this relation of "dependence" was implied in the Biblical concept: the world was created *ex nihilo,* i.e., it did not exist "eternally." In retrospect one was bound to discover its "beginning"—*post nihilum,* as it were. The tension between the two visions, Hellenic and Biblical, was sharp and conspicuous. Greeks and Christians, as it were, were dwelling in different worlds. Accordingly, the categories of Greek philosophy were inadequate for the description of the world of Christian faith. The main emphasis of Christian faith was precisely on the radical contingency of the Cosmos, on its contingency precisely in the order of existence. Indeed, the very existence of the world pointed, for Christians, to the Other, as its Lord and Maker. On the other hand, the Creation of the world was conceived as a sovereign and "free" act of God, and not as something which was "necessarily" implied or inherent in God's own Being. Thus, there was actually a double contingency: on the side of the Cosmos— which could "not have existed at all," and on the side of the Creator—who could "not have created" anything at all. In the fine phrase of Etienne Gilson, "it is quite true that a Creator is an eminently Christian God, but a God whose very

existence is to be a creator is not a Christian God at all."[2]
The very existence of the world was regarded by the Christians as a mystery and miracle of Divine Freedom.

Christian thought, however, was maturing but gradually and slowly, by a way of trial and retraction. The early Christian writers would often describe their new vision of faith in the terms of old and current philosophy. They were not always aware of, and certainly did not always guard against, the ambiguity which was involved in such an enterprise. By using Greek categories Christian writers were forcing upon themselves, without knowing it, a world which was radically different from that in which they dwelt by faith. Thus they were often caught between the vision of their faith and the inadequacy of the language they were using. This predicament must be taken quite seriously. Etienne Gilson once suggested that Christianity has brought the new wine, but the old skins were still good enough, i.e., the skins of Greek Philosophy. "La pensée chrétienne apportait du vin nouveau, mais les vieilles outres étaient encore bonnes."[3] It is an elegant phrase. But is it not rather an optimistic overstatement? Indeed, the skins did not burst at once, but was it really to the benefit of nascent Christian thought? The skins were badly tainted with an old smell, and the wine acquired in them had an alien flavor. In fact, the new vision required new terms and categories for its adequate and fair expression. It was an urgent task for Christians "to coin new names," τὸ καινοτομεῖν τὰ ὀνόματα, in the phrase of St. Gregory of Nazianzus.

Indeed, the radical contingency of the created world was faithfully acknowledged by Christian writers from the very beginning. The Lordship of God over all His Creation was duly emphasized. God alone was mighty and eternal. All created things were brought into existence, and sustained in existence, solely by the grace and pleasure of God, by His sovereign will. Existence was always a gift of God. From this point of view, even the human soul was "mortal," by

its own "nature," i.e. contingent, because it was a creature,
and was maintained only by the grace of God. St. Justin was
quite explicit at this point—in opposition to Platonic arguments for "immortality." Indeed, "immortal" would mean
for him "uncreated."[4] But it was not yet clear how this
creative "will" of God was related to His own "being." And
this was the crucial problem. In early Christian thinking the
very idea of God was only gradually released out of that
"cosmological setting," in which it used to be apprehended
by Greek philosophical thought. The mystery of the Holy
Trinity itself was often interpreted in an ambiguous cosmological context—not primarily as a mystery of God's own
Being, but rather in the perspective of God's creative and
redemptive action and self-disclosure in the world. This was
the main predicament of the Logos-theology in the Apologists, in Hippolytus, and in Tertullian. All these writers
could not distinguish consistently between the categories of
the Divine "Being" and those of Divine "Revelation"
ad extra, in the world. Indeed, it was rather a lack of preci-
sion, an inadequacy of language, than an obstinate doctrinal
error. The Apologists were not just pre-Arians or pro-Arians.
Bishop George Bull was right in his *Defensio Fidei Nicenae*
against the charges of Petavius. And yet, as G. L. Prestige
has pointed out, "the innocent speculations of Apologists
came to provide support for the Arian school of thought."[5]

The case of Origen is especially significant. He also failed
to distinguish between the ontological and cosmological
dimensions. As Bolotov has aptly stated, "the logical link
between the generation of the Son and the existence of the
world was not yet broken in the speculation of Origen."[6] It
can be even contended that this very link has been rather
reinforced in Origen's thinking. The ultimate question for
Origen was precisely this: Is it possible or permissible to
think of God without conceiving Him at once as Creator?
The negative answer to this question was for Origen the
only devout option. An opposite assumption would be sheer

blasphemy. God could never have become anything that He has not been always. There is nothing simply "potential" in God's Being, everything being eternally actualized. This was Origen's basic assumption, his deepest conviction. God is always the Father of the Only Begotten, and the Son is co-eternal with the Father: any other assumption would have compromised the essential immutability of the Divine Being. But God also is always the Creator and the Lord. Indeed, if God is Creator at all—and it is an article of faith that He is Lord and Creator—we must necessarily assume that He had always been Creator and Lord. For, obviously, God never "advances" toward what He had not been before. For Origen this implied inevitably also an eternal actualization of the world's existence, of all those things over which God's might and Lordship were exercised. Origen himself used the term παντοκράτωρ, which he borrowed surely from the Septuagint. Its use by Origen is characteristic. The Greek term is much more pointed than its Latin or English renderings: *Omnipotens,* "Almighty." These latter terms emphasize just might or power. The Greek word stresses specifically the actual exercise of power. The edge of Origen's argument is taken off in Latin translation. "Παντοκράτωρ is in the first place an active word, conveying the idea not just of capacity but of the actualization of capacity."[7] Παντοκράτωρ means just κύριος, the ruling Lord. And God could not be παντοκράτωρ eternally unless τὰ πάντα also existed from all eternity. God's might must have been eternally actualized in the created Cosmos, which therefore appears to be an eternal concomitant or companion of the Divine Being. In this context any clear distinction between "generation" and "creation" was actually impossible—both were eternal relations, indeed "necessary" relations, as it were, intrinsic for the Divine Being. Origen was unable, and indeed reluctant and unwilling, to admit anything "contingent" about the world itself, since, in his conception, this would have involved also a certain "change" on the Divine

level. In Origen's system the eternal being of the Holy
Trinity and the eternal existence of the world are indivisibly
and insolubly linked together: both stand and fall together.
The Son is indeed eternal, and eternally "personal" and
"hypostatic." But He is eternally begotten in relation to the
eternally created world.[8]

Origen's argument is straight and consistent, under his
basic assumptions. It would be flagrantly impious to admit
that God could ever have existed without His Wisdom,
even for a single moment—*ad punctum momenti alicujus.*
God is always the Father of His Son, who is born of Him,
but "without any beginning"—*sine ullo tamen initio.* And
Origen specifies: "not only of that kind which can be distinguished by intervals of time—*aliquibus temporum spatiis,*
but even of that other kind which the mind alone is wont
to contemplate in itself and to perceive, if I may say so,
with the bare intellect and reason"—*nudo intellectu.* In
other words, Wisdom is begotten beyond the limit of any
imaginable "beginning"—*extra omne ergo quod vel dici vel
intelligi potest initium.* Moreover, as Origen explained elsewhere, the "generation" of Wisdom could not be interpreted
as an accomplished "event," but rather as a permanent and
continuous relationship—a relation of "being begotten," just
as radiance is perpetually concomitant with the light itself,
and Wisdom is, in the phrase of *Sap. Sal.* 7, 26, an
ἀπαύγασμα φωτὸς ἀϊδίου (*In Jerem. hom.* IX 4: οὐχὶ
ἐγέννησεν ὁ πατὴρ τὸν υἱὸν . . . ἀλλ᾿ ἀεὶ γεννᾷ αὐτόν,
70 Klostermann; cf. Latin translation in the "Apology" of
Pamphilus, *PG* 17, 564). Now, according to Origen, in
the very subsistence of Wisdom the whole design of creation
is already implied. The whole creation, *universa creatura,* is
pre-arranged in Wisdom (*De princ.* I 2, 2; 29—30 Koetschau). The text of this important passage might have
been somewhat edited by the Latin translator, but surely
the main argument was faithfully reproduced (cf. the frag-
ment in Greek, in Methodius, *De creatis,* quoted by Photius,

Cod. 235). Origen spoke of "prevision": *virtute praescientiae.*
But, according to his own basic principle, there could
be no temporal order or sequence. The world as "pre-viewed"
in Wisdom had to be also eternally actualized.⁹ It is in
this direction that Origen continued his argument. And
here the terms "Father" and *"Pantokrator"* are conspicuously
bracketed together. "Now as one cannot be father apart
from having a son, nor a lord apart from holding a possession or a slave, so we cannot even call God almighty if
there are none over whom He can exercise His power.
Accordingly, to prove that God is Almighty we must assume
the existence of the world." But, obviously, God is Lord from
all eternity. Consequently, the world, in its entirety, also
existed from all eternity: *necessario existere oportet* (*De
princ.* I 2, 10; 41—42 Koetschau; cf. the Greek quotation
in Justinian, *Epist. ad Mennam,* Mansi IX 528). In brief, the
world must be always co-existent with God and therefore
co-eternal. Of course, Origen meant the primordial world
of spirits. Actually, in Origen's conception there was but
one eternal hierarchical system of beings, a "chain of being."
He could never escape the cosmological pattern of Middle
Platonism.¹⁰

Moreover, Origen seems to have interpreted the Generation of the Son as an act of the Father's will: ἐκ τοῦ θελή-
ματος τοῦ πατρὸς ἐγεννήθη (quoted by Justinian, Mansi
IX 525). On the other hand he was utterly suspicious of
the phrase: ἐκ τῆς οὐσίας πατρός, and probably even
formally repudiated it. For him it was a dangerous and
misleading phrase, heavily overloaded with gross "material-
istic" associations, and suggesting division and separation in
the Divine substance (*In Ioh.* XX 18; 351 Preuschen; *De
princ.* IV 4, 1; 348 Koetschau; cf. the quotation by Marcellus,
given in Eusebius, *c. Marcellum* I 4; 21 Klostermann). The
textual evidence is confused and inconclusive.¹¹ It may be
true that at this point Origen was opposing the Gnostics,
especially the Valentinian conception of προβολή, and only

wanted to vindicate the strictly spiritual character of every-thing Divine.[12] Yet, there was a flagrant ambiguity. Both the generation of the Son and the creation of the world are equally attributed to the will or counsel of the Father. "And my own opinion is that an act of the Father's will—*voluntas Patris*—ought to be sufficient to ensure the subsistence of what He wills. For in willing He uses no other means than that which is produced by the deliberation of His will—*nisi quae consilio voluntatis profertur*. Thus, it is in this way that the existence of the Son also is begotten of Him—*ita ergo et filii ab eo subsistentia generatur*" (*De princ.* I 2, 6; 35 Koetschau). The meaning of this passage is rather obscure, and we have no Greek text.[13] But, in any case, once again the Son is explicitly bracketed together with creatures.[14]

There was an unresolved tension, or an inner contradic-tion, in the system of Origen. And it led to an inner conflict, and finally to an open split, among those theologians who were profoundly influenced by his powerful thought. It may be contended, indeed, that his trinitarian theology was intrinsically orthodox, that is, pro-Nicene, so that the inter-pretation of his views by St. Athanasius and the Cappa-docians was fair and congenial to his ultimate vision. Indeed, Origen strongly defended the eternity of the Divine Genera-tion and, at this point, was definitely anti-Arian. If we can trust St. Athanasius, Origen explicitly denounced those who dared to suggest that "there was when the Son was not," ἦν ποτε ὅτε οὐκ ἦν ὁ υἱός, whosoever these people might have been (see the quotation from Origen in St. Athan-asius, *De decretis* 27). Yet, on the other hand, the general scheme of his theology was utterly inadequate at many crucial points. In any case, the controversies of the fourth century can be properly understood only in the perspective of Origen's theology and its problematic. The crucial philosophical prob-lem at the bottom of that theological controversy was precisely that of time and eternity. Within the system itself there were but two opposite options: to reject the eternity of the world or to contest the eternity of the Logos. The latter option was taken by Arius and all those who, for various reasons, sympathized with him. His opponents were bound to insist on the temporality of the world. The problem of creation was the crucial philosophical problem in the dispute. No clarity could be reached in the doctrine of God until the problem of creation had been settled. Indeed, the essence of the controversy was religious, the ultimate issue was theological. But faith and piety themselves could be vindicated at this historic juncture only by philosophical weapons and arguments. This was well understood already by St. Alexander of Alexandria: φιλοσοφῶν ἐθεολόγει, says Socrates of him (I 5). St. Alexander made the first attempt to disentangle the doctrine of God out of the traditional cosmological context, while keeping himself still close to the tenets of Origen.[15]

Arius himself contended that the Logos was a "creature," a privileged creature indeed, not like others, but still no more than a κτίσμα originated by the will of God. Accordingly, God for him was primarily the Creator, and apart from that, little, if anything, could be said of the unfathomable and incomprehensible Being of God, unknown even to the Son. Actually, there was no room for "theology" in his system. The only real problem was that of "cosmology"—a typically Hellenic approach. Arius had to define the notion of creation. Two major points were made: (a) the total dissimilarity between God and all other realities which "had beginning," beginning of any kind; (b) the "beginning" itself. The Son had a "beginning," simply because He was a son, that is—originated from the Father, as His ἀρχή : only God (the Father) was ἄναρχος in the strict sense of the word. It seems that with Arius the main emphasis lay on the relation of dependence as such, and the element of time was comparatively irrelevant for his argument. Indeed, in his famous letter to Eusebius of Nicomedia, Arius stated plainly that the Son came into existence "before all times and ages"—

πρὸ χρόνων καὶ πρὸ αἰώνων (apud Epiph., *Haeres.* LXIX 6; 156 Holl, and Theodoret, *Hist. eccl.* I 4, 63; 25 Parmentier). St. Athanasius himself complained that the Arians evaded the term χρόνος (*Contra Arianos* I 13). Yet, they obviously contended that all things "created" did somehow "come into existence," so that the state of "being" has been preceded, at least logically, by a state of "non-being" out of which they have emerged, ἐξ οὐκ ὄντων. In this sense "they did not exist before they came into existence"— οὐκ ἦν πρὶν γεννηθῇ. Obviously, "creatureliness" meant for the Arians more than just "dependence": it implied also an "essential" dissimilarity with God, and a finitude, that is—some limitation in retrospect. On the other hand, it was strongly stressed that all Creation was grounded in the will and deliberation of God: θελήματι καὶ βουλῇ, as Arius himself wrote to Eusebius. The latter motive was Origenistic. Indeed, Arius went much further than Origen: Origen rejected only the Gnostic προβολή, but Arius repudiated any "natural" affinity of Logos with God. Arius simply had nothing to say about the life of God, apart from His engagement in Creation. At this point his thought was utterly archaic.

It is highly significant that the Council of Antioch in 324/5—that is, before Nicaea—took up all these major points. The Son is begotten "not from that which is not but from the Father," in an ineffable and indescribable manner, "not as made but as properly offspring," and not "by volition." He existed everlastingly and "did not at one time not exist." Again, "He is the express image, not of the will or anything else, but of His Father's very hypostasis."[16] For all these reasons the Son could not be regarded as "creature." Nothing has been said about Creation. But one can easily guess what "Creation" and "creatureliness" meant for the Fathers of the Council. All elements, of which the later clear distinction between "begetting" and "creating" (or "making") has been construed, are already implied in the conciliar statement.

St. Athanasius made a decisive contribution at the next stage of the dispute.

II

Already in his early writings, before the outbreak of the Arian strife, St. Athanasius was wrestling with the problem of Creation. For him it was intimately related to the crucial message of the Christian faith: the redemptive Incarnation of the Divine Word. Indeed, his interpretation of Redemption, as it was expounded in *De Incarnatione Verbi,* is grounded in a distinctive conception of the Cosmos. There was, in the vision of St. Athanasius, an ultimate and radical cleavage or *hiatus* between the absolute Being of God and the contingent existence of the World. There were actually two modes of existence, radically different and totally dissimilar. On the one hand—the Being of God, eternal and immutable, "immortal" and "incorruptible." On the other— the flux of the Cosmos, intrinsically mutable and "mortal," exposed to change and "corruption." The ultimate ontological tension was precisely between the Divine ἀφθαρσία and the φθορά of the Cosmic flux. Since the whole Creation had once begun, by the will and pleasure of God, "out of nothing," an ultimate "meonic" tendency was inherent in the very "nature" of all creaturely things. By their own "nature," all created things were intrinsically unstable, fluid, impotent, mortal, liable to dissolution: Τῶν μὲν γὰρ γενητῶν ἡ φύσις, ἅτε δὴ ἐξ οὐκ ὄντων ὑποστᾶσα, ρευστή τις καὶ ἀσθενὴς καὶ θνητὴ καθ' ἑαυτὴν συγκρινωμένη τυγχάνει. Their existence was precarious. If there was any order and stability in the Cosmos, they were, as it were, super-imposed upon its own "nature," and imparted to created things by the Divine Logos. It was the Logos that ordered and bound together the whole Creation—συνέχει καὶ συσφίγγει—counter-acting thereby, as it were, its inherent leaning toward disintegration. Indeed, the creaturely "nature" itself is also God's creation. But it was inwardly limited by its creaturely condition: it was inescapably "mortal" and mutable. St. Athanasius formally disavowed the notion of seminal λόγοι, immanent and inherent in the things themselves. Creation stood only by the immediate impact of the Divine Logos. Not only was the Cosmos brought into existence "out of nothing," by an initial and sovereign creative *fiat* of God, but it was maintained in existence solely by the continuous action of the Creator. Man also shared in this "natural" instability of the Cosmos, as a "composite" being and originated "out of the non-existing": ἐκ τοῦ μὴ ὄντος γενόμενοι. By his very "nature," man also was "mortal" and "corruptible"—κατὰ φύσιν φθαρτός—and could escape this condition of mortality only by God's grace and by participation in the energies of the Logos: χάριτι δὲ τῆς τοῦ Λόγου μετουσίας τοῦ κατὰ φύσιν ἐκφυγόντες. By himself man was unable "to continue forever"—οὐχ ἱκανὸν εἴη κατὰ τὸν τῆς ἰδίας γενέσεως λόγον διαμένειν ἀεί (*Contra gentes* 40 to 43; *De incarn.* 2, 3, 5). The pattern of this exposition is conspicuously "Platonic." But St. Athanasius used it judiciously. The cosmic or "demiurgic" function of the Logos was strongly stressed in his conception. But His Divine transcendence was also vigorously stressed. Indeed, the Divine character of the Logos was the main presupposition of the whole argument. The Logos was, in the phrase of St. Athanasius, "the Only-begotten God," originating eternally from the Father as from a spring, a πηγή. There was an absolute dissimilarity between the Logos and the creatures. The Logos is present in the world, but only "dynamically," that is, by His "powers." In His own "substance" He is outside of the world: ἐκτὸς μέν ἐστι τοῦ παντὸς κατ' οὐσίαν, ἐν πᾶσι δέ ἐστι ταῖς ἑαυτοῦ δυνάμεσι (*De incarn.* 17). Now, this distinction between "essence" and "powers" can be traced back to Philo and Plotinus, and, indeed, to the Apologists and

Clement of Alexandria. But in St. Athanasius it has a totally new connotation. It is never applied to the relationship between God and Logos, as had been done even by Origen. It serves now a new purpose: to discriminate strictly between the inner Being of God and His creative and "providential" manifestation *ad extra,* in the creaturely world. The world owes its very existence to God's sovereign will and goodness and stands, over the abyss of its own nothingness and impotence, solely by His quickening "Grace"—as it were, *sola gratia.* But the Grace abides in the world.[17]

In his struggle with the Arians St. Athanasius proceeded from the same presuppositions. The main demarcartion line passes between the Creator and the Creation, and not between the Father and the Son, as Arians contended. Indeed, the Logos is Creator. But He is Creator precisely because He is fully Divine, an "undistinguishable Image" of the Father, ἀπαράλλακτος εἰκών. In creation He is not just an "instrument," ὄργανον. He is its ultimate and immediate efficient cause. His own Being is totally independent of creation, and even of the creative design of the world. At this point St. Athanasius was quite formal. The crucial text is in *Contra Arianos* II 31: Ὁ τοῦ Θεοῦ γὰρ Λόγος οὐ δι' ἡμᾶς γέγονεν, ἀλλὰ μᾶλλον ἡμεῖς δι' αὐτὸν γεγόναμεν, καὶ 'ἐν αὐτῷ ἐκτίσθη τὰ πάντα'· οὐδὲ διὰ τὴν ἡμῶν ἀσθένειαν οὗτος, ὢν δυνατός, ὑπὸ μόνου τοῦ Πατρὸς γέγονεν, ἵν' ἡμᾶς δι' αὐτοῦ ὡς δι' ὀργάνου δημιουργήσῃ· μὴ γένοιτο! οὐκ ἔστιν οὕτως. Καὶ γὰρ καὶ εἰ δόξαν ἦν τῷ Θεῷ μὴ ποιῆσαι τὰ γενητά, ἀλλ' ἦν οὐδὲν ἧττον ὁ Λόγος 'πρὸς τὸν Θεόν', καὶ ἐν αὐτῷ ἦν ὁ Πατήρ. Τὰ μέντοι γενητὰ ἀδύνατον ἦν χωρὶς τοῦ Λόγου γενέσθαι· οὕτω γὰρ καὶ γέγονε δι' αὐτοῦ, καὶ εἰκότως. Ἐπειδὴ γὰρ Λόγος ἐστὶν ἴδιος φύσει τῆς οὐσίας τοῦ Θεοῦ ὁ Υἱός, ἐξ αὐτοῦ τέ ἐστι, καὶ 'ἐν αὐτῷ' ἐστιν, ὡς εἶπεν αὐτός· οὐκ ἠδύνατο μὴ δι' αὐτοῦ γενέσθαι τὰ δημιουργήματα.—*Even supposing that the Father had never been disposed to create the world, or a part of it, nevertheless the Logos would have been with God and the Father in Him* . . . This was the core of the argument. In fact, St. Athanasius carefully eliminates all references to the οἰκονομία of creation or salvation from his description of the inner relationship between the Father and the Son. This was his major and decisive contribution to Trinitarian theology in the critical situation of the Arian dispute. And this left him free to define the concept of Creation properly. Θεολογία, in the ancient sense of the word, and οἰκονομία must be clearly and strictly distinguished and delimited, although they could not be separated from each other. But God's "Being" has an absolute ontological priority over God's action and will.

God is much more than just "Creator." When we call God "a Father," we mean something higher than His relation to creatures (*Contra Arianos* I 33). "Before" God creates at all, πολλῷ πρότερον, He is Father, and He creates through His Son. For the Arians, actually, God was no more than a Creator and Shaper of creatures, argued St. Athanasius. They did not admit in God anything that was "superior to His will," τὸ ὑπερκείμενον τῆς βουλήσεως. But, obviously, "being" precedes "will," and "generation," accordingly, surpasses the "will" also: ὑπεραναβέβηκε δὲ τῆς βουλήσεως τὸ πεφυκέναι (II 2). Of course, it is but a logical order: there is no temporal sequence in Divine Being and Life. Yet, this logical order has an ontological significance. Trinitarian names denote the very character of God, His very Being. They are, as it were, ontological names. There are, in fact, two different sets of names which may be used of God. One set of names refers to God's deeds or acts—that is, to His will and counsel—the other to God's own essence and being. St. Athanasius insisted that these two sets of names had to be formally and consistently distinguished. And, again, it was more than just a logical or mental distinction. There was a distinction in the Divine reality itself. God is what He *is*: Father, Son, and the Holy Spirit. It is an ultimate reality, declared and manifested in the Scriptures. But Creation is a deed of the Divine will, and this will is common to and identical in all Three Persons of the One God. Thus, God's Fatherhood must necessarily precede His Creatorship. The Son's existence flows eternally from the very essence of the Father, or, rather, belongs to this "essence," οὐσία. The world's existence, on the contrary, is, as it were, "external" to this Divine essence and is grounded only in the Divine will. There is an element of contingency in the exercise and disclosure of the creative will, as much as His will reflects God's own essence and character. On the other hand, there is, as it were, an absolute necessity in the Trinitarian being of God. The word may seem strange and startling. In fact, St. Athanasius did not use it directly. It would have embarassed Origen and many others, as offensive to God's perfection: does it not imply that God is subject to certain "constraint" or fatalistic determinism? But, in fact, "necessity" in this case is but another name for "being" or "essence." Indeed, God does not "choose" His own Being. He simply *is*. No further question can be intelligently asked. Indeed, it is proper for God "to create," that is, to manifest Himself *ad extra*. But this manifestation is an act of His will, and in no way an extension of His own Being. On the other hand, "will" and "deliberation" should not be invoked in the description of the eternal relationship between Father and Son. At this point St. Athanasius was definite and explicit. Indeed, his whole refutation of Arianism depended ultimately upon this basic distinction between "essence" and "will," which alone could establish clearly the real difference in kind between "Generation" and "Creation." The Trinitarian vision and the concept of Creation, in the thought of St. Athanasius, belonged closely and organically together.[18]

Let us examine now in detail some few characteristic passages in the famous Athanasian *Discourses against the*

Arians. The accurate dating of these "Discourses" is irrelevant for our present purpose.

I 19: God is described in the Scripture as the Fountain of Wisdom and Life. The Son is His Wisdom. Now, if one admits with the Arians that "there was when He was not," this would imply that once the Fountain was dry, or, rather, that it was not a fountain at all. The spring from which nothing flows is not a spring at all.—The simile is characteristic of St. Athanasius. It reappears often in the *"Discourses."* See, for instance, II 2: if the Word was not the genuine Son of God, God Himself would no longer be a Father, but only a Shaper of creatures. The fecundity of the Divine nature would have been quenched. The nature of God would be sterile, and not fertile: ἔρημος ... μὴ καρπογόνος. It would be a barren thing, a light without shining, a dry font: ὡς φῶς μὴ φωτίζον καὶ πηγὴ ξηρά. See also I 14: ἄγονος ἦν ἡ πηγὴ καὶ ξηρά, φῶς χωρὶς αὐγῆς; or II 33: ἥλιος χωρὶς τοῦ ἀπαυγάσματος.— Both the argument and the imagery can be traced back to Origen. *Otiosam enim et immobilem dicere naturam Dei impium est simul et absurdum* (*De princ.* III 5 2; 272 Koetschau). But, as we have already seen, in Origen the argument was ambiguous and misleading. It was ambiguous because there was no room for any clear discrimination between "being" and "acting." It was misleading because it coupled "generation" and "creation" so closely and intimately together as not to allow any demarcation line. This ambiguity is avoided carefully by St. Athanasius. He never uses this argument—from the Divine "fertility"—in reference to the will of God. On the contrary, he formally refuses to follow Origen at this point,—of course, without quoting him.

I 20: God was never without anything that is His own: Πότε γοῦν τοῦ ἰδίου χωρὶς ἦν ὁ Θεός; On the other hand, created things have no affinity or similarity with the Creator: οὐδὲν ὅμοιον κατ' οὐσίαν ἔχει πρὸς τὸν πεποιηκότα. They are outside God: ἔξωθεν αὐτοῦ. They have received their existence by the grace and appointment of the Word: χάριτι καὶ βουλήσει αὐτοῦ τῷ λόγῳ γενόμενα. And, St. Athanasius characteristically adds, "they could again cease to exist, if it pleased their Creator"—ὥστε πάλιν δύνασθαι καὶ παύεσθαί ποτε, εἰ θελήσειεν ὁ ποιήσας. For, he concludes, "such is the nature of created things"—ταύτης γάρ ἐστι φύσεως τὰ γενητά. See also II 24 and 29: πάντων ἐκ τοῦ μὴ ὄντος ἐχόντων τὴν σύστασιν. Now, at this very point St. Athanasius had to face an objection of his opponents. They said: Is it not so that God must be Creator always, since the "power of creating" could not have come to God, as it were, subsequently? οὐκ ἐπιγέγονεν αὐτῷ τοῦ δημιουργεῖν ἡ δύναμις. Therefore, all creatures must be eternal. It is significant that this counter-argument of the Arians was actually Origen's famous argument, based on the analysis of the term παντοκράτωρ. Only the conclusion was different. Origen's conclusion was that, indeed, creatures were eternal. For the Arians that was blasphemy. By the same argument they wanted to reduce *ad absurdum* the proof of the eternal generation. It was an attack both on Origen and on St. Athanasius. St. Athanasius meets the charge on his own ground. Is there really such a "similarity" between generation and creation—τί ὅμοιον—that what must be said of God as Father must also be said of Him as Creator: ἵνα τὰ ἐπὶ τοῦ πατρὸς ταῦτα καὶ ἐπὶ τῶν δημιουργῶν εἴπωσι? This is the sting of the Athanasian rejoinder. In fact, there is total disparity. The Son is an offspring of the substance: ἴδιον τῆς οὐσίας γέννημα. Creatures are, on the contrary, "external" to the Creator. Accordingly, there is no "necessity" for them to exist eternally: οὐκ ἀνάγκη ἀεὶ εἶναι. But generation is not subject to will (or deliberation): τὸ δὲ γέννημα οὐ βουλήσει ὑπόκειται. It is, on the contrary, a property of the substance: ἀλλὰ τῆς οὐσίας ἐστὶν ἰδιότης. Moreover, a man can be called "a maker," ποιητής, even before he has made anything. But nobody can be called "a father" before he has a son. This is to say that God could be described as Creator even "before" Creation came into existence. It is a subtle but valid point in the argument. St. Athanasius argues that, although God could, indeed, have created things from all eternity, yet created things themselves could not have existed eternally, since they are "out of nothing," ἐξ οὐκ ὄντων, and consequently did not exist before they were brought into existence: οὐκ ἦν πρὶν γένηται. "How can things which did not exist before they originated be co-eternal with God?"—Πῶς ἠδύνατο συνυπάρχειν τῷ ἀεὶ ὄντι Θεῷ; This turn of the argument is highly significant. Indeed, if one starts, as Origen did, with the eternity and immutability of God, it is difficult to see, how anything truly "temporal" could have existed at all. All acts of God must be eternal. God simply could not "have started." But in this case the proper "nature" of temporal things is ignored and disregarded. This is precisely what St. Athanasius wanted to say. "Beginning" belongs to the very "nature" of temporal things. Now, it is the beginning of temporal existence, of an existence in time and flux. For that reason creatures cannot "co-exist" with the Eternal God. There are two incomparable modes of existence. Creatures have their own mode of subsistence: they are outside God. Thus creatures, by their very nature, cannot "co-exist" with God. But this inherent limitation of their nature does not, in any sense, disparage the power of the Creator. The main point of St. Athanasius was precisely this. There is an identity of nature in generation, and a disparity of natures in creation (cf. I 26).

I 36: Since created beings arise "out of nothing," their existence is bound to be a state of flux: ἀλλοιουμένην ἔχει τὴν φύσιν. Cf. I 58: Their existence is precarious, they are perishable by nature: τὰ δυνάμενα ἀπολέσθαι. This does not imply that they will actually and necessarily perish. Yet, if they do not actually perish, it is only by the grace of the Creator. The Son alone, as an offspring of the substance, has an intrinsic power "to co-exist" eternally with the Father: ἴδιον δὲ τὸ ἀεὶ εἶναι καὶ συνδιαμένειν σὺν τῷ Πατρί. See also II 57: The being of that which has existence "according to a beginning" can be traced back to a certain initial instant.

In the later part of his third "Discourse" St. Athanasius discusses at great length the Arian contention that the Son has been begotten by "the will and deliberation" of the Father: βουλήσει καὶ θελήσει γεγενῆσθαι τὸν Υἱὸν ὑπὸ τοῦ Πατρὸς (III 59). These terms, protests St. Athanasius, are quite out of place in this connection. Arians simply attempt to hide their heresy under the cover of these ambiguous words. St. Athanasius suggests that they borrowed their ideas at this point from the Gnostics and mentions the name of Ptolemy. Ptolemy taught that God first thought, and then willed and acted. In a similar way, St. Athanasius contends, Arians claim that the will and deliberation of the Father preceded the generation of the Word. He quotes Asterius at this point.[19] In fact, however, these terms—"will" and "deliberation"—are only applicable to the production of creaturely things. Now, Arians claim that unless the Son's existence depended upon the "deliberation" of the Father, it would appear that God has a Son "by necessity" and, as it were, "unwillingly"—ἀνάγκῃ καὶ μὴ θέλων. This kind of reasoning, St. Athanasius retorts, only shows their inability to grasp the basic difference between "being" and "acting." God does not deliberate with Himself about His own being and existence. Indeed, it would be absurd to contend that God's goodness and mercy are just His voluntary habit, and not a part of His nature. But does it mean that God is good and merciful unwillingly? Now, what is "by Nature" is higher than that which is only "by deliberation"—ὑπέρκειται καὶ προηγεῖται τοῦ βου-λεύεσθαι τὸ κατὰ φύσιν. The Son being an offspring of the Father's own substance, the Father does not "deliberate" about Him, since it would mean "deliberation" about His

own being: τὸν δὲ ἴδιον Λόγον ἐξ αὐτοῦ φύσει γεννώ-
μενον οὐ προβουλεύεται. God is the Father of His Son
"by nature and not by will—οὐ βουλήσει ἀλλὰ φύσει τὸν
ἴδιον ἔχει Λόγον. Whatever was "created," was indeed
created by the good will and deliberation of God. But the
Son is not a deed of will, like creatures, but by nature is an
offspring of God's own substance: οὐ θελήματός ἐστι
δημιούργημα ἐπιγεγονώς, καθάπερ ἡ κτίσις, ἀλλὰ
φύσει τῆς οὐσίας ἴδιον γέννημα. It is an insane and
extravagant idea to put "will" and "counsel" between the
Father and the Son (III 60, 61, 62).

Let us summarize. The theological writings of St. Athanasius were mainly occasional tracts, tracts for the time. He
was always discussing certain particular points, the burning
issues of the current debate. He was interpreting controversial texts of the Scripture, pondering and checking phraseology, answering charges, meeting objections. He never had
time or opportunity for a dispassionate and systematic exposition. Moreover, the time for systems had probably not
yet come. But there was a perfect consistency and coherence
in his theological views. His theological vision was sharp
and well focused. His grasp of problems was unusually
sure and firm. In the turmoil of a heated debate he was
able to discern clearly the real crux of the conflict. From
tradition St. Athanasius inherited the catholic faith in the
Divinity of the Logos. This faith was the true pivot of his
theological thought. It was not enough to correct exegesis,
to improve terminology, to remove misunderstandings. What
needed correction, in the age of St. Athanasius, was the
total theological perspective. It was imperative to establish
"Theology," that is—the doctrine of God, on its proper
ground. The mystery of God, "Three in One," had to be
apprehended in itself. This was the main preoccupation of
St. Athanasius in his great *"Discourses."* Père Louis Bouyer,
in his admirable book on St. Athanasius, has rightly stated
that, in the *"Discourses,"* St. Athanasius forces the reader

"to contemplate the Divine life in God Himself, before it is communicated to us." This was, according to Père Bouyer, the main emphasis in the book. In this perspective one can see the radical difference between the Divine and the creaturely. One sees the absoluteness of the Divine transcendence: God does not need His creatures. His own Being is perfect and complete in itself. And it is this inner Being of God that is disclosed in the mystery of the Trinity.[20] But the actual mystery is double. There is, indeed, the mystery of the Divine Being. But there is another concomitant mystery, the mystery of Creation, the mystery of the Divine οἰκονο-μία. No real advance can be achieved in the realm of "Theology" until the realm of "Oikonomia" had been properly ordered. This, surely, was the reason why St. Athanasius addressed himself to the problem of Creation even in his early treatises, which constituted, in a sense, his theological confession. On the one hand, the meaning of the redemptive Incarnation could be properly clarified only in the perspective of the original creative design of God. On the other, in order to demonstrate the absolute sovereignty of God it was necessary to show the ultimate contingency of the created Cosmos, fully dependent upon the Will of God. In the perspective of the Arian controversy two tasks were closely related to each other: to demonstrate the mystery of the Divine Generation as an integral feature of the Divine Being itself, and to emphasize the contingency of the creaturely Cosmos, which contingency can also be seen in the order of existence. It was precisely in the light of this basic distinction—between "Being" and "Will"— that the ultimate incommensurability of the two modes of existence could be clearly exhibited. The inner life of God is in no way conditioned by His revelatory self-disclosure in the world, including the design of Creation itself. The world is, as it were, a paradoxical "surplus" in the order of existence. The world is "outside" God; or rather it is precisely this "outside" itself. But it does exist, in its own mode and dimension. It arises and stands only by the will of God. It has a beginning precisely because it is contingent, and moves toward an end for which it has been designed by God. The Will of God is manifested in the temporal process of the Divine Οἰκονομία. But God's own Being is immutable and eternal. The two modes of existence, the Divine and the creaturely, can be respectively described as "necessary" and "contingent," or "absolute" and "conditional," or else, in the apt phraseology of a distinguished German theologian of the last century, F. A. Staudenmeier, as *das Nicht-nicht-seyn-könnende* and *das Nicht-seyn-könnende*. This corresponds exactly to the distinction between the Divine Being and the Divine Will.[21] This distinction was made and consistently elaborated, probably for the first time in the history of Christian thought, in the heat of the Arian debate by St. Athanasius of Alexandria. It was a step beyond Origen. St. Athanasius was not only an expert controversialist, but a great theologian in his own right.

III

The Athanasian distinction between "Generation" and "Creation," with all its implications, was already commonly accepted in the Church in his own time. A bit later, St. Cyril of Alexandria simply repeated his great predecessor. Indeed, his *Thesaurus de sancta et consubstantiali Trinitate* depended heavily upon the Athanasian "Discourses."[22] Only instead of "will" and "deliberation," St. Cyril spoke of Divine "energy": τὸ μὲν ποιεῖν ἐνεργείας ἐστί, φύσεως δὲ τὸ γεννᾶν· φύσις δὲ καὶ ἐνέργεια οὐ ταὐτὸν (*Thesaurus,* ass. 18, PG 75, 313; cf. ass. 15, PG 75, 276: τὸ γέννημα... ἐκ τῆς οὐσίας τοῦ γεννῶντος πρόεισι φυσικῶς—(τὸ κτίσμα) ...ἔξωθέν ἐστιν ὡς ἀλλότριον; also ass. 32, PG 75, 564-565). And finally, St. John of Damascus, in his great *Exposition of the Orthodox*

Faith, repeated St. Cyril. "For we hold that it is from Him, that is, from the Father's nature, that the Son is generated. And unless we grant that the Son co-existed from the beginning with the Father, by Whom He was begotten, we introduce change into the Father's subsistence, because, not being the Father, He subsequently became the Father. For the creation, even though it originated later, is nevertheless not derived from the essence of God, but is brought into existence out of nothing by His will and power, and change does not touch God's nature. For generation means that the begetter produces out of his essence offspring similar in essence. But creation and making mean that the creator and maker produces from that which is external, and not of his own essence, a creation which is of an absolutely dissimilar nature." The Divine Generation is an effect of nature, τῆς φυσικῆς γονιμότητος. Creation is, on the contrary, an act of decision and will—θελήσεως ἔργον (*De fide orth.* I 8, PG 94, 812-813). This antithesis: γονιμότης and θέλησις or βούλησις is one of the main distinctive marks of Eastern theology.[23] It was systematically elaborated once more in late Byzantine theology, especially in the theology of St. Gregory Palamas (1296-1359). St. Gregory contended that unless a clear distinction had been made between the "essence" and "energy" in God, one could not distinguish also between "generation" and "creation."[24] And once again this was emphasized, somewhat later, by St. Mark of Ephesus.[25] It was a true Athanasian motive, and his arguments again came to the fore.

Now, the question arises: Is the distinction between "Being" and "Acting" in God, or, in other terms, between the Divine "Essence" and "Energy," a genuine and ontological distinction—*in re ipsa;* or is it merely a mental or logical distinction, as it were, κατ' ἐπίνοιαν, which should not be interpreted objectively, lest the Simplicity of the Divine Being is compromised.[26] There cannot be the slightest doubt that for St. Athanasius it was a real and ontological difference. Otherwise his main argument against the Arians would have been invalidated and destroyed. Indeed, the mystery remains. The very Being of God is "incomprehensible" for the human intellect: this was the common conviction of the Greek Fathers in the Fourth century—the Cappadocians, St. John Chrysostom, and others. And yet there is always ample room for understanding. Not only do we distinguish between "Being" and "Will"; but it is not the same thing, even for God, "to be" and "to act." This was the deepest conviction of St. Athanasius.

The Patristic Age and Eschatology: An Introduction

I

FOUR "LAST THINGS" are traditionally listed: Death, Judgment, Heaven, and Hell. These four are "the last things of man." And there are four "last things" of mankind: the Last Day, the Resurrection of the Flesh, the Final Judgment, and the End of the World.[1] The major item, however, is missing in this listing, namely "the Last Adam," Christ Himself, and His Body, the Church. For indeed Eschatology is not just one particular section of the Christian theological system, but rather its basis and foundation, its guiding and inspiring principle, or, as it were, the climate of the whole of Christian thinking. Christianity is essentially eschatological, and the Church is an "eschatological community," since she is the New Testament, the ultimate and the final, and, consequently, "the last."[2] Christ Himself is the last Adam because He is "the New Man" (Ignatius, *Ephes.* 20. 1). The Christian perspective is intrinsically eschatological. "The

This article originally appeared in *Studia Patristica,* Vol. II, ed. Kurt Aland and F. L. Cross (Berlin: Akademie Verlag, 1956), 235-250. Reprinted by permission of the author.

Old has passed away. Behold, the New has come." It was precisely "in these last days" that God of the Fathers had ultimately acted, once for all, once for ever. The "end" had come, God's design of human salvation had been consummated (John 19.28, 30: τετέλεσται). Yet, this ultimate action was just a new beginning. The greater things were yet to come. The "Last Adam" was coming again. "And let him who heareth say, Come." The Kingdom had been inaugurated, but it did not yet come in its full power and glory. Or, rather, the Kingdom was still to come,—the King had come already. The Church was still *in via,* and Christians were still "pilgrims" and strangers in "this world." This tension between "the Past" and "the Coming" was essential for the Christian message from the very beginning. There were always these two basic terms of reference: the Gospel and the Second Advent. The story of Salvation was still in progress. But more than a "promise" had been granted unto the Church. Or, rather, "the Promise of the Father" was the Holy Spirit, which did come and was abiding in the Church for ever. The Kingdom of the Spirit had been already inaugurated. Thus, the Church was living in two dimensions at once. St. Augustine describes this basic duality of the Christian situation in a remarkable passage of his "Commentary" on the Gospel of St. John, interpreting the XXIst chapter. "There are two states of life that are known to the Church, preached and commended to herself from heaven, whereof one is of faith, the other of sight. One—in the temporal sojourn in a foreign land, the other in the eternity of the (heavenly) abode. One—on the way, the other—in the fatherland. One—in active work, the other—in the wages of contemplation . . . The one is anxious with the care of conquering, the other is secure in the peace of victory . . . The whole of the one is passed here to the end of this world, and then finds its termination. The other is deferred for its completion till after the end of this world, but has no end in the world to come" (*in Johan. tr.* 124.5). Yet, it is essentially the same Church that has this dual life, *duas vitas.* This duality is signified in the Gospel story by two names: Peter and John.

II

Christianity was recently described as an "experience of novelty," a "*Neuheitserlebnis.*" And this "novelty" was ultimate and absolute. It was the Mystery of the Incarnation. Incarnation was interpreted by the Fathers not as a metaphysical miracle, but primarily as the solution of an existential predicament in which mankind was hopelessly imprisoned, i.e. as the Redemptive act of God. It was "for us men and for our salvation" that the Son of God came down, and was made man.[3] Redemption has been accomplished, once for all. The union, or "communion," with God has been re-established, and the power of becoming children of God has been granted to men, through faith. Christ Jesus is the only Mediator and Advocate, and His sacrifice on the Cross, *in ara crucis,* was "a full, perfect, and sufficient sacrifice, oblation, and satisfaction." The human situation has been radically changed, and the status of man also. Man was re-adopted as the son of God in Christ Jesus, the Only Begotten Son of God Incarnate, crucified and risen. The catholic doctrine of the Incarnation, elaborated by the Fathers, from St. Irenaeus to St. John of Damascus, emphasizes first of all this aspect of finality and uniqueness, of accomplishment and achievement. The Son of God "was made man" for ever. The Son of God, "One of the Holy Trinity," is man, by the virtue of the Incarnation, for ever and ever. The Hypostatic Union is a permanent accomplishment. And the victory of the Cross is a final victory. Again, the Resurrection of the Lord is the beginning of the general resurrection. But precisely for these reasons the "History of Salvation" should go and is going on. The doctrine of Christ finds its fulness and completion in the doctrine of the Church, i.e. of "the Whole Christ,"—*totus Christus, caput et corpus,* to use the glorious phrase of St. Augustine. And this immediately introduces the historical duration. The Church is a growing body, till she comes to "mature manhood," εἰς ἄνδρα τέλειον. In the Church the Incarnate is unfailingly "present." It was precisely this awareness of His abiding presence that necessitated the orientation towards the future. It was in the Church, and through the Church, that God was still pursuing His redemptive purpose, through Jesus Christ, the Lord. Again, the Church was a missionary body, sent into the world to proclaim and to propagate the Kingdom, and the "whole creation" was expected to share or to participate in that ultimate "re-novation," which was already inaugurated by the Incarnate Lord, and in Him. History was theologically vindicated precisely by this missionary concern of the Church. On the other hand, history, i.e. the "History of Salvation," could not be regarded as an endless process. The "End of times" and the "Consummation" were faithfully anticipated. "The End" was clearly predicted in the Scriptures, as the Early Christians read them. The goal was indeed "beyond history," but history was inwardly regulated and organized precisely by this super-historical and transcendent goal, by a watchful expectation of the Coming Lord. Only an ultimate and final "con-summation," an ultimate and final re-integration or "re-capitulation" could have given meaning to the flux of happenings and events, to the duration of time itself. The strong corporate feeling compelled the Early Christians to look for an ultimate and inclusive integration of the Redemptive process in the Kingdom to come. This was plainly stated already by Origen. *"Omne ergo corpus Ecclesiae redimendum sperat Apostolus, nec putat posse quae perfecta sunt dari singulis quibusdam membris, nisi universum corpus in unum fuerit congregatum"* (*in Rom.* VII. 5). History goes on because the Body has not yet been completed. "The fulness of the Body" implies and presupposes a re-integration of history, including the Old dispensation, i.e. "the end." Or, in the phrase of St. John Chrysostom, "then is the Head filled up, then is the Body rendered perfect, when we are all together, all knit together and united" (*in Ephes. hom.* III, *ad* I. 23). *Erit unus Christus, amans seipsum* (St. Augustine, *in Ps.* 26, *sermo* 2, n. 23). The other reason for looking forward, to a future consummation, was the firm and fervent belief in the Resurrection of the dead. In its own way it was to be a "re-integration" of history. Christ is risen indeed, and the sting of death has been taken away. The power of death was radically broken, and Life Eternal manifested and disclosed, *in Christo*. The "last enemy," however, is still active in the world, although death does not "reign" in the world any more. The victory of the Risen Christ is not yet fully disclosed. Only in the General Resurrection will Christ's redemptive triumph be fully actualized. *"Expectandum nobis etiam et corporis ver est"* (Minucius Felix, *Octavius,* 34). This was the common conviction of the Patristic age, from Athenagoras and St. Irenaeus and up to St. John of Damascus. St. Athanasius was most emphatic on this point, and St. Gregory of Nyssa also. Christ had to die in order to abrogate death and corruption by His death. Indeed, death was that "last enemy" which he had to destroy in order to redeem man out of corruption. This was one of the main arguments of St. Athanasius in his *De Incarnatione*. "In order to accept death He had a body" (*de incarn.* 21). And St. Gregory of Nyssa says the same: "if one inquires into the mystery, he will say rather, not that death happened to Him as a consequence of birth, but that birth itself was assumed on the account of death" (*orat. cat.* 32). Or in the sharp phrase of Tertullian: *Christus mori missus, nasci quoque necessario habuit, ut mori posset* (*de carne Christi,* 6). The bodily Resurrection of man was one of the main aims of Redemption. The coming and general Resurrection will not be just a "re-statement" to the previous condition. This would have been rather an "immortalization of death," as St. Maximus sharply pointed out (*epist.* 7). The coming Resurrection was conceived rather as a new creative act of God, as an integral and comprehensive "re-novation" of the whole Creation. "Behold, I make all things new." In the phrase of St. Gregory of Nazianzus, it was to be the third and final "transformation" of human life ("μετάστασις"), completing and superseding the two previous, the Old and the New testaments, a concluding eschatological σεισμός (*orat. theol.* V. 25).

III

The new vision of human destiny, in the light of Christ, could not be accurately and adequately expressed in the terms of the current philosophies of that time. A new set of concepts had to be elaborated before the Christian belief could be fully articulated and developed into a coherent system of theological propositions. The problem was not that of adjustment, but rather of a radical change of the basic habits of mind. Greek Philosophy was dominated by the ideas of permanence and recurrence. In spite of the great variety of trends, a common pattern can be detected in all systems. This was a vision of an "eternal" Cosmos. Everything which was worthy of existence had to have actually existed in the most perfect manner before all time, and nothing could be added to this accomplished fulness. No basic change was possible, and no real "novelty" could ever emerge. The whole, the Cosmos, was perfect and complete, and nothing could be perfected or completed. There could be but a disclosure of the pre-existing fulness. Aristotle made this point with a complete frankness. "What is 'of necessity' coincides with what is 'always', since that which 'must be' cannot possibly 'not-be'. Hence a thing is eternal if its 'being' is necessary; and if it is eternal, its 'being' is necessary. And if, therefore, the 'coming-to-be' of a thing is necessary, its 'coming-to-be' is eternal; and if eternal, necessary. It follows that the 'coming-to-be' of anything, if it is absolutely necessary, must be cyclical, i.e. must return upon itself . . . It is in circular movement therefore, and in cyclical 'coming-to-be', that the 'absolutely necessary' is to be found" (*de gen. et corr.* II. 2, 338a). The argument is perfectly clear. If there is any "sufficient reason" for a certain thing to exist ("necessity"), this reason must be "eternal," i.e. there can be no reason whatever, why this thing should not have existed "from eternity," since otherwise the reason for its existence could not have been "sufficient" or "necessary." And consequently "being" is simply "necessary." No increase in "being" is conceivable. Nothing truly real can be "innovated." The true reality is always "behind" ("from eternity"), and never "ahead." Accordingly, the Cosmos is a periodical being, and there will be no end of cosmic "revolutions." The highest symbol of reality is exactly the recurrent circle. The cosmic reality, of which man was but a part, was conceived as a permanent cyclical process, enacted, as it were, in an infinite series of self-reproducing instalments, of self-reiterating circles. Only the circle is perfect.[4] Obviously, there was no room for any real "eschatology" in such a scheme. Greek Philosophy indeed was always concerned rather with the "first principles" than with the "last things." The whole conception was obviously based on astronomical experience. Indeed, the celestial movements were periodical and recurrent. The whole course of rotation would be accomplished in a certain period ("the Great Year"), and then will come a "repetition," a new and identical cycle or circle. There was no "pro-gress" in time, but only eternal returns, a "cyclophoria."[5] Time itself was in this scheme but a rotation, a periodical reiteration of itself. As Plato put it in the *Timaeus,* time "imitates" eternity, and rolls on according to the laws of numbers (38a, b), and in this sense it can be called "a mobile image of eternity" (37 d). In itself, time is rather a lower or reduced mode of existence. This idea of the periodical succession of identical worlds seems to be traditional in Greek Philosophy. The Pythagoreans seem to have been the first to profess an exact repetition. With Aristotle this periodical conception of the Universe took a strict scientific shape and was elaborated into a coherent system of Physics. Later on this idea of periodical returns was taken up by the Stoics. They professed the belief in the periodical dissolution and "rebirth" of all things, παλιγ-γενεσία, and then every minute detail will be exactly reproduced. This return was what the Stoics used to call the "Universal Restoration," ἀποκατάστασις τῶν πάντων. And this was obviously an astronomical term.[6] There was a kind of a cosmic *perpetuum mobile,* and all individual existences were hopelessly or inextricably involved in this cosmic rotation, in these cosmic rhythms and "astral courses" (this was precisely what the Greeks used to call "destiny" or fate, ἡ εἱμαρμένη, *vis positionis astrorum*). The Universe itself was always numerically the same, and its laws were immutable and invariable and each next world therefore will exactly resemble the earlier ones in all particulars. There was no room for history in this scheme. "Cyclical motion and the transmigration of souls is not history. It was a history built on the pattern of astronomy, it was indeed itself a kind of astronomy."[7] Already Origen protested most vigorously against this system of cosmic bondage. "If this be true, then free will is destroyed" (*contra Celsum,* IV. 67 etc.; cf. V. 20-21). Oscar Cullmann, in his renowned book, *Christus und die Zeit,* has well depicted the radical divergence between the "circular" concept of time in Greek thought and the "linear" concept in the Bible and in Christian doctrine. The ancient Fathers were fully aware of this divergence. *Circuitus illi jam explosi sunt,* exclaims St. Augustine. Let us fellow Christ, "the right way," and turn our mind away from the vain circular maze of the impious.—*Viam rectam sequentes quae nobis est Christus. Eo duce et salvatore, a vano et inepto impiorum circuitu iter fidei mentemque avertamus* (*de Civ. Dei,* XII. 20).—Now, this circular conception of the Universe, as "a periodical being," was closely connected with the initial conviction of the Greeks that the Universe, the Cosmos, was "eternal," i.e. had no beginning, and therefore was also "immortal," i.e. could have no end. The Cosmos itself was, in this sense, "Divine." Therefore, the radical refutation of the cyclical conception was possible only in the context of a coherent doctrine of Creation. Christian Eschatology does inextricably depend upon an adequate doctrine of Creation. And it was at this point that Christian thought encountered major difficulties.[8] Origen was probably the first to attempt a systematic formulation of the doctrine of Creation. But he was, from the outset, strongly handicapped by the "hellenistic" habits of his mind. Belief in Creation was for him an integral article of the Apostolic faith. But from the absolute "perfection" of God he felt himself compelled to deduce the "eternity" of the world. Otherwise, he thought, it would be necessary to admit some changes in God Himself. In Origen's conception, the Cosmos is a kind of an eternal companion of God. The Aristotelian character of his reasoning at this point is obvious. Next, Origen had to admit "cycles" and a sort of rotation, although he plainly rejected the iterative character of the sucessive "cycles." There was an unresolved inconsistency in his system. The "eternity" of the world implied an infinite number of "cycles" in the past, but Origen was firmly convinced that this series of "cycles" was to come to an end, and therefore there had to be but a finite number of "cycles" in the future. Now, this is plainly inconsistent. On the other hand, Origen was compelled to interpret the final "con-summation" as a "re-turn" to the initial situation, "before all times." In any case, history was for him, as it were, unproductive, and all that might be "added" to the preexistent reality had to be simply omitted in the ultimate summing up, as an accidental alloy or vain accretion. The fulness of Creation had been realized by the creative *fiat* "in eternity"

once for all. The process of history could have for him but
a "symbolic" meaning. It was more or less transparent for
these eternal values. All links in the chain could be interpreted as signs of a higher reality. Ultimately, all such signs
and symbols will pass away, although it was difficult to see
why the infinite series of "cycles" should ever end. Nevertheless, all signs have their own function in history. Events,
as temporal happenings, have no permanent significance.
The only valid interpretation of them is "symbolical." This
basic assumption led Origen into insuperable difficulties in
Christology. Could the Incarnation itself be regarded as a
permanent achievement, or rather was it no more than an
"episode" in history, to be surpassed in "eternity"? Moreover, "manhood" itself, as a particular mode of existence,
was to be interpreted precisely as an "episode," like all
differentiation of beings. It did not belong to the original
plan of Creation and originated in the general disintegration
of the Fall. Therefore, it was bound to disappear, when the
whole of Creation is restored to its initial integrity, when
the primordial world of pure spirits is re-stated in its original
splendor. History simply has nothing to contribute to this
ultimate "apocatastasis."—Now, it is easy to dismiss this
kind of Eschatology as an obvious case of "acute Hellenization." The true historical situation, however, was much
more complex. Origen was wrestling with a real problem.
His "aberrations" were in fact the birth-pangs of the Christian
mind. His own system was an abortive birth. Or, to change
the metaphor, his failures themselves were to become sign-
posts on the road to a more satisfactory synthesis. It was in
the struggle with Arianism that the Fathers were compelled
to a clear conception of "Creation," as distinguished from
other forms of "becoming" and "being." The contribution
of St. Athanasius was decisive at this point. St. Augustine,
from another point of view, was wrestling with the same
problem, and his discovery that Time itself had to be
regarded as a creature was one of the most relevant achieve-

ments of Christian thought. This discovery liberated this thought from the heavy heritage of Hellenistic habits. And a safe foundation was laid for the Christian theology of History.

IV

No comprehensive integration of human existence is possible without the Resurrection of the dead. The unity of mankind can be achieved only if the dead rise. This was perhaps the most striking novelty in the original Christian message. The preaching of the Resurrection as well as the preaching of the Cross was foolishness and a stumbling-block to the Gentiles. The Christian belief in a coming Resurrection could only confuse and embarrass the Greeks. It would mean for them simply that the present imprisonment in the flesh will be renewed again and forever. The expectation of a bodily resurrection would befit rather an earthworm, suggested Celsus, and he jeered in the name of common sense. He nicknamed Christians "a flesh-loving crew," φιλο-σώματον γένος, and treated the Docetists with far greater sympathy and understanding (apud Origen, *contra Celsum,* V. 14; VII. 36, 39). Porphyrius, in his *"Life of Plotinus,"* tells that Plotinus, it seemed, "was ashamed to be in the flesh," and with this statement he begins his biography. "And in such a frame of mind he refused to speak either of his ancestors or parents, or of his fatherland. He would not sit for a sculptor or painter." "It was absurd to make a permanent image of this perishable frame. It was already enough that we should bear it now" (*Life of Plotinus,* 1). This philosophical asceticism of Plotinus should be distinguished from Oriental dualism, Gnostic or Manichean. Plotinus himself wrote very strongly "against Gnostics." Yet, it was rather a difference of motives and methods. The practical

issue in both cases was one and the same—a "flight" or
"retreat" from this corporeal world, an "escape" from the
body. Plotinus himself suggested the following simile. Two
men live in the same house. One of them blames the builder
and his handiwork because it is made of inanimate wood
and stone. The other praises the wisdom of the architect
because the building is so skillfully constructed. For Plotinus
this world was not evil, it was the "image" or reflection of
the world above, and probably the best of images. Still, one
had to aspire beyond all images, from the image to the
prototype. One should cherish not the copy, but the pattern
(V. 8.8). "He knows that when the time comes, he will go
out and will no longer have any need of a house." It is to
say that the soul was to be liberated from the ties of the body,
to be disrobed, and then only it could ascend to its proper
sphere (II. 9. 15). "The true awakening is the true resurrection from the body, and not with the body," ἀπὸ σώματος, οὐ μετὰ σώματος ἀνάστασις,—since the body is
by nature opposite to the soul (τὸ ἀλλότριον). A bodily
resurrection would be just a passage from one "sleep" to
another (III. 6. 6). The polemical turn of these phrases is
obvious. The concept of the bodily resurrection was quite
alien and unwelcome to the Greek mind. The Christian
attitude was just the opposite. "Not that we would be
unclothed, but that we would be clothed, so that what is mortal
may be swallowed up by life" (2 *Cor.* 5.4). St. Paul was
pleading for an ἀπολύτρωσις τοῦ σώματος (*Rom.*
8.23).* As St. John Chrysostom commented on these passages,
one should clearly distinguish the body itself and "corruption." The body is God's creation, although it had been
corrupted. The "strange thing" which must be put off is
not the body, but corruption (*de resurr. mortuor.* 6). There
was a flagrant "conflict in anthropology" between the
Christian message and Greek wisdom. A new anthropology had to be elaborated in order to commend the Christian hope of Resurrection to the Gentiles. In the last resort it

was Aristotle and not Plato who could offer help to Christian philosophers. In the philosophical interpretation of its eschatological hope, Christian theology from the very beginning clings to Aristotle.[10] Such a biased preference may appear to be unexpected and strange. For, strictly speaking, in Aristotle there was no room for any "after-death" destiny of man. In his interpretation man was entirely an earthly being. Nothing really human passes beyond the grave. Man is mortal through and through. His singular being is not a person and does not survive death. But yet in this weakness of Aristotle was his strength. He had a real understanding of the unity of human existence. Man was to him, first of all, an individual being, a living unit. Man was one just in his duality, as an "animated body," and two elements in him exist only together, in a concrete and indivisible correlation. Soul and body, for Aristotle they are not even two elements, which are combined or connected with each other, but rather simply two aspects of the same concrete reality. "Soul and body together constitute the animal. Now it needs no proof that the soul cannot be separated from the body" (*de anima,* 413a). Once the functional unity of the soul and body has been broken by death, no "organism" is there any more, the corpse is no more a body, and a dead man can hardly be called man at all (*meteor.* IV. 12, 389b: νεκρὸς ἄνθρωπος ὁμώνυμος; cf. *de part. anim.* 641a). No "transmigration" of souls to other bodies was possible for Aristotle. Each soul abides in its "own" body, which it creates and forms, and each body has its "own" soul, as its vital principle, *"eidos"* or form. This anthropology easily lends itself to a biological simplification when man is almost completely equated with any other living being. Such indeed was the interpretation of many followers of the Stagirite, including the famous Alexander of Aphrodisias. Aristotle himself has hardly escaped these inherent dangers of his conception. Of course, man was for him an "intelligent being," and the faculty of thinking was his distinctive mark. But the

doctrine of νοῦς does not fit very well into the general
frame of Aristotelian psychology, and probably is a
survival of his early Platonism. It was possible to adapt the
Aristotelian conception for Christian purposes, and this was
just what was done by the Fathers, but Aristotle himself
obviously "was not a Moslem mystic, nor a Christian theologian."[11] The real failure of Aristotle was not in his
"naturalism," but in that he could not admit any permanence
of the individual. But this was rather a common failure
of Greek philosophy. Beyond time Greek thought visualized only the "typical," and nothing truly personal. Hegel
suggested, in his *Aesthetics,* that Sculpture gives the true key
to the whole of Greek mentality.[12] Recently, a Russian
scholar, A. Th. Lossev, pointed out that the whole of Greek
philosophy was just "a sculptural symbolism." He was
thinking especially of Platonism, but his suggestion has a
wider relevance. "Against a dark background, as a result
of an interplay of light and shadow, there stands out a
blind, colorless, cold, marble and divinely beautiful, proud
and majestic body, a statue. And the world is such a statue,
and gods are statues; the city-state also, and the heroes, and
the myths, and ideas; all conceal underneath them this
original sculptural intuition . . . There is no personality, no
eyes, no spiritual individuality. There is a 'something', but
not a 'someone', an individualized 'it', but no living person
with his proper name . . . There is no one at all. There are
bodies, and there are ideas. The spiritual character of
ideas is killed by the body, but the warmth of the body is
restrained by the abstract idea. There are here beautiful,
but cold and blissfully indifferent statues."[13] And yet Aristotle
did feel and understand the individual more than anyone
else in his tradition. He provided Christian philosophers
with all the elements out of which an adequate conception
of personality could be built up. His strength was just in
his understanding of the empirical wholeness of human
existence. Aristotle's conception was radically transformed

in this Christian adaptation, for new perspectives were opened, and all the terms were given a new significance. And yet one cannot fail to acknowledge the Aristotelian origin of the main anthropological ideas in early Christian theology. Such a christening of Aristotelianism we find already in Origen, to a certain extent in St. Methodius of Olympus as well, and later in St. Gregory of Nyssa, who in his thrilling *De Anima et Resurrectione* attempted a daring synthesis of Origen and Methodius. The break between the "Intellect," impersonal and "eternal," and the soul, individual but mortal, was overcome and healed in the new self-consciousness of a spiritual personality. The idea of personality itself was probably the greatest Christian contribution to philosophy. And then the tragedy of death could be visualized in its true dimension. For Plato and Platonists death was just a welcome release out of the bodily bondage, "a flight to the fatherland." For Aristotle and his followers it was a natural end of earthly existence, a sad but inevitable end, "and nothing is thought to be any longer either good or bad for the dead" (*ethic. Nicom.* III. 6, III. 5a). For Christians it was a catastrophe, a frustration of human existence, a reduction to a sub-human state, abnormal and rooted in the sinful condition of mankind, out of which one is now liberated by the victory of Christ. The task of Christian theologians was now to relate the hope of Resurrection to the new conception of man. It is interesting to observe that the problem was clearly seen and stated in the first theological essay on the Resurrection which we possess. In his brief treatise *De resurrectione mortuorum,* Athenagoras of Athens begins with the plain statement that "God gave independent being and life neither to the nature of the soul itself, nor to the nature of the body separately, but rather to men, composed of soul and body." There would no longer be a man, if the completeness of this structure were broken, for then the identity of the individual would be broken also. "And if there is no resurrection, human

nature is no longer human" (*de resurr. mort.* 13, 15).
Aristotle concluded from the mortality of the body to the
mortality of the soul, which was but the vital power of the
body. Both go down together. Athenagoras, on the contrary,
infers the resurrection of the body from the immortality of
the reasonable soul. Both are kept together.[14] Thus, a safe
foundation was laid for further elaboration.

V

The purpose of this brief paper was not to give a complete summary of the eschatological thought and teaching of
the Fathers. It was rather an attempt to emphasize the main
themes and the main problems with which the Fathers
had to wrestle. Again, it was also an attempt to show how
deeply and closely all eschatological topics are related to
the core of the Christian message and faith, to the Redemption of man by the Incarnate and Risen Lord. Only in this
wider perspective, in the total context of Christian doctrine,
can one fully and faithfully understand all the variations
of Patristic thought. The eschatological hope is rooted in
the faith, and cannot be understood except in this context.
The Fathers never attempted a systematic exposition of
Eschatology, in a narrow and technical sense. But they were
fully aware of that inner logic which had to lead from
the belief in Christ the Redeemer to the hope for the age to
come: the end of the world, the final consummation, the
resurrection of the dead, and life everlasting.

St. John Chrysostom:
The Prophet of Charity

CHRYSOSTOM was a powerful preacher. He was fond of preaching, and regarded preaching as the duty of a Christian minister. Priesthood is authority, but it is authority of word and conviction. This is the distinctive mark of Christian power. Kings compel, and pastors convince. The former act by orders, the latter by exhortations. Pastors appeal to human freedom, to human will and call for decisions. As Chrysostom used to say himself, "We have to accomplish the salvation of men by word, meekness, and exhortation." The whole meaning of human life for Chrysostom was in that it was, and had to be, a life in freedom, and therefore a life of service. In his preaching he spoke persistently about freedom and decision. Freedom was for him an image of God in man. Christ came, as Chrysostom used to remind, precisely to heal the will of man. God always acts in such a way as not to destroy our own freedom. God Himself acts by calls and exhortations, not by compulsion. He shows the right way, calls and invites, and warns against the dangers of wickedness, but does not

This article originally appeared in *St. Vladimir's Seminary Quarterly*, IV, Nos. 3/4 (1955), 37-42. Reprinted by permission of the author.

constrain. Christian pastors must act accordingly. By tempera-
ment, Chrysostom was rather a maximalist, sharp and
rigoristic, but he was always against compulsion, even in
the struggle with heretics. Christians are forbidden, he used
to insist, to apply violence even for good aims: "Our
warfare does not make the living dead, but rather makes
the dead to live, because it is conducted in the spirit of
meekness and humility. I persecute by word, not by acts. I
persecute heresy, not heretics. It is mine more to be persecuted, than to persecute. So Christ was victorious as a
Crucified, and not as a crucifier." The strength of Christianity was for him in humility and toleration, not in power.
One had to be strict about oneself, and meek to the others.

Yet, Chrysostom was in no sense a sentimental optimist.
His diagnosis of the human situation was stern and grim. He
lived in a time when the Church was suddenly invaded by
crowds of nominal converts. He had an impression that he
was preaching to the dead. He watched the lack of charity
and the complacent injustice and saw them almost in an
apocalyptic perspective: "We have quenched the zeal, and
the body of Christ is dead." He had an impression that
he was speaking to people for whom Christianity was just
a conventional fashion, an empty form, a manner and little
more: "Among the thousands one can hardly find more
than a hundred of them who are being saved, and even
about that I am doubtful." He was rather embarrassed by the
great number of alleged Christians: "an extra food for fire."

Prosperity was for him a danger, the worst kind of
persecution, worse than an open persecution. Nobody sees
dangers. Prosperity breeds carelessness. Men fall asleep, and
the devil kills the sleepy. Chrysostom was disturbed especially
by an open and deliberate lowering of standards and requirements, even among the clergy. Salt was losing its savour. He
reacted to this not only by a word of rebuke and reprimand,
but by deeds of charity and love. He was desperately
concerned with the renewal of society, with the healing of

social ills. He was preaching and practising charity, founding hospitals and orphanages, helping the poor and destitute. He wanted to recover the spirit of practising love. He wanted more activity and commitment among Christians. Christianity for him was precisely "the Way," as it had been sometimes described in Apostolic times, and Christ Himself was "the Way." Chrysostom was always against all compromises, against the policy of appeasement and adjustment. He was a prophet of an integral Christianity.

Chrysostom was mainly a preacher of morality, but his ethics was deeply rooted in the faith. He used to interpret Scripture to his flocks, and his favorite writer was St. Paul. It was in his epistles that one could see this organic connection between faith and life. Chrysostom had his favorite dogmatic theme, to which he would constantly return— first of all, the theme of the Church, closely linked to the doctrine of Redemption, being the sacrifice of the High-Priest Christ; the Church is the new being, the life in Christ, and the life of Christ in men. Secondly, the theme of Eucharist, a sacrament and a sacrifice. It is but fair to call Chrysostom, as he was actually called, "the teacher of Eucharist," *doctor eucharisticus.* Both themes were linked together. It was in the Eucharist, and through it, that the Church could be alive.

Chrysostom was a witness of the living faith, and for that reason his voice was so eagerly listened to, both in the East and in the West; but for him, the faith was a norm of life, and not just a theory. Dogmas must be practised. Chrysostom was preaching the Gospel of Salvation, the good tidings of the new life. He was not a preacher of independent ethics. He preached Christ, and Him crucified and risen, the Lamb and the High Priest. Right life was for him the only efficient test of right beliefs. Faith is accomplished in the deeds, the deeds of charity and love. Without love faith, contemplation, and the vision of the mysteries of God are impossible. Chrysostom was watching the desperate struggle for truth in the society of his own days. He was always concerned with living soults; he was speaking to men, to living persons. He was always addressing a flock, for which he felt responsibility. He was always discussing concrete cases and situations.

One of his constant and favorite subjects was that of wealth and misery. The theme was imposed or dictated by the setting in which Chrysostom had to work. He had to face the life in great and overcrowded cities, with all the tensions between the rich and the poor. He simply could not evade social problems without detaching Christianity from life, but social problems were for him emphatically religious and ethical problems. He was not primarily a social reformer, even if he had his own plans for Christian society. He was concerned with the ways of Christians in the world, with their duties, with their vocation.

In his sermons we find, first of all, a penetrating analysis of the social situation. He finds too much injustice, coldness, indifference, and suffering and sorrow in the society of his days. And he sees well to what extent it is connected with the *acquisitive* character of the contemporary society, with the *acquisitive* spirit of life. This *acquisitive* spirit breeds inequality, and therefore injustice. He is not only upset by fruitless luxury of life; he is apprehensive of wealth as a standing temptation. Wealth seduces the rich. Wealth itself has no value. It is a guise, under which the real face of man is concealed, but those who hold possessions come to cherish them, and are deceived; they come to value them and rely on them. All possessions, not only the large ones, are dangerous, in so far as man learns to rely upon what is, by its very nature, something passing and unreal.

Chrysostom is very evangelical at this point. Treasures must be gathered in heaven, and not on earth, and all earthly treasures are unreal and doomed to corruption. "A love for wealth is abnormal," says Chrysostom. It is just a burden for the soul, and a dangerous burden. It enslaves the soul; it distracts it from the service to God. The Christian spirit is a spirit of renunciation, and wealth ties man to inanimate things. The *acquisitive* spirit distorts the vision, perverts the perspective. Chrysostom is closely following the injunctions of the Sermon on the Mount. "Do not be anxious for your life, what you shall eat, nor for your body, what you shall put on..." Life is greater than clothing or food, but it is anxiety which is the prevailing temper of the *acquisitive* society.

Christians are called to renounce all possessions and to follow Christ in full confidence and trust. Possessions can be justified only by their use: feed the hungry, help the poor, and give everything to the needy. Here is the main tension, and the main conflict, between the spirit of the Church and the mood of the worldly society. The cruel injustice of actual life is the bleeding wound of this society. In a world of sorrow and need, all possessions are wrong— they are just proofs of coldness, and symptoms of little faith. Chrysostom goes so far as to denounce even the splendor of the temples. "The Church," he says, "is a triumphant company of angels, and not a shop of a silversmith. The Church claims human souls, and only for the sake of the souls does God accept any other gifts. The cup which Christ offered to the disciples at the Last Supper was not made of gold. Yet it was precious above all measure. If you want to honor Christ, do it when you see Him naked, in the person of the poor. No use, if you bring silk and precious metals to the temple, and leave Christ to suffer cold and nakedness in the outside. No use, if the temple is full of golden vessels, but Christ himself is starving. You make golden chalices, but fail to offer cups of cold water to the needy. Christ, as a homeless stranger, is wandering around and begging, and instead of receiving Him you make decorations."

Chrysostom was afraid that everything kept aside was in a sense stolen from the poor. One cannot be rich, except at the cost of keeping others poor. The root of wealth is always in some injustice. Yet, poverty was not for Chrysostom just a virtue by itself. Poverty meant for him first of all need and want, and suffering and pain. For this reason Christ can be found among the poor, and he comes to us in the guise of a beggar, and not in that of a rich man. Poverty is a blessing only when it is cheerfully accepted for Christ's sake. The poor have less anxiety than the rich and are more independent—or at least may be. Chrysostom was fully aware that poverty can be tempting too, not only as a burden, but as an incentive of envy or despair. For that very reason he wanted to fight poverty, in order not only to ease the suffering, but to remove temptations also.

Chrysostom was always concerned with ethical issues. He had his own vision of a just society, and the first prerequisite was, in his opinion, equality. It is the first claim of any genuine love. But Chrysostom would go much further. He felt that there was but one owner of all things in the world—God Himself, the Maker of all. Strictly speaking, no private property should exist at all. Everything belongs to God. Everything is loaned rather than given by God in trust to man, for God's purposes. Chrysostom would add: Everything is God's except the good deeds of man—it is the only thing that man can own. As everything belongs to God, our common Master, everything is given for common use. Is it not true even of worldly things? Cities, market-places, streets—are they not a common possession? God's economy is of the same kind. Water, air, sun and moon, and the rest of creation, are intended for common use. Quarrels begin usually when people attempt to appropriate things which, by their very nature, were not intended for the private possession of some, to the exclusion of others.

Chrysostom had serious doubts about private property. Does not strife begin when the cold distinction between "mine" and "thine" is first introduced? Chrysostom was concerned not so much with the results, as with causes—with the orientation of the will. Where is man going to gather his treasures? Chrysostom was after justice in defense of human dignity. Was not every man created in God's image? Did God not wish salvation and conversion of every single man, regardless of his position in life, and even regardless of his behavior in the past? All are called to repentance, and all can repent. There was, however, no neglect of material things in his preaching. Material goods come also from God, and they are not bad in themselves. What is bad, is only the unjust use of goods, to the profit of some, while others are left starving. The answer is in love. Love is not selfish, "is not ambitious, is not self-seeking." Chrysostom was looking back to the primitive Church. "Observe the increase of piety. They cast away their riches, and rejoiced, and had great gladness, for greater were the riches they received without labor. None reproached, none envied, none grudged; no pride, no contempt. No talk of 'mine' and 'thine.' Hence gladness waited at their table; no one seemed to eat of his own, or another's. Neither did they consider their brethren's property foreign to themselves; it was a property of the Master; nor again deemed they ought their own, all was the brethren's." How was this possible, Chrysostom asks: By the inspiration of love, in recognition of the unfathomable love of God.

In no sense was Chrysostom preaching "communism." The pattern itself may be deceitful and misleading as any other. The real thing is the spirit. What Chrysostom was preaching in the cities, monks were fervently practising in their communities, professing by deeds that God was the only Master and owner of everything. Chrysostom did not regard monastic life just as an advanced course for the select, but rather as a normal *evangelical* pattern intended for all Christian. At this point he was in full agreement with the main tradition of the early Church, from St. Basil and St. Augustine up to St. Theodore of Studium in the later times. But the strength of monasticism is not in the pattern itself, but in the spirit of dedication, in the choice of a "higher calling." Was this calling only for the few? Chrysostom was always suspicious of inequality. Was it not dangerous to discriminate between the "strong" and the "weak"? Who could judge and decide in advance? Chrysostom was always thinking about real men. There was some kind of individualism inherent in his approach to people, but he valued *unanimity* most highly—the spirit of solidarity, of common care and responsibility, the spirit of service. No person can grow in virtue, unless he serves his brethren. For that reason he always emphasized charity. Those who fail *to do* charity will be left outside the bridal chamber of Christ. It is not enough, he says, to lift our hands to heaven—stretch them to the needy, and then you will be heard by the Father. He points out that, according to the Parable of the Last Judgment, the only question which will be asked then is that about charity. But again it was not just a moralism with him. His ethics had an obvious mystical depth. The true altar is the body of men itself. It is not enough to worship at the altars. There is another altar made of living souls, and this altar is Christ Himself, His Body. The sacrifice of righteousness and mercy should be offered on this altar too, if our offerings are to be acceptable in God's sight. The deeds of charity had to be inspired by the ultimate dedication and devotion to Christ, who came into the world to relieve all want, and sorrow, and pain.

Chrysostom did not believe in abstract schemes; he had a fiery faith in the creative power of Christian love. It was for that reason that he became the teacher and prophet for all ages in the Church. In his youth he spent some few years in the desert, but would not stay there. For him monastic solitude was just a training period. He returned to the world to proclaim the power of the Gospel. He was a missionary by vocation; he had an apostolic and evangelistic zeal. He wanted to share his inspiration with his brethren. He wanted to work for the establishment of God's Kingdom.

He prayed for such things in common life so that nobody would need to retire to the wilderness in search for perfection, because there would be the same opportunity in the cities. He wanted to reform the city itself, and for that purpose he chose for himself the way of priesthood and apostolate.

Was this a utopian dream? Was it possible to reshape the world, and to overrule the wordliness of the world? Was Chrysostom successful in his mission? His life was stormy and hard, it was a life of endurance and martyrdom. He was persecuted and rejected not by the heathen, but by false brethren, and died homeless as a prisoner in exile. All he was given to endure he accepted in the spirit of joy, as from the hand of Christ, Who was Himself rejected and executed. The Church gratefully recognized that witness and solemnly acclaimed Chrysostom as one of the "ecumenical teachers" for all ages to come.

There is some unusual flavor of modernity in the writings of Chrysostom. His world was like ours, a world of tensions, a world of unresolved problems in all walks of life. His advice may appeal to our age no less than it did to his own. But his main advice is a call to integral Christianity, in which faith and charity, belief and practice, are organically linked in an unconditional surrender of man to God's overwhelming love, in an unconditional trust in His mercy, in an unconditional committment to His service, through Jesus Christ, our Lord.

The Anthropomorphites
in the Egyptian Desert

Part I

IN HIS TENTH *"Conference"* John Cassian tells the story of a certain Sarapion, a monk of high distinction: *antiquis-simae distinctionis atque in actuali disciplina per omnia consummatus.* By inadvertence, however, he lapsed into the errors of the "Anthropomorphites." It was a great scandal in the community. All efforts were made to restore Sarapion to the right way. It appears that the main issue involved was that of certain devotional practices. But some points of exegesis were also implied. At that time, a certain Photinus, a deacon from Cappadocia and a man of profound learning, was staying with the brethren. His testimony was sought concerning the meaning of the scriptural phrase: man was created *"in the image and likeness of God."* In an eloquent and elaborate speech, Photinus explained that in the East "all leaders of the churches" used to interpret this phrase "spiritually"—*non secundum humilem litterae sonum, sed*

This article originally appeared in *Akten des XI Internationalen Byzantinistenkongresses* (Munich: Verlag C. H. Beck, 1958), 154-159. Reprinted by permission of the author.

spiritualiter. Finally, Sarapion was persuaded to discontinue his erroneous practices in worship. Yet he was sorely distressed by the new method. He felt himself utterly confounded and frustrated, when, as it is stated, "the anthropomorphic image of the Godhead, which he used to set before him in prayer, was removed from his heart." In great despair, prostrating himself on the ground, weeping and groaning, he complained: "they have taken my God from me, and I have now none to behold, and whom to worship and address I know not"—*tulerunt a me Deum meum, et quem nunc teneam non habeo vel quem adorem aut interpellem jam nescio (Coll.* X. 3, p. 288-289 Petschenig).

What is the meaning of this striking episode? What were, in fact, those "anthropomorphite" practices to which the unfortunate Sarapion had been addicted, and which he was dissuaded from employing? What was the point of his distress and confusion?

Our information about the disputes in the Desert, between the "Origenists" and the alleged "Anthropomorphites," is scarce and biased. Indeed, it comes mainly from the "Origenistic" side. Cassian himself was strongly prejudiced in his description of monastic Egypt. His great treatises, the *"Institutions"* and the *"Conferences,"* were written in order to present a particular doctrine of spirituality, "Origenistic" and Evagrian. The story in Socrates (VI. 7) and Sozomen (VIII. 11-12) was derived probably from the oral reports, and also gossip, circulated in Constantinople by the refugees from Egypt, including the Tall Brothers, and also by Theophilus and his group (cf. Palladius, *Dialogus,* VII). These reports, of course, were tendentiously unfair to the "Anthropomorphites." Indeed, the name itself was a polemical slogan, a derogatory label, invented in the heat of the strife and used as a demagogical weapon. As Owen Chadwick has said recently, "in Egypt 'anthropomorphite' is a malicious term applied by their Origenistic opponents to the literalist Egyptian majority."[1] Its purpose was not to define a group properly, but to discredit it in advance. Indeed, the "Anthropomorphite" monks in the Desert in no sense were a "sect." They had no relation whatever to the heretical sect of Audians, which had spread in Mesopotamia and Syria and by the time of John Cassian was already in steady decay (see Epiphanius, *Haeres.* LXX). Nor should the "literalism" of the alleged "Anthropomorphites" be attributed to their "ignorance" and "simplicity." We are told, in the sources available, about rude and rustic monks who, misled by their crude understanding of certain passages of the Scripture, came to conceive of God in material shape. This aspect of the controversy is grossly misrepresented in our sources. No doubt, "simple" and rustic people were numerous in the monastic ranks, especially among those of Coptic origin, hardly touched at all by any Greek learning. And certain abuses, indeed, might have crept into their practices. But the actual problem was much deeper and more complex than that. The "Anthropomorphites" could quote in their support an old and venerable tradition, which could not be summarily discarded by the charge of "ignorance."

The story of Sarapion, in fact, is an integral part of that great treatise on Prayer which Cassian presents in his ninth and tenth *"Conferences,"* on behalf of the Abbot Isaac. The "Origenistic" character of this treatise is obvious, and close parallels in Origen's writings can be easily found to every point of the discourse. There are stages and grades in spiritual growth. There is an ascension from earthly things to the heavenly. There is an alternative between beholding Jesus "still in His humility and in the flesh"—*humilem adhuc et carneum*—and contemplating Him in His Divine glory and majesty. The former attitude is described as a kind of "Judaic weakness"—*quodammodo Iudaica infirmitate detenti.* At this point II Cor. 5. 16 is quoted: "Those cannot see Jesus coming in His Kingdom who are still kept in a state of Jewish weakness, and cannot say with the Apostle: 'and if we have known Christ after the flesh, yet now we know Him so no

more.' But only those can look with purest eyes on His
Godhead, who rise with Him from low and earthly works
and thoughts and go apart in the lofty mountain of solitude,
which is free from the disturbance of all earthly thoughts
and troubles." The main emphasis in the argument is precisely at this point: "no more in the flesh" (*Coll.* I. 6, 291-
292 P). Accordingly, not only all "images" of the Godhead
must be eliminated from prayer (*nullam divinitatis effigiem*
—"which it is a sin even to mention"), but "one should not
admit any memory of something said, or any kind of a
deed, or an outline of any character"—*ne ullam quidem in se
memoriam dicti cujusque vel facti speciem seu formam
cujuslibet characteri admittet* (X. 5, p. 291 P). The phrase
is by no means clear. It refers primarily, of course, to the
katharsis of the mind, which must be ever cleansed from the
flux of fleeting thoughts and "images,"—and this, indeed,
was Cassian's permanent concern in the whole system of
spiritual discipline. But more than that was obviously implied in these strictures. No *memoria dicti cujusque,* and no
species facti,—these injunctions, if carried out strictly and consistently, would exclude from prayer, especially at its climax,
also any reference to, and any link with, the scriptural
"image" of Christ Jesus, His own *dicta* and *facta,* His saving
oikonomia "in the flesh." *No more in the flesh* . . . This
seems to have been the root of Sarapion's perplexity, which
could not be easily solved or calmed down by any exegetical
arguments. "They have taken away my God from me,"
he complained. Presumably, he was urged to abstain from
using in his devotions any mental image of "Jesus after the
flesh," as he was accustomed to do previously in order to
fix his attention in prayer and to know "whom to adore."
Such practice of his was, from the strict "Origenistic" point
of view, just a "Judaic weakness," a mark of imperfection.
But to dismiss this "anthropomorphic" image of the Saviour
meant for Sarapion to lose ground in prayer. "Whom should
I invoke now?"—*quem interpellem nescio.* Indeed, no crude

"anthropomorphism" was involved at this point. The basic alternative in the argument of Abbot Isaac was between the *infirmitas Judaica* and the *jam non*. The main question seems to have been about the Christological orientation in prayer. To what extent, and in what manner, should prayer be constantly anchored in the "memory" of the historic Jesus, of Jesus "in the flesh"? In what manner, and to what extent, should this historic "image" be permissibly "transcended" in devotional practice and exercise? And this was, indeed, the crucial problem of "Origenistic" spirituality, beginning with Origen himself.

Now, Origen himself never denied that "history" had to be *the starting point,* both in theology and in devotion. But it had to be no more than a starting point. And one inevitably moves away from the start more and more, while one really progresses. The past events, even the events of the Gospel story, must be left behind in this process of spiritual climbing—to the mountain of solitude. These "images" must be transcended in the new "spiritual" vision. One must not look back any more, but steadily forward, to the glorious things to come. The ultimate goal of contemplation, according to Origen, is the knowledge of the Father,—indeed, through the knowledge of the Son. But His historic *oikonomia,* in "the flesh," must be transcended at this point. In spite of all his ardent love for the Crucified Jesus, and all his emphasis on the mystery of the Incarnation, on the higher stages of contemplation Origen claims to move beyond the Incarnation, in order that the Divine glory of the Son would not be obscured by His *oikonomia.*[2] In this sense, the "Christ-mysticism" was for Origen just a stage on the road toward the "God-mysticism." *"Die Christusmystik ist also Durchgangsstadium zur Gottesmystik,"* as Walter Voelker has well stated.[3] And here lies the major danger of "Origenism." This danger is especially acute in the realm of devotion. "Origenism" tends towards a certain "de-christologization" of worship. Devotion is no more focussed on the historic *oikonomia* of salvation. This tendency is obvious in John Cassian. As Owen Chadwick rightly observes, Cassian is so much concerned with the method of contemplation that he has but little to say about its actual object. "In these monastic books we hear little, surprisingly little, of the Gospel, of the earthly life of Jesus Christ, of the revelation of God."[4] The "simple," the *simpliciores* of Origen, utterly resisted this tendency to move away from the "historic" Gospel. And this was, probably, the true core of the "Anthropomorphite" movement, or rather the "resistance-movement," in the Egyptian Desert. It was a striking example of that conflict between the "faith of the people" and "learned theology" which was one of the distinctive features of Christian life in the third century.[5] This tension continued in the Nicene age. The ultimate mystery of the Christian faith is, indeed, in that "God was manifest *in the flesh.*" The truth of this crucial "manifestation" is in no way contradicted by that other truth that Christ "was received up into glory" (I Tim. 3. 16).

The struggle against the "Anthropomorphites" was initiated already by Origen himself: *qui in Ecclesia positi imaginem corpoream hominis Dei esse imaginem dicunt* (*Comm. in Rom.* 1. 19, MG XIV, c. 870-871). In his commentary on Genesis Origen quotes Melito, as one of those who were committed to this erroneous view. Judging by Origen's rejoinder, we must conclude that Melito's main argument was derived from the fact of corporeal theophanies of the Old Testament and from the "anthropomorphic" phraseology of the Bible (*Selecta in Gen.,* ad 1. 26, quoted by Theodoret, Lomm. VIII. 49-52). There is no text in the extant writings of Melito to support that charge. And it seems highly improbable that Melito was really so crudely "anthropomorphite" as Origen's remarks seem to suggest. He was probably close to that view which has been so emphatically expounded by St. Irenaeus.[6] According to Origen, that man which was created "in the image of God" was not a "bodily man": *hunc sane hominem . . . non intelligimus corporalem.* There is no "image of God" in the body, but only in the soul of man. Only the "inner man" was made "in the image": *interior homo noster est, invisibilis, et incorporalis, et incorruptus atque immortalis.* Otherwise, one might be tempted to attribute corporeal features to God himself, as has been actually done by certain carnal men: *carnales isti homines qui intellectum divinitatis ignorant.* Indeed, the "image" in which man has been created was the Son of God, our Saviour, who is "the firstborn of every creature" (*In Genes. hom.* 1. 13, p. 15-18 Baehrens). For Origen it only meant that all intellectual or "logical" beings were made in the shape of the Divine Logos.[7] The same idea has been quite differently elaborated by St. Irenaeus. Here we have a clear opposition of two different views and approaches. According to St. Irenaeus, man was indeed shaped in the image of the Word. But Irenaeus refers here to the Word Incarnate. Man was created in the image of the Incarnate Word, as it were, by anticipation, or proleptically. Accordingly, the bodily figment is also included in the "image": *caro quae est plasmata secundum imaginem Dei . . . imaginem habens in plasmate.* The whole man is created in the "image of God" (*Adv. haeres.* V. 6. 1). "In the times long past, it was said that man was created after the image of God, but it was not yet manifested. For the Word was as yet invisible, after whose image man was created. Wherefore also man has easily lost the similitude. When, however, the Word of God became flesh, He confirmed both these: for He showed forth the true image, since He became Himself what was His image; and He re-established the similitude after a sure manner, by assimilating man to the invisible Father through the means of the visible Word" (*Adv. haeres.* V. 16. 2). This text is of capital importance. The "image of God" in man has been fully manifested precisely through the Incarnation, in the exemplary manhood of the Incarnate God. In his catechetical treatise, St. Irenaeus is quite formal and precise. "He gave his frame the outline of His own form in order that even the visible appearance should be Godlike —for it was as an image of God that man was fashioned and set on earth" (*Demonstr.* II, p. 54 Smith's translation). "And the 'image' is the Son of God, in whose image man was made. And therefore He was manifested in the last times to show that the image was like unto Himself" (*Demonstr.* 22, p. 61 Smith). The concept of "image" has in St. Irenaeus an obvious *"somatic"* connotation,—"a strongly physical emphasis," in the phrase of David Cairns.[8] This emphasis is not accidental for Irenaeus. It is directly related to his basic idea of recapitulation. Indeed, the Word Incarnate, the God-Man, is the center of his theological vision and scheme. This emphasis encourages the use of "visible" and *"somatic"* images in theological thought and language, without committing Christians to any "anthropomorphite" conception of Divinity. The "image" is in the total structure of man; "likeness" is confined to his spiritual sphere.[9]

The "Anthropomorphite" monks stood in a venerable tradition. The conflict in the Desert was not just a clash between the "ignorant" and the "learned." It was the conflict between the two traditions: Evangelical realism and "Origenistic" symbolism.

Theophilus of Alexandria
and Apa Aphou of Pemdje

The Anthropomorphites in the Egyptian Desert

Part II

I

T HE "LIFE OF BLESSED APHOU," an Egyptian hermit and eventually Bishop of Pemdje, or Oxyrhynchus, was published for the first time by Eugene Revillout in 1883 from a Turin manuscript. Revillout was aware of the historical value of this hagiographical document and intended to discuss it in detail. But his essay was never completed. He only printed the Coptic text (in Sahidic), with a brief preface.[1] The "Life" was republished again in 1886 by Francesco Rossi, from the same Turin manuscript, together with an Italian translation, but without any commentary or notes.[2] In the same year V.V. Bolotov published a Russian translation of

From the *Harry Austryn Wolfson Jubilee Volume* (Jerusalem: American Academy for Jewish Research, 1965), Vol. I, pp. 275-310. Reprinted by permission of the author.

Revillout's text, with an extensive introduction. Bolotov
stressed the interest of the document. "A modest hagiological
document of the Egyptian Church, the 'Life of Blessed
Aphou' must occupy, in our opinion, an important place in
the history of dogma: it throws a totally new and peculiar
light on the Anthropomorphite controversy (which developed
later into the Origenistic struggle).... Only now the history
of the Anthropomorphites becomes really comprehensible."
Bolotov planned a special excursus on this particular topic,
but the second part of his article never appeared, and we
do not know what this great master had actually to say.[3]
The only special study of the "Life" of Aphou is by E.
Drioton. He was interested primarily in the story of the
Anthropomorphites. In his article Drioton reprinted the
relevant part of the Coptic text, following Rossi's edition,
and also supplied a French translation.[4] Unfortunately,
Drioton was misguided by his gratuitous assumption that
Egyptian "Anthropomorphites" were actually Audians, and
this assumption marred considerably and distorted his analysis
of the text itself.

There is no adequate paleographic description of the Turin
papyri, even in the catalogue of Rossi.[5] The date of the
manuscripts remains uncertain, and their origin is still rather
obscure. Indeed, the same may be said of many other collections. Already Zoëga, in his famous Catalogue of the
Borgian collection, complained: *Quibus Aegypti locis quibusve
in bibliothecis olim adservati fuerint codices, quorum frag-
menta sunt in museo Borgiano, plane ignoratur ... Arabes ex
monasteriis (eos) rapuisse videntur vel potius in dirutorum
olim monasteriorum ruderibus invenisse... Hujusmodi fasci-
culi vere chaotici cum subinde ex Aegypto adveherentur
mihique ordinandi traderentur.*[6] In fact, the Turin papyri
were acquired somewhere by Bernardino Drovetti, the French
consul in Egypt, and then purchased for the Turin museum.[7]
Amedeo Peyron, the first to handle the manuscripts, soon
after they were brought to Turin in 1821, had very little to

say. They were in miserable condition, sorely mutilated and even torn to small pieces—*piccolissimi pezzi*. For transportation they were carelessly packed in a box—*quam cum aperuissem infandam vidi ac deploravi papyrorum cladem*, exclaims Peyron. Peyron was able, however, to fit the scattered fragments together, and fixed them on transparent sheets.⁸ Unfortunately, varnish used for fixation deteriorated with time, the paper grew even more fragile, and the text did not read easily. This was one of Rossi's reasons for precipitating the publication.⁹

Among the papyri—*en tête de la masse de ces papyres*—Revillout found an interesting note, on a separate scrap of paper. It appears that these papers were once deposited by a certain pious lady, whose name is known to God, "in this place of St. John the Baptist," with the intention that prayers should be said for her and for her family. No date is given, and it is not certain at all whether this note refers to the whole collection or only to some particular documents in it. One must recall that the documents came to Turin in a poor and confused state, and in complete disorder. Revillout, however, took for granted that the whole collection, as we know it now, was deposited at St. John's already in the first decades of the fifth century, or, in any case, before the Schism.¹⁰ The Church of St. John in Alexandria is, of course, the famous Serapeum. It was made into a church under Theophilus, and in 398 the relics of St. John the Baptist were transferred to the new *martyrion*. For that reason the church came to be known under the name of St. John. There was a library in this church.¹¹ Now, it seems that the Turin papyri are of a later date, probably of the seventh century.¹² In this case the dating of Revillout is untenable.

Bolotov contested the early dating for other reasons. Certain documents in the collection seem to be of a later date, as, for instance, a spurious "Life" of St. Athanasius. Again, it is hardly probable that numerous homilies of St. John Chrysostom (authentic or spurious) could be included

in an Alexandrinian collection in the times of St. Cyril and
Dioscoros. Bolotov suggested that the Drovetti collection was,
in fact, a part of a Coptic *Menologion,* or Lectionary, compiled in some monastery. The part preserved covers the
months *tout* and *paopi,*—that is, the first months of the
liturgical year. The "Life of Blessed Aphou" is to be read
on the 21st day of the month *tout,* which corresponds to
September 18. Now, Zoëga already has shown that most of
the Memphitic (or Bohairic) documents in the Borgian and
Vatican collections were actually but *disjecta membra* of a
Lectionary, which originated in the monastery of St. Macarius
in Scete: *olim pertinuisse videantur ad lectionarium, quod
secundum menses diesque digestum adservabatur in mon-
asterio S. Macarii in Scetis.*[13] Bolotov suggested that a similar
Lectionary, or *Menologion,* existed also in Sahidic. In its
content and composition it seems to have differed considerably from the Macarian version. In any case, the names of
Aphou and some others do not occur at all in the later
Synaxaria of the Coptic Church in Arabic.[14] At any rate,
particular documents in the *Menologion* can easily be of
quite different dates, including some early material. But the
whole collection, the *Menologion* as such, could hardly have
been completed by 444 or 451, as Revillout contended.[15]

Thus, the date of each particular document must be
examined separately. The date of the collection may only
provide the ultimate *terminus ante quem.* And, in our case,
when precisely this date is doubtful and uncertain, it is
rather irrelevant.

Now, the "Life of Blessed Aphou" was written some
time after his death, but hardly by a close contemporary,
although still at a time when memories of the saint were
fresh. The style of the writer is both naive and pathetic, but
plain and sober, without legendary adornments and without
any emphasis on the miraculous, which are so characteristic
of later Coptic hagiography. Bolotov regarded the "Life"
as generally reliable.[16] Drioton was of the same opinion: *le*

papyrus porte en lui-même un cachet indubitable d'historicité.
Drioton suggested that the unknown hagiographer might
have had at his disposal certain official documents; his
description of the dispute between Aphou and Theophilus
was based probably on an official record taken formally by
an episcopal clerk: *un procès-verbal de quelque notaire
épiscopal.* On the other hand, the writer was unaware of that
complex and controversial situation in which the dispute had
taken place and therefore had no incentive to be tendentious:
he had a "blind accuracy"—*une exactitude aveugle,* as Drioton
puts it.[17] It may be added that his description of Aphou's
episcopate, in the final section of the "Life," has the character
of an historic narrative.

The only safe date in the biography of Aphou is that
of his disputation with Theophilus. It could have taken
place only in 399. At that time Aphou was already an aged
man, a renowned hermit. According to the "Life," three years
later he was made bishop by Theophilus, and his episcopate
seems to have been of considerable duration. He died as an
old man. This would bring us at least into the second decade
of the fifth century. The "Life" seems to have been written
in a day when the turbulent events of the times of Theophilus
had been forgotten in monastic circles. Some time must have
elapsed before the "Life" could be included in a *Menologion.*
Thus, it seems most probable that the whole collection was
completed in the later part of the fifth century.

II

Aphou was conspicuously a simple and rustic man: his
conversation was "with the wild beasts." He did not dwell
with the people and rigorously avoided their company. Only
on the day of Easter he used to appear in the city, at
Oxyrhynchus, "to hear the preaching" in the church. He led
a solitary life, among the beasts, and they were friends to-

gether—the hermit and the beasts. The beasts were even looking after him. In winter time they would gather around him and warm him with their breathing. They would even bring him food. When, later in life, Aphou was nominated by Theophilus for the episcopal office in Oxyrhynchus, he could not be found. People in the city did not know him. They asked local monks about him, and one of the monks happened to have known him before. He suggested that Aphou must be in the wilderness, as "he did not dwell with men, but with the beasts," and warned in advance that Aphou, surely, would run away if he was told the reason for which he was sought. Finally, Aphou was caught in the net which hunters had set for the beasts. So much we learn from the "Life of Blessed Aphou." The picture is at once coarse and idyllic.

An interesting episode is included in the *Narratio Eze-chielis monachi de vita magistri sui Pauli*. The Coptic text was published already by Zoëga with a Latin paraphrase, from a Borgian manuscript, and was republished once more by Amélineau, who also supplied a French translation.[18] Apa Paul of Tamwah (or Thmoui) was notorious for his ascetical excesses, of an almost suicidal character. He dwelt on the Mount of Antinoe. In his later years Paul was intimately associated with Apa Bishai (= Psois), one of the earliest settlers in Scete and the founder of one of the main monasteries there.[19] Ezechiel, a close disciple of Apa Paul, wrote a description of their common journey in the desert, in the course of which they met Aphou. Amélineau was inclined to disavow the narrative as a fiction, *un livre de pure imagina-tion.* The name of Ezechiel was just a disguise, and the story was compiled much later. Amélineau admitted, however, that certain features in the story were of real interest for the history of ideas.[20] Now, whatever may be said about the literary form of the narrative, there is no valid reason to deny its realistic core. The journey in the desert may be a literary device, a means to chain together various *dicta* and episodes, but *dicta* and episodes may still be genuine and authentic. At the present we are concerned only with one episode in the story of Ezechiel, the meeting of Apa Paul with Apa Aphou. We have here a close parallel to the "Life."

> We travelled southward from Mount Terab until we came to Mount Terotashans, south of Kos. We found some antelopes down in the valley, and in their midst was a monk. My father went forward, greeted him, and said to him, "What is your name?" He said, "My name is Aphou. Remember me, my father, Apa Paul, and may the Lord bring my life to a good finish." My father said to him, "How many years have you been in this place?" He said, "Fifty-four years." My father then said, "Who placed the scheme upon you?" He said, "Apa Antonios of Scete." My father said to him, "How have you lived, travelling with these antelopes?" He said, "My nourishment and that of these antelopes is the same nourishment, namely the plants of the field and these vegetables." My father said to him, "Do you not freeze in the winter or roast in the summer?" He said to him, "When it is winter, I sleep in the midst of these antelopes, and they warm me with the vapor which is in their mouth. When it is summer, they gather together and stand and make shade for me, so that the heat should not bother me." My father said to him, "Truly are you given the epithet: Apa Aphou the Antelope." At that moment a voice came to us saying, "This is his name unto all the rest of the eternities of the earth." We were amazed at what had happened so suddenly and we greeted him. Then we left."[21]

Aphou was not the only one in the Egyptian desert to practise this peculiar form of ascetical estrangement, ξενιτεία. Hermits dwelling with the beasts in the wilderness are mentioned often in hagiographical documents of that time.[22] Now, Wilhelm Bousset contended that all these stories were but legends or novels. The paradisiac hermits, wandering with the beasts, existed only in poetical imagination, not in real life: "nur in der Gestalt legendarischer Erzählungen und nicht in greifbarer Wirklichkeit." The monks of Scete were more sound and sober in their ascetical endeavor and did not approve of wandering monks.[23] This peculiar and rough manner of asceticism—"das tierartige Umherschweifen in der Wüste," in the phrase of Bousset,— originated probably in Syria and Mesopotamia, and for that area it is so well attested in the authentic sources that no reasonable doubts can be raised about its historicity. Sozomen speaks of hermits in Syria and in the adjacent part of Persia which were called βοσκοί, because of their manner of life: they had no houses and dwelt constantly on the mountains. "At the usual hours of meals, they each took a sickle, and went to the mountains to cut some grass on the mountains, as though they were flocks in pasture—καθάπερ νεμόμε-νοι." Sozomen enumerates by names those who have chosen this kind of "philosophy" (VI, 33). The primary meaning of the word βοσκός was herdsman or shepherd. But in this connection it was used rather in the sense of βοσκόμενος νεμόμενος.[24] In Palestine also there were numerous ascetics who practiced this or a similar way of life. There were those who dwelt in mountains, dens, and caves of the earth, and others used to live with the beasts—σύνοικοι θηρίοις γενό-μενοι. Again, some others led even a harder life—νέμονται δὲ τὴν γῆν, βοσκοὺς καλοῦσι... ὥστε τῷ χρόνῳ καὶ θηρίοις συναφομοιοῦσθαι (Evagrius Schol., *hist. eccl.,* I, 21).

There are good reasons to assume that the same rigid and radical method of ascetical retirement was practiced also in Egypt. It is curious to know that Apa Aphou was not the only one to be given the nickname "the Antelope." According to John Cassian, the same nickname was given also to Apa Paphnutius, who was, in any case, a historical personality. The passage must be quoted in full. *Coll.* III. I). *Ubi rursum tanto fervore etiam ipsorum anachoretarum virtutes superans desiderio et intentione jugis ac divinae illius theoriae cunctorum devinabat aspectus, vastiora et inaccessibilia solitudinis penetrans loca multoque in eis tempore delitescens, ut ab ipsis quoque anachoretis difficulter ac rarissime deprehensus angelorum cotidiano consortio delectari ac perfrui crederetur, atque ei merito virtutis hujus ab ipsis inditum fuerit Bubali cognomentum.* The last sentence is rather puzzling: what is the link between the *consortium angelorum* and *Bubali cognomentum?* Obviously, there must be another reason for this peculiar nickname. Paphnutius used to retire in the *inaccessibilia solitudinis loca,* beyond the reach of hermits themselves. Would it be too much to suggest that there he was dwelling with the beasts?—in this case the *cognomentum* would be well motivated. It should be added at this point that the story of a journey in the wilderness, known as the "Life and Conversation" of Apa Onouphrius, in which "naked hermits" were encountered, is attributed to Paphnutius. On the other hand, Apa Paphnutius of Scete was the only leader there who, according to John Cassian, opposed the monks revolting against Theophilus in connection with his Epistle of 399 against the Anthropomorphites.

In fact, the basic principles of the anchorites was: φεῦγε τοὺς ἀνθρώπους καὶ σώζη (*Apophthegmata*, Arsenius I, Cotelerius, *Ecclesiae Graecae Monumenta*, I, p. 353). Retirement and renunciation was usually justified by Biblical examples: the images of Elijah and other prophets, of St. John the Baptist, and even of the Apostles were often recalled and their names quoted.[25] The Epistle to the Hebrews could be also recalled. The way of the anchorites was the way of prophets and apostles. It was precisely in this manner that Apa Aphou used to explain his strange and peculiar mode of life. He was asked by people, in his later years, when he was already bishop, about the reasons of his peculiar life. In reply he simply quoted Scripture. Is it not said in the

Gospel about Christ himself that He was in the wilderness "with the wild beasts" (Mk 1:13)? Did not the blessed David say about himself: "I was as a beast before Thee" (Ps. 73:22)? Did not Isaiah, by the Lord's command, walk naked and barefoot (Is. 20:2)? Now, if Christ himself and His great saints had so condescended and humbled themselves, it was much more imperative for him to do the same—a poor and weak man.

A simple and rustic man, Aphou was a man of genuine piety, of resolute will, and of penetrating mind. According to the "Life" Theophilus was much impressed by Aphou: he appeared before him as a "common man," an ἰδιώτης, but his speech was that of a wise man. In his later years, when he was made bishop—indeed, against his own will, Aphou displayed an unusual pastoral wisdom and zeal. The image depicted in the "Life of Blessed Aphou" is quite impressive. Aphou was an active and efficient bishop, although he accepted this charge reluctantly. He still maintained his peculiar habits. He did not reside in the city, but in a "monastery" outside—in this connection the word "monastery" means obviously just a solitary cell, which was actually the primary meaning of this word.[26] Only on weekends did he appear in the city. On Saturdays he used to gather people into the church and instruct them the whole day. Then he would spend the night in prayer and psalmody, till the time of celebration. And after the service he used to continue instruction till the close of the day. Then, in the evening he would retire to his own place, till the next weekend. In this way he endeavored to combine his *anachoresis* with the episcopal duties. It should be kept in mind that Oxyrhynchus was at that time a very peculiar city. According to Rufinus, there *multo plura monasteria quam domus videbantur* (*Hist. monach.,* ch. V,—of course, in this text *monasterium* denotes the solitary cells; cf. the Greek text, ed. Festugière, *Subsidia Hagiographica,* 34 [1961], 41-43). The city was rather a monastic city: *sed nec portae ipsae, nec turres*

*civitatis, aut ullus omnino angulus ejus, monachorum habita-
tionibus vacat, quique per omnem partem civitatis, die ac
nocte hymnos ac laudes Deo referentes, urbem totam quasi
unam Dei ecclesiam faciunt.* And it was a large city: according to Rufinus, there were 20,000 virgins and 10,000 monks.[27]

Aphou was especially concerned with the poor and the
needy, and also with all those who have suffered from injustice. He organized the material life of his church, by ap-
pointing a special officer for this task, in such a way that
he always had means to help the needy, and he almost
abolished poverty in his flock altogether.[28] He enforced strict
discipline in the church: no woman was allowed to receive
communion if she appeared in a colored dress or wearing
jewels. Aphou was concerned not only with the offended
but also with the offenders, as they were transgressing
the law of God and were in peril of damnation. He was quite
strict about the order of the divine service. From his candi-
dates for ordination he used to require a solid knowledge
of Scripture, and examined them himself. Occasionally he had
raptures, and in this manner used to learn what was going
on in the city. His last admonition to his clergy, already on
his death-bed, was not to seek high positions. He could hardly
himself preserve that which he had achieved as a hermit,
when he became bishop, and, while being bishop, he did not
achieve anything. Obviously, it is not just an idealized portrait,
but a picture of a living person, with distinctive individual
features.

There is an interesting pericope concerning Aphou in the
alphabetic *Apophthegmata,* a close parallel to that last
admonition of his which is recorded in the "Life."[29] As a
hermit, Aphou led a severe life. He wanted to continue the
same after he had become bishop, but was unable to do so
—οὐκ ἴσχυσε. In despair, he prostrated himself before God
and asked, whether it was because of his episcopacy that
grace had departed from him: μὴ ἄρα διὰ τὴν ἐπισκοπὴν
ἀπῆλθεν ἡ χάρις ἀπ' ἐμοῦ. No, was the answer in a

revelation. But, when he was in the desert, and there was no man—μὴ ὄντος ἀνθρώπου—God was helping him: ὁ Θεὸς ἀντελαμβάνετο. Now, when he is in the world, people are taking care of him (Cotelerius, pp. 398-399; cf. *Verba Seniorum,* XV. 13, ML LXXIII, c. 956). The emphasis is here on the antithesis: ἔρημος and κόσμος. This episode is quoted, without the name of Aphou, by St. Isaac of Nineveh, and this shows its popularity. The context in which the quotation appears in St. Isaac helps to grasp its full meaning. It appears in the "Treatise in Questions and Answers," concerning the life of those who dwell in the wilderness, or in solitude. The question is asked: why are "visions and revelations" sometimes given to certain people, while to others they are not given at all, although they may have labored more. Now, visions and visitations are granted often to those who on account of their fervent zeal have fled from the world, "abandoning it entirely in despair and retiring from any part inhabited by men, following God, naked, without hope or help from anything visible, assailed by the fear of desolation or surrounded by the peril of death from hunger or illness or any other evil whatever, and near to dejection." On the other hand, "as long as a man receives consolation from his fellowmen or from any of these visible things, such (heavenly) consolation does not happen to him." This is the answer; and then follow the illustrations. The second is the story of Aphou (but the name is not given). "Another witness to this is he who led a solitary life in reclusion, *and often tasted of consolations granted by grace, and divine care often became visible to him in manifest apperception;* but when he came *near the inhabited world* and sought these things as usual, *he did not find them.* He besought God that the truth concerning this matter might become known to him, saying: perhaps, my Lord, grace has been withdrawn from me on account of my episcopal rank? It was said to him: No. But then, *there was the desert,* there were no men, and God provided for thee. Now, there is *the inhabited world,* and men provide for thee."[30]

In this context the pericope of the *Apophthegmata* comes into a clearer light. The "grace" which had been granted to Aphou in the wilderness was actually a *charisma,* or rather *charismata*—of visions and consolations. The term "grace" is ambiguous in this context, meaning at once "help" and "consolation." With Divine help Aphou was able, in the wilderness, to afford his rigid σκληραγωγία. But now it became impossible—"in the inhabited world," in a community of men. Aphou was a charismatic, a πνευματικός, but charismatics must dwell in solitude, or in the desert and not "in the world." It is interesting to note that the author of the "Life" of Aphou mentions his "ecstasies" only in passing. He is much more interested in his pastoral exploits. Was this author a monk himself?

According to the "Life," in his early years Aphou lived "in obedience" with certain chosen and faithful people— some of them taught by the "disciples of the Apostles." After their death Aphou alone was left, except for one brother, probably a novice, whom he was instructing in the ways to heaven. Thus, originally Aphou lived in a community, and only later chose the solitary life. It is possible, however, that he lived in a company of hermits. It was not unusual at that time that even members of a coenobitical community would retire to the solitary life. There was nothing peculiar in the change. Unfortunately, at this very point the Coptic text is deficient: there is a lacuna of an indefinite length. But we have additional information in the "Life of Apa Paul": Aphou was made monk by Apa Antonius of Scete and stayed in the desert for fifty-four years.

Now, at this very point Drioton makes a hasty conclusion that it was an Audian community in which Aphou had been reared. His argument is strained and peculiar, vague and shaky.[31] First, he contends that teachers of Aphou are so "mysteriously" designated in the "Life" as to give an im-

pression that they were a "separate" group: "ces hommes
que le papyrus désigne si mysterieusement donnent bien
l'impression d'être des séparés." In fact, there is simply
nothing "mysterious" in the text at all. The phrasing is
rather trivial and conventional: Aphou came from the company of venerable and "faithful" masters. These masters
themselves were instructed by the "Apostolic disciples." This
phrase may seem, at the first glance, rather peculiar. For
Drioton it is a conspicuous Audian link: "un trait bien
Audien." In this connection Drioton recalls the Audian claim
to follow the "Apostolic tradition" concerning the Paschal
practices. He admits himself, however, that actually there is
no slightest hint in the "Life" of Aphou (which is, indeed,
the only document in which Aphou's teachers are mentioned)
of any peculiar Paschal usages. It is evident, on the contrary,
that Aphou himself followed the regular calendar of the
Church of Alexandria. Moreover, in the "Life" there is no
reference to any Apostolic *tradition*. It is only stated that
Aphou's own masters were instructed by the *disciples* of
the Apostles, the *mathetai*. The question arises as to what
connotation this term has had, or may have had, in the
ecclesiastical or monastic idiom of the fourth century. And
it is not difficult to find it out.

In fact, early monasticism, in Egypt and elsewhere, always
claimed to have followed the Apostolic pattern, and the
term "apostolic" was used, widely and persistently, to denote
ascetical endeavor—renunciation, poverty, the wandering life,
and the like. The term was applied especially to hermits.
The retreat from the world itself was regarded as an
apostolic action, as an imitation of the disciples who left
everything and followed Christ (cf. Luke 5:11—ἀφέντες
πάντα). This idea is plainly implied in the great "Life of
Anthony," although the term itself is not used.[32] Eusebius
reports that Origen emphatically insisted on the evangelical
command of poverty—not to possess anything (VI, 3, 10).
Speaking of the Therapeutai, Eusebius uses the term: ἀπο-

στολικοὶ ἄνδρες, precisely because they were committed to ascetical practices (II, 17, 2). Richard Reitzenstein already has shown that for Eusebius the term "apostolic life" had a definite and established meaning: it meant asceticism.[33] And asceticism also implied a pneumatic endowment. In the phrase of Reitzenstein, "der vollkommene Asket ist ἐμπνευσθεὶς ὑπὸ ᾿Ιησοῦ ὡς οἱ ἀπόστολοι, er ist der ἀνὴρ ἀποστολικός."[34] Hermits in particular are the Apostolic people, and their life is apostolic. It was a commonplace in the literature of the fourth and fifth centuries.[35] Two examples will suffice at this point. Speaking of the persecutions under Valens, Socrates mentions the Novatian bishop Agelius: "he had led *an apostolic life*—βίον ἀποστολικὸν βιούς—because he always walked barefoot, and used but one coat, observing the injunctions of the Gospel" (IV, 9). Epiphanius uses the term in the same sense: ἀποταξάμενοι καὶ ἀποστολικὸν βίον βιοῦντες. Renunciation and "apostolic life" are equated. Actually Epiphanius was discussing the encratite sect of Apostolics: this name emphasizes their commitment to the Apostolic pattern of life. Epiphanius sharply exposes their exclusiveness and intolerance, but admits that the pattern of renunciation is truly apostolic. Apostles had no possessions: ἀκτήμονες ὑπάρχοντες. And the Saviour himself, while in the flesh never acquired anything earthly: οὐδὲν ἀπὸ τῆς γῆς ἐκτήσατο (*Panar.*, haeres. XLI, al. LXI, c. 3, 4).

It is safe to conclude that the expression "the disciples of the Apostles" is used in the "Life of Blessed Aphou" only to denote their strict ascetical manner of life. They were ἀποστολικοὶ ἄνδρες. Surely, there is nothing *"bien Audien"* in the phrase, and the whole argument of Drioton is based on a sheer misunderstanding.

Finally, Drioton calls attention to the fact that the community of Aphou's teachers probably came to its end approximately at the time in which, according to Epiphanius, Audian communities declined. It is a lame argument: a mere coincidence in time does not prove anything, neither identity nor even connection. Moreover, there is no evidence that the Audian movement ever expanded to Egypt. It is significant that no enemy of the Egyptian "Anthropomorphites" ever suggested that they had any sectarian connection, even in the heat of strife, although, of course, it would have been a good argument in the struggle. Drioton simply begins with the assumption that Audians were the only source from which "Anthropomorphite" convictions could have come. He does not consider the possibility that the allegedly "Anthropomorphite" arguments could be derived from some other source. Drioton is compelled to admit that Aphou's own position was much more qualified than that of the historic Audians. And yet he finds his position to be "heretical," although it is not clear what exactly he regards as heretical in the exposition given in the "Life."

To sum up, Drioton's arguments cannot substantiate his claim that Aphou came from the Audian background, that his teachers were but "authentic adherents of a disappearing sect"—"les adhérents authentiques d'un schisme finissant." One cannot but regret that Drioton put his unwarranted assumption into the very title of his otherwise competent and interesting article: "La discussion d'un moine anthropomorphite audien. . . ." This assumption so blinded Drioton that he failed to grasp the true subject of this "discussion" and to discern its actual theme and its internal structure.

III

The theological discussion between Apa Aphou and Archbishop Theophilus is the crucial and most significant part of the "Life." Let us, first of all, quote the relevant part of the document in full.[36]

And it came to pass, then, that, while yet abiding

with the wild beasts, he went out for the preaching of Holy Easter. And he heard an expression (λέξις) which was not in accord with the knowledge of the Holy Spirit, so that he was much troubled by that discourse. And, indeed, all those who heard it were afflicted and troubled. But the angel of the Lord commanded the blessed Aphou not to disregard the word, saying to him: "Thou art ordered by the Lord to go to Alexandria to set this word aright." And that word was as follows: the preacher, as if he were exalting the glory of God in his address, had recalled the weakness of man and had said: "*It is not the image of God which we men bear.*"

When he heard that, the blessed Aphou was filled with the Holy Spirit and departed for the city of Alexandria, wearing a wornout tunic. Blessed Aphou stood at the bishop's gate for three days, and no one let him in, for they took him for a common man (ἰδιώτης). Then one of the clerics took notice of him, observing his patience and perceived that he was a man of God. He entered within and informed the archbishop, saying, "Behold, a poor man is at the gate and says that he wishes to meet you, but we have not dared to take him to you, for he has not suitable clothing upon him." But immediately, as though he had been impelled by God, the archbishop ordered that they bring him to him. And when the latter was before him, he asked him to state his case. He answered: "May my Lord bishop bear the word of his servant with love and patience (ἐν ἀγάπῃ καὶ ἀνοχῇ)." He said to him: "Speak." Blessed Aphou replied: "I know of your soul's kindness (χρηστότητα) and that you are a thoughtful man. That is the reason for my approaching your highness. I am certain that you will not contemn the word of piety, even though it come from such a poor man as I." And

Theophilus, the archbishop, said to him: "How
reprobate is he who shall be mad enough to reject
God's word for the sake of a trifle."

Aphou answered him: "Let my Lord command
that the original (ἴσον) of the sermon be read
to me, wherein I heard the sentence (λέξις) that
was not in agreement with the Scriptures inspired
by God. Personally, I did not believe (οὐ
πιστεύω) that it had come from you, but I thought
that the clerk (συγγραφεὺς) had committed a
scribal error, regarding which a goodly number of
pious people blunder to the point of being greatly
troubled."[37] Then Apa Theophilus, the archbishop,
gave an order. The original (ἴσον) of the sermon
was brought to him. When the reading had begun,
that phrase was reached. Then Apa Aphou bowed
down, saying: "This sentence like that is not correct; I, on the other hand, will maintain that it is
in the image of God that all men have been
created." The Archbishop replied: "How is it
that you alone have spoken against this reading,
and that there has not been anyone in agreement
with you?" Apa Aphou said: "But indeed I am
sure that you will be in agreement with me and
will not argue with me."

The Archbishop said: "How could you say of an
Ethiopian that he is the image of God, or of a leper,
or of a cripple, or of a blind man?"

Blessed Aphou replied: "If you proclaim that in
such fashion, you will be denying that which He
said, namely, 'Let us make man in our likeness and
in our image' (Gen. 1:26)."

The Archbishop replied: "Far be it! but I believe
that Adam alone was created in His likeness and
image, but that his children whom he begot after

him do not resemble him." Apa Aphou replied,
saying: "Moreover, after God had established the
covenant with Noah following the flood, He said
to him: 'whoever sheds human blood, his own will
be shed in return, for man had been created in the
image of God' (Gen. 9:6)."

The Archbishop said: "I hesitate to say of an ailing
man or . . . that he bears the image of God, Who
is impassible and self-sufficient, while (the former)
squats outside and performs his necessities (παρα-
σκευάζει—cf. I Sam. 24:4, LXX). How could
you think of him (as being one) with God, the
true light whom nothing can surpass?"

Aphou said to him: "If you mention this too, one
may say of the body of Christ that it is not what
you say it is. For the Jews will claim: 'How do you
take a bit of bread which the earth had so labori-
ously produced, and then believe and say that this
is the body of the Lord?' " The Archbishop said
to him: "That is not the case, for it is truly bread
before we elevate it above the altar (θυσιαστή-
ριον); only after we have elevated it above the
altar and have invoked God upon them, does the
bread become the body of Christ and the cup become
the blood, according as He said to His disciples:
'Take ye and eat, this is my body and my blood'.
And then do we believe." Apa Aphou said to him:
"Just as it is necessary to have faith in that, it is
necessary to have faith . . . that man has been created
. . . in the likeness (and) image (of) God. For He
Who said, 'I am the bread which is come from
heaven', is also He Who said, 'whoever will shed
human blood, his own will be shed in return, for
man has been created in the image of God'. Because
of the glory of God's greatness, whoever. . . capable
of arranging that something. . . to him. . . his. . .
(will establish) it. . . and because of the weakness

of man's insignificance according to the natural frailty of which we are aware. If we think, for example, of a king who will give orders and a likeness (εἰκὼν) will be painted, and all will proclaim that it is the image of the king, but at the same time all know that it is wood and colors, for it does not raise its nose (head), like man, nor are its ears like those of the king's countenance, nor does it speak like the king. And all these weaknesses which belong to it nobody remembers out of respect for the king's judgment, because he has proclaimed: 'it is my image'. On the contrary, if anyone dare deny it (ἀρνεῖν), on the plea that it is not the king's image, he will be executed (killed) for having slighted it. Furthermore, the authorities are mustered concerning it and give praise to bits of wood and to colors, out of respect to the king. Now, if such things happen to an image which has no spirit, neither does it stir, being... delusive (ἀντίθετος), how much more, then, (to) man, in whom abides the Spirit of God, and who is active and honored above all the animals which are upon the earth; but because of the diversity of elements and colors . . . and of weaknesses which in us are... for us on account of our salvation; for it is not possible for any one of these latter to slight the glory which God has given us, according to the word of Paul: 'As for man, it is not proper that he cover his head (because he is the image and glory of God)' (I Cor. 11:7)."

When he heard these words, the blessed Archbishop arose and bent his head, saying: "This is fitting that instruction come from those who search in solitude, for, as for us, the reasonings of our hearts are mixed in us, to the point that we err completely in ignorance."

And immediately he wrote within all the country,

> retracting that phrase, saying: "It is erroneous and proceeds from my lack of intelligence in this respect."

It is not difficult to put this episode in a proper chronological setting. The preaching which Aphou attended on Easter day was, obviously, the reading of that Festal "Epistle" of Theophilus, which, according to Sozomen, so strongly offended and irritated the Desert monks. In this epistle, says Sozomen, Theophilus "took occasion to state that God ought to be regarded as incorporeal, and alien to human form" (VIII. 11). To the same effect he preached himself in his church (cf. also Socrates, VI. 7). This Festal Epistle of Theophilus—for the year 399—is not preserved. Yet, Gennadius gives an extensive resumé of it: *sed et Adversum Anthropomorphitas haereticos, qui dicunt Deum humana figura et membris constare, disputatione longissima confutans, et divinarum Scripturarum testimoniis arguens et convincens, ostendit Deum incorruptibilem et incorporeum juxta fidem Patrum credendum, nec ullis omnino membrorum lineamentis compositum, et ob id nihil ei in creaturis simile per substantiam, neque cuiquam incorruptibilitatem suae dedisse naturae, sed esse omnes intellectuales naturas corporeas, omnes corruptibiles, omnes mutabiles, ut ille solus corruptibilitati et mutabilitati non subjacet, "qui solus habet immortalitatem"* (*de scriptoribus ecclesiasticis*, XXXIV, p. 74 Richardson). The same Epistle is mentioned by John Cassian. *Coll.* X. 2: *Theophili praedictae urbis episcopi solemnes epistulae commearunt, quibus cum denuntiatione paschali ineptam quoque Anthropomorphitarum haeresim longa disputatione disseruit eamque copioso sermone destruxit.* Cassian then proceeds to the description of the commotion produced in monastic circles by this sharp and heavy epistle, especially *in heremo Scitii:* in no monastery there, except one, was this epistle permitted to be read, publicly or privately: *legi- aut recitari.* The Archbishop himself was suspected and

condemned—*velut haeresi gravissima depravatus:* he contradicted the Holy Scripture—*impugnare sanctae scripturae
sententiam videretur.* Was it not written that man was
created in the image of God?

The meeting between Aphou and Theophilus took place,
surely, *before* that tumultuous intervention of angry monks
which is so vividly described both by Socrates and Sozomen.[38]
Indeed, it is difficult to conceive that such a peaceful interview as is described in the "Life of Blessed Aphou" could
have taken place at a time when a hectic controversy was
already raging everywhere in the monastic colonies of Egypt.
Moreover, this interview would have been superfluous after
Theophilus had changed his attitude. Again, according to the
"Life," Aphou was the first to present objections to Theophilus concerning his "preaching." Aphou's intervention was
his individual move, based on a private revelation. At that
time Aphou was dwelling, apparently, somewhere in the
neighborhood of Oxyrhynchus—he calls himself "a man of
Pemdje," which refers rather to his residence than to his
origin. It was in Oxyrhynchus that he heard the reading of
Theophilus's epistle. Aphou's intervention had no direct connection with that general commotion *in eremo Scitii* of which
John Cassian spoke.

There is an obvious discrepancy between our sources.
Socrates and Sozomen present the story as that Theophilus
was frightened by the monks and then yielded to their pressure—to condemn Origen. The name of Origen does not
occur in the "Life" of Aphou. The hagiographer insists that
Theophilus was moved by Aphou's arguments and "immediately" retracted his unfortunate statement—"has written
to all in the country." It is reasonable to assume that Theophilus had various contacts with individuals before the
monastic multitudes arrived. In any case, Aphou is nowhere
mentioned in this connection, apart from the "Life." On
the other hand, it is highly improbable that the whole episode
of the monastic tumult could be completely omitted by a

· close contemporary of the event. It is more probable that the
"Life of Blessed Aphou" was written much later, when the
memories of the trouble had faded away, and by a writer
who was interested only in the ascetical exploits of his saintly
hero and in his pastoral work in the community of Oxyrhynchus. Aphou's visit to Theophilus is presented in the
context of his biography, and not in the perspective of the
history of his time.

It is both curious and significant that, according to the
"Life," Aphou took exception to one particular expression,
or a λέξις, in the epistle of Theophilus. In his conversation
with the Archbishop he was concerned solely with the concept of God's image in man. He did not develop or defend
any "Anthropomorphite" thesis. The sting of his argument
was directed against the denial of God's image *in man,* and
there was no word whatever about any "human form" *in
God.* Aphou only contended that man, even in his present
condition and in spite of all his misery and destitution, had
to be regarded still as being created in the image of God,
and must be, for that reason, respected. Aphou was primarily
concerned with man's dignity and honor. Theophilus, on the
other hand, was embarrassed by man's misery and depravity:
could an Ethiopian or a cripple be regarded as being "in the
image of God," he asked.

Theophilus appears to have held the view that the "image
of God" had been lost by man in the Fall and that, accordingly, the children of Adam were not (pro)created in the
image. It is precisely this opinion which was sharply exposed
and refuted by Epiphanius, both in his *Ancoratus* and in the
Panarion, in the section on the Audians. Let us recall that
both works were written in the seventies, that is, long before
the outbreak of the Origenistic and the Anthropomorphite
troubles in Egypt.[39] Epiphanius's own position in this matter
was balanced and cautiously qualified. Man was created in
the image of God, κατ᾽ εἰκόνα,—this is a Scriptural truth
which cannot be doubted or ignored. But one should not

attempt to decide in which part of man this κατ' εἰκόνα is situated, nor should one restrict this image to one part or aspect of the human constitution, to the exclusion of others. One has to confess faithfully the presence of this "image" in man, lest we despise the Divine grant and appear unfaithful to Him: ἵνα μὴ τὴν χάριν τοῦ Θεοῦ ἀθετήσωμεν καὶ ἀπιστήσωμεν Θεῷ. What God has said is truth, even if it escapes our understanding in certain respects: εἰ καὶ ἐξέφυγε τὴν ἡμῶν ἔννοιαν ἐν ὀλίγοις λόγοις. In any case, to deny the κατ' εἰκόνα is contrary to Catholic faith and to the mind of the Holy Church: οὐ πιστὸν οὔτε τῆς ἁγίας τοῦ Θεοῦ ἐκκλησίας (*Ancoratus,* 55; *Panarion, haeres. LXX, al. L,* ch. 2). Now, proceeds Epiphanius, there are many who would attempt to localize the image, either only in the soul, or in the body alone, or else in the virtues of man. All these attempts go astray from tradition. The κατ' εἰκόνα is not exclusively in the soul, nor exclusively in the body, but it would be wrong to deny that it is also in the body and in the soul: ἀλλ' οὔτε λέγομεν τὸ σῶμα μὴ εἶναι κατ' εἰκόνα οὔτε τὴν ψυχήν. In other words, the "image" is in the whole man: man is created κατ' εἰκόνα Θεοῦ, and not just one part of man. Finally, there are also those who concede that God's image was in Adam, but it was lost when Adam was expelled from Paradise: ἀπώλεσε. Great is the licentious phantasy of those people, exclaims Epiphanius: πολλὴ τίς ἐστι τῶν ἀνθρώπων μυθοποιία. Indeed, we are obliged to believe that τὸ κατ' εἰκόνα is still in man, and in the whole man: ἐν παντὶ δὲ μάλιστα καὶ οὐχ ἁπλῶς (ἔν τινι μέρει). But how and where exactly it resides is known to God alone, Who has granted it by His grace, κατὰ χάριν. The "image" does not perish, although it may be polluted and marred by sins. Then Epiphanius gives his Scriptural references: Gen. 2:6, I Cor. 11:4, Jas. 3:8 (*Panar. LXX,* ch. 3; cf. *Ancor.,* 56, 57). It should be noted at this point that the same texts (except for Jas.) were quoted also by Aphou, in his conversation with

Theophilus. Even more significant is the fact that in his *Ancoratus* Epiphanius uses the same Eucharistic analogy which we find in the "Life" of Aphou. The κατ' εἰκόνα is the grant of God, and God must be trusted. The κατ' εἰκόνα can be understood by analogy: ἀπὸ τῶν ὁμοίων. Then comes a brief description of the Institution. Now, says Epiphanius, ὁρῶμεν ὅτι οὐκ ἴσον ἐστὶν οὐδὲ ὅμοιον οὐ τῇ ἐνσάρκῳ εἰκόνι οὐ τῇ ἀοράτῳ Θεότητι οὐ τοῖς χαρακτῆρσι τῶν μελλῶν. But we simply trust the words of Christ (*Ancoratus, 57*).

Epiphanius takes a firm stand: according to Scripture man is created "in the image" of God, and it is against the Catholic rule of faith to doubt or to deny that. But this "image," τὸ κατ' εἰκόνα, is, as it were, a mystery, a gracious gift of God, and this mystery must not be rationalized—it must be apprehended by faith. From this point of view Epiphanius objects both to "Anthropomorphite" literalism in exegesis, and to the vagaries of Origenistic spiritualism. This was the position he maintained at Jerusalem in 394. He stated plainly his argument in his letter to John, which is extant only in the Latin translation of St. Jerome. Among various errors of Origen Epiphanius mentions also this: *ausus est dicere perdidisse imaginem Dei Adam... et illum solum factum esse ad imaginem Dei qui plasmatus esset ex humo et uxorem ejus, eos vero qui conciperentur in utero et non ita nascerentur ut Adam Dei non habere imaginem.* Against this "malicious interpretation"—*maligna interpretatione*—Epiphanius quotes Scripture: an array of texts follows: Gen. 9:4-6; Ps. 38:7; Sap. 2:23; Jas. 3:8-9; I Cor. 11:7. Epiphanius concludes: *nos autem, dilectissime, credimus his quae locutus est Dominus, et scimus quod in cunctis hominibus imago Dei permaneat, ipsique concedimus nosse in qua parte homo ad imaginem Dei conditus est* (Epiph. *ad Iohannem episcopum,* inter *epist. Hieronymi,* LI, 6.15-7.4). It was but natural that John suspected Epiphanius of an "Anthropomorphite" leaning, as Jerome informs us: *volens illum suspectum facere stultissimae haereseos.* Jerome recalls the dramatic clash between John and Epiphanius, and the sermon of John directed against the Bishop of Cyprus. Epiphanius had to restate his position: *cuncta (inquit) quae locutus est collegio frater, aetate filius meus, contra Anthropomorphitarum haeresin, bene et fideliter locutus est, quae mea quoque damnantur voce; sed aequum est, ut quomodo hanc haeresin condemnamus, etiam Origenis perversa dogmata condemnemus* (Hieron., *Contra Iohannem Hierosolymitanum,* cap. II). Although Jerome wrote some years after the events and his treatise is an emotional and venomous invective, we may assume that the position of Epiphanius was stated correctly. It should be added that Theophilus was originally suspicious of Epiphanius too, and "accused him of entertaining low thoughts of God, by supposing Him to have a human form." He reconciled himself and even allied with Epiphanius, but later, after 399, when he changed his position (*Socr.* VI. 10).

Now, let us return to the "Life of Blessed Aphou." Aphou's position in the dispute appears to be very similar to that of Epiphanius. His crucial emphasis is simply this: the reality of the "image" in general is not compromised by its factual inadequacy. An image of the king, which is itself lifeless and material, is still the king's image, the image of a living person, and must be, accordingly, respected. Moreover, man is not a lifeless image, but in him abides the Spirit of God. Again, an official image of the king must be regarded as such on account of the king's declaration, "this is my image." And, in regard to man, this is warranted by God himself, according to the Scriptures. Unfortunately, the text of the "Life" is in this passage corrupt and deficient, but it seems that Aphou had here also a reference to the Incarnation. Aphou's Eucharistic argument was to the same effect: do not trust appearances, but trust the word of God. In the Eucharist we actually see bread, but by faith we behold the Body, and believe it in obedience to the Dominical witness: "this is my Body." In the same way has God declared concerning man: "he is created in My image." In fact, Aphou does not go beyond this statement and does not try to locate the image or to rationalize the mystery. There is nothing specifically "Anthropomorphite" in his exposition. On the other hand, Aphou's reasoning is so close to that of Epiphanius that it may suggest a direct dependence. It is fair to assume that Epiphanius' writings and letters had considerable circulation at that time, and that, if certain people in the Egyptian communities were reading at that time Origen, others read his opponents, of which Epiphanius was the most venerable and conspicuous.

We have to identify now those people denying τὸ κατ' εἰκόνα in man after the Fall whom Epiphanius was so sharply and angrily refuting already in the *Panarion*. He probably had in view Origen and his followers, those especially among the hermits in Egypt. In the section of the *Panarion* on Origen Epiphanius accused him briefly of the contention that Adam had lost the κατ' εἰκόνα (*haeres. LXIV, al. XLIV, cap. 4*). In fact, the thought of Origen was more complex and qualified than a blunt denial. Moreover, one finds in his writings certain passages in which Origen strongly insisted that the "image" simply cannot have been totally lost or effaced and remains even in the soul, in which a "terrestrial image" is, by ignorance or resistance, superimposed over the κατ' εἰκόνα Θεοῦ (*Contra Celsum*, IV. 83; *Homil. in Gen.*, XIII. 3, 4). However, Origen spoke primarily of the "interior man"—the κατ' εἰκόνα was restricted to the νοῦς or the ἡγεμονικόν, and the body was emphatically excluded.[40] In the Greek theology of the fourth century there was an unresolved ambiguity concerning the image of God. One must be very careful at this point: the writers of that time did not claim that man *was an image*, but rather that he was created or shaped *in the image*. Thus, the emphasis was on conformity: an image is a true image when it actually mirrors or reflects adequately that reality of which it is held or expected to be the image. Accordingly, there was always a strong dynamic stress in the concept of the image. The question could not fail to arise, in what sense and to what extent could this dynamic relationship continue or persist when the conformity was conspicuously broken, and fallen man went astray and frustrated his vocation. This ambiguity could be obviated by distinguishing carefully the "image" and the "likeness," or "similitude." But this was never done consistently, nor by all. In fact, the theology of the image was intimately related to the theology of Sin and Redemption, and, again, the theology of Sin was not yet adequately elaborated at that time, either in the East or in the West. There was an obvious tension between different motives in the thought of St. Athanasius, especially in his early period. In the *de Incarnatione* St. Athanasius presents the Fall as a total and radical catastrophe: τὸ μὲν τῶν ἀνθρώπων γένος ἐφθείρετο. Ὁ δὲ λογικὸς καὶ κατ᾽ εἰκόνα γενόμενος ἄνθρωπος ἠφανίζετο (6. I). Fallen man was, as it were, reduced to a sub-human status: ἡ γὰρ παράβασις τῆς ἐντολῆς εἰς τὸ κατὰ φύσιν αὐτοὺς ἐπέστρεφεν, ἵνα ὥσπερ οὐκ ὄντες γεγόνασιν (4. 4). The κατ᾽ εἰκόνα was a grant of grace, and this grant was lost or withdrawn. The κατ᾽ εἰκόνα had to be restored or even re-created: the verbs used by St. Athanasius were: ἀνακαινίζειν and ἀνα-κτίζειν. According to St. Athanasius, τὸ κατ᾽ εἰκόνα was, as it were, superimposed over the "nature" in man which was intrinsically mutable and fluid—φύσις ρευστὴ καὶ δια-λυομένη. The stability of human composition was insured, in the state of innocence, by its "participation" in the Logos. In the state of estrangement, which was the root of sin, this participation was discontinued.[41] Actually, St. Athanasius wanted to emphasize the depth and radicalness of sin: fallen man is no more man in the full sense, and this is manifested most conspicuously in his actualized mortality, an inherent consequence of the estrangement, the ultimate sting of corruption, on the very verge of annihilation.[42] The same ambiguity remains in the theology of St. Cyril of Alexandria.

In a sense, according to his interpretation, man still is κατ᾽ εἰκόνα, as a "rational" creature endowed with freedom. But other basic aspects or features of the "image," and above all—incorruptibility, were lost, and the "image" itself was distorted or "falsified"—παρεχαράττετο, like a counterfeit coin or seal. Like St. Athanasius, St. Cyril uses the ambiguous word: ἀφανίζειν to characterize the impact of sin on τὸ κατ᾽ εἰκόνα, and it is difficult to detect his proper intention, since the word may mean both a superficial obliteration and total destruction.[43]

It is beyond the scope of the present study to analyze at full length the problem of the κατ᾽ εἰκόνα in the Greek theology of the fourth and following centuries. This brief and rather sketchy survey will suffice, however, for our immediate objective: to explain the position of Theophilus. Obviously, he followed St. Athanasius, just as St. Cyril did later. The brief summary of his controversial epistle given by Gennadius, which we have quoted earlier, is helpful. The emphasis of Theophilus was the same as that of St. Athanasius: the basic contrast between God, Eternal and "Immortal," and man, mutable, corruptible, and unstable, in man's fallen condition. He is no longer "in the image" after the Fall. Moreover, the Alexandrinian Fathers always tended to restrict τὸ κατ᾽ εἰκόνα to the "interior man," to the spiritual aspect of his existence. This was, undoubtedly, an inheritance from Origen.

To sum up: in the conversation between Aphou and Theophilus we have a confrontation of two different conceptions concerning τὸ κατ᾽ εἰκόνα Θεοῦ, that is, concerning the nature and character of "the image of God in man." And we may guess that this was the major issue in that violent conflict which came to be known as the "Anthropomorphite Controversy." No doubt, there were in Egypt also rustic monks who were addicted to literal interpretation of Scriptural images—*simplicitate rustica,* in the phrase of St. Jerome, which refers, however, to the situation in Palestine. But there was a deeper core of theological contention: there was an opposition to the whole tradition of Origen. W. Bousset observed rightly: *"Wenn des Theophilus Bekämpfung des Anthropomorphismus eine so grosse Erregung bei den sketischen Mönchen hervorruft* (Cassian, *Coll.* X), *so handelt es hier eigentlich nicht um das Dogma, sondern um eine Lebensfrage für die von der Gottesschau lebende enthusiastische Frömmigkeit."[44] The story of Sarapion, told by Cassian (*Coll.* X. 3), is illuminating in this respect.[45]

In the light of the information we can derive from the "Life of Blessed Aphou" we can understand that rather enigmatic phrase with which Theophilus, according to both Socrates and Sozomen, managed to placate the angry monks. "Going to the monks, he in a conciliatory tone thus addressed them: 'In seeing you, I behold the face of God'. The utterance of this saying moderated the fury of these men and they replied: if you really admit that God's countenance is such as ours, anathematize Origen's book" (Socr. VI. 7—οὕτως ὑμᾶς, ἔφη, εἶδον ὡς Θεοῦ πρόσωπον; cf. Sozom. VIII. 11). Indeed, it could be no more than a flattering compliment, as Tillemont has interpreted it.[46] And, of course, it was a Biblical phrase: Gen. 33:10—Jacob meeting Esau—"for therefore I have seen thy face, as though I had seen the face of God." But it does seem to be more than just a compliment. Let us remember now the phrase in the epistle of Theophilus to which Aphou took exception: "It is not the image of God which we men bear." In his rejoinder Aphou insisted that the glory of God could be perceived even in that inadequate image which is man. It seems strange that angry monks be placated by the address of Theophilus, if it was no more than a courteous phrase. In fact, it was just to the point, it was a disguised retraction of his offensive phrase in the controversial epistle that had irritated the monks. It seems that the monks understood it.[47]

According to the "Life" of Aphou, Theophilus was impressed by his arguments, admitted his error, and issued a new encyclical. No such encyclical epistle is known. In his later Festal Epistles, which are preserved only in the Latin translation of Jerome, Theophilus did not discuss the problem of the image at all. They were concerned mainly with the refutation of Origen.[48] But we can trust the "Life" and admit that Theophilus was impressed by Aphou himself. This rustic anchorite was a wise man. Aphou, on his side, praised the humility of Theophilus which allowed him to acknowledge his error. The story may be embellished a bit. Aphou declined the invitation to stay in Alexandria for a longer time and went back to his own place. After three years the see of Pemdje became vacant and Theophilus appointed Aphou, although another candidate had been nominated by the community. There is nothing improbable in that. Already in the time of St. Athanasius it was usual to appoint monks to episcopal position. Theophilus had done this not once. The best known case is, of course, that of Dioscurus, one of the Tall Brothers, whom he made bishop of Hermopolis.

The "Life of Blessed Aphou" comes, obviously, from Coptic circles.

The information on the Anthropomorphite Controversy which we derive from Greek and Latin sources is biased and onesided. This is true especially of John Cassian, a "pious journalist," as René Draguet has labelled him.[49] He was on the Origenist side in the conflict. He wrote from the Evagrian point of view: "noi in Cassiano rileggiamo Evagrio," rightly says a modern student of John Cassian.[50] The picture of Egyptian monasticism presented in the *Historia Lausiaca* is also drawn from the Greek point of view, "in the spirit of Evagrius," as Draguet puts it.[51] The case of the "Anthropomorphites" has been polemically misrepresented since that time. The controversy was presented as a clash between the rustic *simpliciores* and the learned. This aspect of the case should not be ignored or denied. But there was much more than that: there was also a clash of theological traditions, and a clash of spiritual conceptions. The "Life" of Aphou

helps us to grasp this theological perspective of the controversy, and this constitutes the high historical value of this
peculiar hagiological document.

A Postscript

1.   The valuable book by Antoine Guillaumont, *Les
'Kephalaia Gnostica' d'Evagre le Pontique et l'Histoire de
l'Origénisme chez les Grecs et les Syriens* (= "Patristica
Sorbonensia" 5, Editions du Seuil, Paris, 1962), appeared
after the present article had been delivered for publication.
Guillaumont has a brief paragraph on the Anthropomorphite
controversy (pp. 59-61). He does not believe that the
Anthropomorphites of Egypt had any relation to the Audians:
"Cette filiation est difficile à établir historiquement. Il parait
plus naturel de ne voir dans ce mouvement qu'une réaction
spontanée contre la théorie evagrienne de la prière pure—réaction comprehensible de la part de gens simples qui pouvaient
craindre que le Dieu de la Bible, qui a fati l'homme à son
image, n'ait plus de place dans une piété si haute," p. 61,
note 62. Guillaumont quotes my article of 1960 with general
approval, but regrets that I have limited myself to the text
of Cassian and did not mention Evagrius and his treatise
"On Prayer." In fact, my only purpose in that article of
mine—a brief communication at the Congress in Munich,
sorely restricted in space—was to describe the position of
Sarapion and to stress the importance of the conception of the
"image of God" in man for the understanding of the whole
conflict. On the other hand, Guillaumont refers to the article
of Drioton, but does not seem to have appreciated the
significance of the "Life of Aphou," le "curieux document,"
as he labels it (p. 62, note 63).

2.   βούβαλος (or βούβαλις) is *not a buffalo* (as it has
been often mistranslated, for instance by Dom E. Pichery, in
his edition of the 'Conferences' of Cassian, in the "Sources

Chrétiennes"—*le boeuf sauvage!*), but antelope, *bubalis mauretanica;* see the Lexicon of Liddell-Scott, *sub voce.* In English the word "buffalo" may denote both a kind of African stag or gazelle, and the wild ox (cf. Webster's Dictionary).

The Hagia Sophia Churches

I

THE FIRST TEMPLE in Constantinople dedicated under the name of "Holy Wisdom" was possibly designed by Constantine himself. The building was however completed much later and the "Great Church" was first consecrated only in 360, under Constantius, by an Arian bishop. It is not at all clear when the name "Hagia Sophia" was first given to the church. Socrates says only: "which is now called Sophia" (II, 43). It is quite possible that the "Great Church" in the beginning had no special name, and the name of Sophia came to prominence later; it was probably a current connotation rather than an intentional dedication.

The name, however, by no means was an accident. Some archeologist of old guessed that the name was rather an abstract idea or a Divine attribute, and that Constantine used to dedicate temples to "abstract ideas,"—Wisdom, Power,

"The Hagia Sophia Churches" originally appeared as a résumé of a lecture entitled "Christ, the Wisdom of God, in Byzantine Theology" in *Résumés des Rapports et Communications, Sixième Congrès International d'Études Byzantines* (Paris, 1940), pp. 255-260. Reprinted by permission. This résumé was only an introduction to a larger paper which was to be presented at the Byzantine Congress at Alger in 1939. The Congress, however, did not take place.

131

Peace. All this is but a misunderstanding. The name of
Wisdom is a *biblical* name, and all these three "abstract"
names are used in St. Paul, as names of Christ: Sophia
[Σοφία], Dynamis [Δύναμις], Eirênê [Εἰρήνη]. Passages
in the Old Testament where the Wisdom of God was
described as a person (and specially the VIII-th chapter of
Proverbs) were from an early date regarded as referring
to Christ, the Incarnate Word. We find this in St. Justin.
The other suggestion, that Wisdom meant rather the Holy
Spirit (the Spirit of Wisdom, of course), found in Theophilus
of Antioch and St. Irenaeus, was not used ever by any of the
later writers, and the identification of "Sophia-Wisdom"
as of one of the names of the Second Person of the Holy
Trinity became the common place of Patristic exegesis and
theology. Origen regards the name "Wisdom" as the first
and principal name of the Son (*Comm. in Ioann.* I. 22).
Both "Wisdom" and "Power" are mentionned in the Symbol
of St. Gregory of Neo-Caesarea. In the IV-th century both
Arians and Orthodox agreed that the Holy Wisdom described
in the book of Proverbs was the Son of God. The eighth
chapter of Proverbs was one of the principal topics of dispute
throughout the whole IV-th century, and certainly the name
was known and comprehensible to all and was full of associations. Anyhow it was the name of Christ, and it was but
natural to give this name to the "Great Church."

Hagia Sophia was dedicated to Christ under the name
of Wisdom. There is no reason whatever to suspect any
change of dedication under Justinian. It is obvious that
Sophia was commonly regarded as the temple of Christ. It is
clearly shown in the famous story of the construction of
Justinian's Sophia: "Hagia Sophia," which means the Word
of God (ed. Preger, p. 74: καὶ ἔκτοτε ἔλαβε τὴν προση-
γορίαν ὁ ναὸς ῾Αγία Σοφία, ὁ Λόγος τοῦ Θεοῦ ἑρμη-
νευόμενος). It is hardly possible to speak of any specified
dedication of churches in Justinian's time or even later. A
church was usually dedicated simply to Our Lord or to the

Blessed Virgin, or else to the Saints. But it depended upon some peculiar conditions when any special dedication was stressed. The patronal festival was kept on the Anniversary of the dedication. In St. Sophia it was on the 23-rd of December, because the temple was consecrated under Justinian on the 26-th of December and again on the 24-th. Of course Christmas was chosen as the most suitable season. In the office for the Anniversary, as it is described in the Typik of the Great Church published by Dmitrievsky, there is nothing to suggest any special commemoration for the day; it is rather a general office for any Anniversary. And actually it was recommended for this purpose by Symeon of Salonica.

The churches dedicated to Holy Wisdom were quite numerous both in Byzantium and among the Slavs. On many occasions we have a direct proof that they were regarded as dedicated to Christ, the Word and the Wisdom. And there is no reason or hint whatever to suspect that any other dedication of the Sophia-churches was ever known or used in the Byzantine Church. Scholars were misled or confused by the unexpected and rather startling fact that in Russia the patronal festival in the Sophia-churches was kept on Our Lady's days, on the 8-th of September in Kiev (the Nativity of Our Lady) and on the 15-th of August in Novgorod (the Assumption). This seemed to suggest that these famous Cathedrals were dedicated to the Blessed Virgin, and that the name of Wisdom was applied to Her as well. Some scholars were inclined to see in that a special contribution of Russia to the theology of Wisdom. One has to object first that in earlier times the patronal festival both in Novgorod and Kiev was kept on the Anniversary of the dedication, as it is stated in old calendars. And secondly we are very fortunate to have some formal proofs that the patronal festival was transferred to the new dates quite late. In Kiev this occurred not before the restoration of the Hagia Sophia by Peter Mogila or even later. In Novgorod it took place under Archbishop Gennadius about the close of the XV-th century.

But even after that date the Novgorod Sophia was usually called the temple of the Wisdom and Word.

II

There are two distinct manners to represent the Wisdom of God in Byzantine iconography. First, Christ as Wisdom and Word under the image of an Angel (μεγάλης βουλῆς ἄγγελος, Is. IX. 6). Second, the personification of Wisdom, Divine or human, as a virgin. The first scheme is biblical, the second classical, and they are originally quite independent from each other.

The first one is very rare in early monuments. One has to mention the fresco in the catacombs in Karmuz, where the inscription is emphatic: ΣΟΦΙΑ ΙΣ ΧΣ. The representation is badly described and the whole monument not quite clear. One may interpret the image as a representation of Christ in the Old Testament similitude. One may compare it with the early document as "Shepherd" Hermas, in which the Son of God was described as an Angel and almost confused with Michel the Archangel (ὁ ἔνδοξος ἄγγελος). And one can understand easily why this image could not be very popular in early iconography. The main emphasis was rather on the historicity and reality of the presentation of Our Lord, and it was intended to convey to the worshipers the sound dogmatic idea. Symbolical images were rather definitely discouraged. This was the meaning of the 82nd canon of the Council in Trullo. The image of the Angel of the Great Council becomes popular and usual only in later Byzantine iconography, and is found often in Mistra and Athos, but only as an exception are we warranted to believe that the Angel was meant to represent Wisdom. One can mention only one fresco described by Charles Diehl at St. Stefano in Soleto, probably from the late XIV-th century. The angel has a chalice in his hand, which suggests an eucharistic interpretation (see Prov. IX, 2, which is referred to the Eucharist in the office of Good Thursday). But the inscription is plain: H ΑΓ. ΣΟΦΙΑ Ο ΛΟΓΟΣ. There are some interesting compositions in miniatures. But it is certain that in Byzantine art we never had any canonized scheme for the representation of Divine Wisdom.

The second composition, the personification, can be found first in the miniatures. It is enough to mention the famous Parisin. N. 139 (X-th cent.). But even here the classical motive was possibly amalgamated with the biblical. One can recall the vision of St. Cyril, where Wisdom was seen as a virgin (see Sap. Sal. VIII, 2). In monumental art the composition in Monreale has to be mentioned. All that does not suggest that the image of Wisdom had any special appeal to the Byzantine Christians. But a basis was provided for the further development of the topic in Russian iconography. The famous Novgorod icon of St. Sophia is hardly older than the late XV-th century. It is a peculiar kind of Deisis, where Christ is represented as Wisdom under the image of the Angel, and the Blessed Virgin and St. John the Baptist standing at His sides. The icon belongs to a very interesting series of the new Russian compositions of the XV-th and XVI-th centuries and is a new interpretation of some traditional Byzantine motives.

II
ASPECTS OF RUSSIAN CHURCH HISTORY

Russian Missions:
An Historical Sketch

I

IN A CERTAIN SENSE the whole history of Russia is a process of colonization, the peopling of a country or the settling of inhabitants in different parts of it. In this movement the Church took a creative part and not only did she follow the people but often she led them. Strangely enough, she led them even at the time when she seemed to be deserting them by withdrawing from the outer material world into the world of the spirit, for it frequently happened that the ascetics and hermits were the pioneers on the rough and half-wild virgin soil in the north and north-east of Russia. For them the dense forests served as a desert, but they were followed by the world from which they wished to escape and so they had to depart from their settlements and get away still farther, cutting into the very depths of the primeval forests. Thus the ascetic retreat from the world attracted, as it were, the advance of the world; a process which historians call monastic colonization.

"Russian Missions: An Historical Sketch" appeared in *The Christian East*, Vol. XIV, No. 1 (1933), pp. 30-41. Reprinted by permission of the author.

This was an important factor and moment in the social history of the Russian people, and at the same time it was a missionary process, that is, a geographical propagation and extension of the Church. The baptism of Russia cannot be looked upon as a single fact; it was rather an extensive process spread over centuries, a process of Christian occupation of new lands and territories. For a long time the Russian Church was in a state of constant movement, wandering about, practically leading a nomadic life and always entering into the lands of the unbaptized either simultaneously with the State or often before it. Up to the last the Russian Church was like an island in the midst of a pagan sea, and even inside Russia itself she was always a missionary Church. Missionary work, that is the calling of unbelievers to the faith, was a part of her daily life.

It was from Byzantium that the Russian Church received the request of carrying on this missionary work and to this end it adapted Byzantine methods.

This meant putting in the forefront the use of the vernacular or local dialects in preaching. In other words, it was evangelization as a way of awakening the new peoples to a Christian life, and at the same time it was an adaptation to a tradition of culture, but without any negation or suppression of national differences and peculiarities. By this means the Slavonic people, enlightened and baptized by the Byzantine missionaries, were drawn into the vortex of Byzantine civilization and yet did not lose their Slavonic features. (The history of the Georgian Church should be mentioned in this connection.)

Translation as a method of missionary influence is a major premise of Byzantine missionary work, and that method was adopted by the Russian civilizers and missionaries from the very beginning. In this respect the personality of St. Stephen of Perm, the civilizer of Zirian and a friend of St. Sergius (d. 1396), is most brilliant and expressive. Of his own accord he undertook a missionary journey through the district of Perm. He not only preached but even officiated in the vernacular, with which purpose in view he had to translate the holy scriptures and Church books, and to do this it was first necessary to work out a Zirian alphabet which he probably based upon the local Runic signs.

St. Stephen's idea was to create a local "Perm" Church in which all the spiritual forces of the newly civilized people would have revealed themselves and received their consecration. His immediate successors in the see of Perm were inspired by the same ideal, which, however, was not attained, his Zirian Orthodox Church being finally absorbed by the Russian Orthodox Church. It is indeed possible that St. Stephen wanted to give the Zirians somewhat more than they really needed or were able to absorb and retain. Not all peoples possess their own culture, or indeed can possess it, and that "can" or "cannot" is a bare historical fact. Not every people or tribe has its own spiritual words, its own creative style for biological and spiritual expressions and phenomena of different grades. These facts present great difficulties for missionary work and a missionary must possess great tact and sensitiveness in order to learn and find the right way.

In any case, however, it was the missionary ideal of St. Stephen of Perm that continued to be a typical guide in the Russian Church till quite recently. The Gospel was preached and divine service performed in many tongues.

Particularly noteworthy is the creation of an Orthodox Church for the Tartars with their own native clergy in the Kazan region. But the most brilliant example of that missionary nationalism is the creation of a Japanese Church, which grew up and still remains as one of the dioceses of the Russian patriarchate.

Missionary work must start first of all with translation, as it is always necessary to begin in the vernacular. The Gospel must be translated and reduced to writing, or at any rate related in the tongue of the country; but as the work

goes on questions arise. Is it necessary to translate the whole
Bible and the whole cycle of Church books as well as to
work out in each tongue the theological terminology which
is necessary for the translation of dogmatic formulæ? The
difficulty here lies in the fact that many of the tongues are
still undeveloped and insufficiently flexible and rich in their
vocabulary to be used in mystical and sacred quotations. The
missionaries often have not only to invent an alphabet but,
as it were, to invent and work out the tongue itself. Another
difficulty arises in translating into languages of non-Christian
civilizations, for there are many old associations and a lack
is felt of words to express the new conceptions because the
old words have too many old connotations. In any case a
missionary must have a great philological gift and sensitiveness; a loving and lively sense of the tongue; a desire and
power to penetrate into the foreign soul and understand it;
that is to say, one has in a certain sense to have the faculty
of sympathetic reincarnation.

The same is, no doubt, required from every pastor and
teacher in general, but the claim on these qualities in missionary work is especially acute. Very often missionaries have
to create and build up the civilization of the natives, for it
is often impossible to draw the line between evangelical
doctrines and everyday life. Too often it is necessary to
change or even to break up the whole structure or mode of
life which has become too closely amalgamated with the
pagan past and too firmly a part of daily life. Sometimes
it is necessary to isolate the neophytes from their own people, often for the sake of their own safety. Again, for them
to benefit from the preaching of the Gospel, it is important
to enlarge the mental outlook of a flock that is being sought
for, so as to arouse and elevate its requirements, and this
again is only possible by bringing them into touch with a
higher civilization which has already taken root. It is generally only by the acceptance of this higher civilization that
the hidden forces of a newly enlightened people can be

awakened. In experiments in real life one cannot draw a line between religious and worldly things. According to the inner logic of missionary work itself a missionary ought to enter into the daily life of his people. It is not wrong that a missionary should be involved in worldly business and cares; this is only wrong if he loses the true perspective of the Gospel and yields himself up to the spirit of the world. It is inevitable for the mission to come face to face with the State, *i.e.* to co-operate with it, or at least to work alongside the State's compulsory and organizing institutions, but it is difficult to say which is more difficult, to co-operate or to struggle. Help and facilities from the State generally rather complicate the inner work of a missionary. The application of direct force is not so dangerous, but the strength and power of the State unwittingly overawe, and superiority of culture attracts, with the result that the genuine simplicity of a Christian conversion and its growth is hampered and the *tempo* of missionary work becomes too rapid. Sometimes the mission inevitably enters into controversy with the State; for it may happen that the interest of the State demands delay in the Christianizing movement among younger nations; or sometimes, on the contrary, baptism acquires for the empire the means of forcing them into a central civilized political union. In the case of local dialects, too, the methods of evangelization may appear injurious from the point of view of the State. To find a way through all these difficulties and conflicts in the process of creating the Christian life is only possible by creative inspiration and sagacity.

II

The concrete tasks of Russian missionary activity were defined by the growth of the Empire. At first it was the evangelization of an inhabited country, above all of a Slavonic population. Then the movement spread into the region of the Finnish tribes. Strictly speaking, the conversion of the smaller Finnish tribes has never been completed. The influence of pagan inertia remained strong up to the last and was responsible for the fact of masses falling back to paganism after the Russian Revolution. In this respect the North-East of European Russia may be taken as an example. The religion of these Finnish tribes may be defined as animism with a strongly developed belief in magic and sorcery; in this sorcery and still more in the sorcerers themselves lie the chief causes of pagan stability.

In the sixteenth century the Russian Church came face to face with Islam, and especially in the time of Ivan the Terrible, after his conquests and annexation of the Tartar kingdoms along the river Volga. The meeting with Islam was rather hostile. It is true that many Tartar races accepted baptism at once, but on the whole the mass of the Tartars remained faithful to the traditions of their fathers, and it was only for the sake of preserving their national characteristics that the principle of toleration was advanced against any intrusion of the Orthodox mission into the secluded world of the Tartars. The right course of making missionary influence felt was found here only when the ideal of Tartar Orthodoxy was brought forward openly and fearlessly. But one has to bear in mind that the presence of a Russian mission amongst the local Moslems was only one of the incidents of the great world struggle of Christianity with Islam, and that it was always affected by the broad religious and political perspective. The regions along the river Volga remained the experimental fields for missionary work up to the last. Here the old paganism was still preserved amongst the natives, and all this country overlooked Asia with its religious zeal and inertia.

Here the Orthodox mission for the first time came into touch with the Lamaism of the Kalmuck who migrated to the province of Saratov at the end of the seventeenth century. In the eighteenth century the circumstances of missionary activities were not, in general, favorable: the State interfered too powerfully with the affairs of the mission, pursuing its own interests, that is to say, getting the maximum benefit for itself from the people. Often enough, indeed, the State put obstacles in the way of the missionary work, especially among Moslems, and generally speaking the eighteenth century was a difficult period in the history of the Russian Church, which was somewhat restrained by the supervision of the State and weakened materially by the secularization of her property. Only a few held fast at the period of general indifference and spiritual backwardness. The advance started again only at the beginning of the nineteenth century. This delay is very important to note. With it are bound up the chief difficulties of the mission of the nineteenth century. A new tradition began and was established.

As a matter of fact it was only at the beginning of this nineteenth century that the mission commenced its development in the provinces along the river Volga. This was above all due to the activities of the Bible Society and its branches. In the first decade of the nineteenth century the New Testament was published in the following translations: Nogay, Tartar, Tchuvash, Morduates, Tcheremiss, Kalmuck, Zirian, Votiak and Korel. It must, however, be noted that these translations are far from being always satisfactory and reliable.

At that same time native schools were opened and teaching was commenced in the local dialects. Special courses were organized in ecclesiastical seminaries for the training of teachers and the more serious study of the native environment and the work to be undertaken by the mission were organized in the Kazan Ecclesiastical Academy (founded in 1842). Here a special section of missionary training was opened in 1854. In the year 1867 the missionary brotherhood of St. Gouri was also started, which occupied itself with the external and internal arrangements of the mission and especially with the publishing work and the starting of schools. In 1833 it was generally recognized in principle that the performance of divine services in the local tongues was admissible and desirable. A whole series of brotherhoods came into being in other dioceses and a network of native schools began to spread abroad. The missionary struggle with Islam was particularly difficult because of the well-developed network of Moslem schools and the great zeal of the Moslem clergy. In order to succeed it was generally necessary for the missionaries to break up the primitive form of life and to work out new and independent ways of social life for the neophytes.

One must point out yet another object of missionary activities within the boundaries of European Russia, the enlightenment of the Eskimo who led a nomadic life on marshy plains in the Government of Archangel. Since the twenties of the nineteenth century the whole New Testament and catechism had been translated into the Eskimo tongue, and a grammar and dictionary were compiled (Mission of Archimandrite Veniamin Smirnov).

The missionary activities in Siberia were still more intricate. There they had to preach to pagan Shamanists predominantly small Finnish tribes) and to the Moslems, and, above all, to the Lamaists, and one must strictly distinguish these different spheres of missionary work and the varied methods that they required.

The great extent of territory and the roughness of the climate fully explain the comparative slowness of regular Church and even governmental organization. Small and isolated oases sprang up in the midst of an empty, and, for a long time, inimical world.

At the beginning of the eighteenth century one should draw attention to the activities, full of inspiration (particularly amongst the Finnish tribes) of Phylophei Leshchinski, the missionary who was twice Bishop of Tobolsk, and between these appointments became a monk. In spite of this he carried on the missionary work, personally exposing his life to great risks. He made several journeys to preach the Gospel to the Ostiaks and Voguls, etc. To consolidate the results, he opened schools and organized churches, though for a long time the newly opened churches could only be served by visiting chaplains. The new parishes were at enormous distances from each other, and consequently the chief centers, monasteries and cathedral cities, were of great importance, these providing the constant stream of active workers. It is particularly necessary to note also the missionary expeditions (in the middle of the eighteenth century) to Kamschatka, whence Christianity spread across the islands to the Alaskan shores of North America.

In the eighteenth century, also, there sprang up an Orthodox mission in China, at Peking, principally on behalf of the Russian prisoners of war who had settled there, but also for the purpose of collecting information. But, generally speaking, missionary work in the eighteenth century was very insignificant. Its revival in Siberia begins only in the nineteenth century, and once more we must emphasize the rather unfriendly attitude adopted by the State towards the Orthodox mission. In the eighteenth century, preaching to the Kirgeeses was forbidden, and conversions to Islam were, if anything, patronized. At the beginning of the nineteenth century the Lamaian hierarchy was recognized by the State. The spiritual awakening which followed conversion and baptism troubled the local representatives of the government. The raising of the tone of life meant that the pulse was quickened and strengthened, and that appeared to be troublesome. In the eighteenth century the too zealous missionaries were moved farther on, to places where there was no one to convert. But at last, in the nineteenth century, several outstanding and permanent missionary centers arose in Siberia, amongst which the Altai mission deserves above all to be noted. It was started in 1830 at the initiative of Evgeni Kazantzev, at that time Archbishop of Tobolsk, and at the head of it was placed the Archimandrite Makarios Gloukarev. Archimandrite Makarios was a remarkable man, of great spiritual earnestness and very profound, but rather exalted by eschatological interests and those Utopian ideas which were characteristic, even in the West, at the beginning of the nineteenth century. Undoubtedly a mystic, and the translator of eastern and western mystics (*e.g.,* St. Teresa of of Spain), he knew how to find common expression with others and to sympathize even with the Quakers. He himself led a very rigid, ascetic and evangelical life, and Metropolitan Philaret, who knew him intimately and loved him, called him a "romantic missionary." And, indeed, Makarios introduced into his missionary work a literally romantic zeal and ardor. He looked upon his missionary calling with sincere humility and he tried to arrange it on the principles of a strict communalism. "Let it be our rule that we should possess everything in common, money, food, clothes, books and everything else, and let this be a means of facilitating our inspiration towards unanimity." It is an apostolic rather than a monastic ideal. Makarios had few assistants, but with them he succeeded in achieving unanimity. He did not hurry to baptize, and during the thirteen years of his work he converted only about 650 persons. In his work he laid great stress on the "call to faith." He endeavored to attain spiritual regeneration and to awaken sincere and sparkling faith in sleeping souls. He preached Christ crucified, and great stress was laid on re-education and the achievement of moral ideals. In accordance with his ideas a sisterhood of widows and young women was attached to the mission.

Makarios himself was much occupied with translations, and at one time he was preoccupied with the idea of translating the Bible (especially from the Hebrew), but his work was disapproved by the central authority, and to this resistance he attached great importance. He worked out a general missionary scheme which was called *"Some notes on the means for an intensive propagation of the Christian Faith amongst*

Jews, Moslems and heathen in the Russian Empire" (1839).
For those destined to missionary work he considered it necessary to establish in Kazan an educational missionary center,
a monastery-school for which a more elaborate scheme for
ecclesiastical and ethnographic education was to have been
worked out.

The full significance of Fr. Makarios' enterprise can only
be appreciated when the harsh and rugged nature of the
region of the Altai is borne in mind, and the poverty of the
mission as well (up to 1857 its budget was only 571 roubles
a year).

After Makarios the Altai mission continued to flourish,
particularly under the management of Father Vladimir
Petrov, who later on became a bishop in the Altai, and died
Archbishop of Kazan. Still later another Makarios worked
there, who in the time of the Great War was Metropolitan
of Moscow. Less valuable work was done by the Obdorsk
and Surgut missions in the same diocese of Tobolsk.

In course of time the missionary duties were distributed
amongst the parish clergy, and they had to face the work
unaided by special missionary institutions. This step was
somewhat untimely and indiscreet. The missionary advance
ought to have continued constant and persistent in view of
the general low standard of life, and the absorbing influence of environment.

The second bright page in the history of the Siberian
mission opens with the activities of Archbishop Nilus in
Eastern Siberia (Irkutsk 1838 to 1853, depicted in Leskov's
famous novel *On the Edge of the World*) and in particular
of Innokenti Veniaminov, later Metropolitan of Moscow
after the death of Philaret.

Archbishop Nilus took an interest in mission work while
Bishop of Viatka, even before he was appointed to Siberia.
In Irkutsk and the Trans-Baikal region it was necessary to
preach to the Buriats who belonged to the Lamaian faith.
Nilus worked a great deal on the translation of Church books

into the Mongol-Buriat language and still carried on that work after his reappointment to Yaroslavl'. Innokenti Veniaminov commenced his work on the Aleutian Islands, which at that time belonged to Russia. Here he preached to the Koloshes and the Aleutes for about fifteen years. He studied local dialects, compiled a grammar and a dictionary and began to make translations; he also left us a description of the country and the ways of life there. According to his scheme made in 1840, the mission at that time in the Russian possessions in North America was legally organized and placed under the management of the Bishop of Kamschatka. Innokenti was appointed to the bishop's throne, and for twenty-eight years he worked in this new country, new and yet his by birthright. His diocese covered enormous distances, and most of his time was spent in travelling. His assistants translated the Church books into the Yakut and Tungus tongues.

Mission work against the Lamaian faith in the Trans-Baikal Country was most difficult; yet many improvements were made there by Parpheni Popov, the Archbishop of Irkutsk, and later on by the Archbishop Veniamin Blagonravov. The mission in China never could attain any noticeable growth, though a great work was done in translation, and the mission at Peking was the general center of sinological studies for a long time. The mission workers were in consequence more prominent for their scientific than for their apostolic achievements. China is in general a very difficult country and unfavorable for missionary work.

In a very different way the life of the Russian mission in Japan was progressing. Of course, it was very much owing to the personal qualities and exploits of the first of the Russian missionaries Nikolai Kazatkin, who, later on, became Archbishop of Japan, or rather its apostle in the true sense of the word. He began his work in 1861, soon after Japan opened her doors to Europeans and prior to the declaration of toleration. Yet the mission began to grow very quickly.

Again the method of translation was adopted and many years were spent in the translation of the Christian service books, and a net of Orthodox parishes spread gradually all over Japan.

In the history of the Japanese Orthodox Church one is struck by the astonishing simplicity and strength of the immediate corporate Church feeling. Parish life goes on very actively and intensively. Diocesan meetings with the parishioners participating are organized every year. The work of the catechists goes on slowly and steadily and the cultural level of Japanese Orthodoxy is sufficiently high for it to spread also among educated people. For many years an ecclesiastical seminary existed in Tokyo, and the Japanese Church has long ago become an independent diocese with complete internal status and management and is canonically a member of the Moscow patriarchate.

III

Missionary work does not lend itself well to schemes of management and organization issued from the center. It is, above all, the work of pastoral creative power and inspiration. Therefore it depends much more upon the personality of the individuals who are the active workers than upon plans and programmes, and that is why the history of a mission is bound up closely with names. Therefore, too, missionary work often progresses spasmodically and stops altogether at intervals. And yet it is very important that the personal initiative should find an encouraging response, sympathy and facilities in the whole Church body. Therefore when in 1865 the Orthodox Missionary Society was inaugurated this was considered an event of great importance. Its work, however, became really effective only after its reorganization in 1869, when Innokenti, at that time Metropolitan of Moscow, became its president and its activities became more interwoven with the metropolitan see.

The missionary society had its branches in the centers of work and took the financial cares of the mission and its parishes upon itself. Yet there was another important task which required organized help, the scientific and scholastic training of the missionaries who were in need of good knowledge and understanding of the environment in which they would have to work. It was necessary to know the language of the people, their history and their ways of living, all leading on to an understanding of the soul. It was necessary to see how to approach that soul with the word of Christ's truth, and for this, knowledge of a language and folklore is not alone sufficient. The specific blending of an apostolic divine light and the *pathos* of a stranger's philosophy is essential and these qualities are more easily to be found in natives.

The necessity for a high ecclesiastical missionary school was not realized at once. Only in 1854 was a special missionary section opened in the Kazan Ecclesiastical Academy, and it was left there even after reforms had been introduced in ecclesiastical schools in general in 1870. A specific teaching of missionary subjects had already begun in 1845 with the participation of the professors of the Kazan University, but as a matter of fact the studies were concentrated exclusively on languages.

Names such as Sabloukov, Ilminsky, Bobrovnikov, are important and unforgettable in the history of the Kazan Academy. Sabloukov was a man self-taught in Arabic and Tartar philology. By hard work, fired by scientific enthusiasm and a natural love of work, he attained to profound erudition not only in the languages themselves but in history and archaeology as well. His translation of the Koran is especially well known. Not all the books written by him were published; many of them perished in a fire at his home. His teaching in the Academy and his participation in all missionary undertakings amongst the Tartars meant very much.

Still more important was the work of Ilminsky, who arranged his work of preaching to the Tartars in systematic order. Ilminsky was adverse to the method of polemics. He tried to work out a scheme of preaching for the purpose of conversion. He not only had scholastic and theoretic training, but understood intimately the life and ways of the local Tartars. He visited their villages and lived amongst them for some time in order to penetrate intimately into their manner of life. He also in 1851-3 travelled in the east with many stops along the way, making long stops at Cairo, Lebanon and Constantinople. As the outcome of this practical acquaintance with the mass of the people he came to a very important conclusion with regard to translations. He insisted on the necessity of these being made in the living conversational Tartar language and not in the literary language, and this was of the utmost importance. In the first place the literary language of the Tartars was laden with Arabic and Persian words and had a general flavor of Islam, and by the use of colloquial speech it was possible to escape that hidden Moslem taint. Secondly, the translation into a colloquial tongue requires great creative powers and intensity on the part of the translator and this was exactly what Ilminsky wanted. He was aiming at the formation of a specific Christian Tartar language in opposition to an Islamic one and saw in this an important step in the matter of preaching. The language itself was not to him something already developed and stationary, it was a living spiritual element which it was possible to transmute and transfigure. With this was connected a scheme for working out a whole network of Christian Tartar schools with the teaching carried on in the tongue of the people. Thirdly, there was in view the democratization of the mission, which spread far and wide among the masses, avoiding the book-learned and the aristocrats. Ilminsky's scheme was a complete system for the Christian transformation of the Tartars, yet without the least trace of any Russification. A note should also be made about the Arabic letters which he changed into Russian, as being more convenient, since he saw in the Arabic alphabet the presence of Moslem culture while that of Russia bore the symbols of Christianity. He did not believe in the fruitfulness of any preaching unless done in the people's own tongue. "Christianity as a living principle should work as a leaven in the thoughts and feelings and after having taken shape in men of advanced minds it should come from and through them to others. We believe that the evangelical word of our Saviour Jesus Christ, having become incarnate, so to speak, in the living tongue of the Tartars and through it having associated itself most sincerely with their deepest thoughts and religious consciousness, would produce the Christian revival of this tribe." Nevertheless, Ilminsky's scheme did not spring into being at once nor without some opposition both in the Kazan district and in Turkestan.

A net-work of schools, with a seminary as a center at Kazan, was organized and Ilminsky was appointed director of the seminary. Yet the most important work was still translating. This required great creative power and for it Ilminsky found help amongst the baptized Tartars. Furthermore, the introduction of divine service in the Tartar language proved one of the most effective missionary methods. Of Ilminsky's assistants and followers should be mentioned such persons as the Archpriest Malov, Ostrooumov, and the Tartar Timofeiev. The principles laid down by Ilminsky were also applied to other spheres of missionary enterprise among the natives. In connection with the study of anti-Lamaian controversies, there were no such outstanding organizers in the Kazan Academy as this man.

A. A. Bobrovnikov was a great authority on the Mongol-Buriat dialect and he compiled the first successful Mongol-Kalmuck grammar of that period. A native of the Irkutsk district and the son of a missionary, he felt, when mingling with the Buriats, an intimate nearness to this Mongol people. His book studies were supplemented by his scientific expeditions. Yet he was not a man of initiative and could not find the true methods of translating though he did expose some faults of the previous literary translations. In spite of all its incompleteness the work done by the Kazan Academy was of great importance for the help given to the missionaries to penetrate into the souls of non-Europeans, and it has not even yet been fully appreciated or used to the uttermost.

IV

Russian missionary work amongst the foreign tribes was put an end to forcibly. The Gospel of Christ on Russian soil became an impossibility and as a consequence a return to former beliefs took place especially among the Shamaist tribes in the districts of the river Volga and in Siberia, though at one time for some reason a partial freedom was enjoyed by Islam.

It is not given to us to foresee the future or to make guesses with regard to the fate of the Christian Faith among the native tribes of Russia; but we can, and it is necessary that we should, look back, so as to understand and consider well the lessons of the past which bear on the words: "Whosoever shall do and teach them the same shall be called great in the Kingdom of Heaven." (*Matt.* v. 19.)

Western Influences
in Russian Theology

THE QUESTION concerning Western influences on Orthodox Theology is a complex one. This question is still
often raised today, sometimes sharply and with excitement.
According to Metropolitan Antonii Khrapovitskii (d. 1936),
the whole development of Russian Theology since the 17th
century, as taught in the schools, was but a dangerous borrowing from heterodox Western sources. And, for that
reason, according to him, it must be completely disavowed
and eliminated.

> The system of Orthodox theology is still something
> to seek for, and, for that reason, one must identify
> and examine its genuine sources instead of copying
> systems of heretical doctrines, as it has been our
> custom for 200 years.[1]

This paper was first presented to the First Congress of Orthodox Theology
at Athens in 1936.

This article originally appeared as "Westliche Einflüsse in der Russischen
Theologie" in *Kyrios,* II, No. 1 (Berlin, 1937), 1-22 as well as in *Procès-
Verbaux du Premier Congrès de Theologie Orthodoxe* (Athens, 1939).
Reprinted by permission of the author. Translated from the German by
Thomas Bird and Richard Haugh.

Many got the impression that Russian theology had been entirely *disfigured* by Western influences. Thus the conviction arose that a basic and decisive redirection of the whole theological task was necessary, a radical return to the ignored and forgotten sources of genuine and patristic Orthodoxy. This return implies denial and abrogation. There is a bit of truth in such assertions. "The Struggle against the West" in Russian Theology can be justified. There are certainly enough occasions and reasons to justify this attitude. And it is precisely the history of these Western influences and borrowings in Orthodox Theology which has still not been sufficiently explored. One must, by all means, always start with an exact description of the facts.

In this short essay one must be content with a selection of a limited number of facts, the most important, decisive or distinctive ones. For a fuller presentation of the problem I would refer the reader to my book, *Puti russkogo bogosloviia* [*The Ways of Russian Theology*] (Paris: YMCA-Press, vii, 574 pp. [in Russian]).

I

The traditional view of the complete isolation and enclosure of Ancient Russia was discarded long ago. Ancient "*Rus'*" was never fully cut off from the West. And this connection with the West asserted itself not only in the political or economic sphere but also in the sphere of spiritual development, even in the realm of religious culture.[1] Byzantine influence indeed prevailed, but it was by no means the only influence. One must acknowledge a weakening of Byzantine influence already in the 16th century, a *crisis of Russian Byzantinism*. The Western relations of Novgorod were the most conspicuous and continuous. And precisely in the 14th and 15th centuries this city became the religious and cultural center, the center for the entire Russian North and East. Moscow, rapidly rising at that time, was still for the most part culturally dependent upon sources from Novgorod. Books were supplied precisely from this Northern democracy.[3]

At that time, under the stimulus of Archbishop Gennadii, a most responsible work was initiated—the compiling of the first complete Slavic Biblical Codex. The Bible had not been originally translated into Slavic as a uniform and complete book but rather as a collection of liturgical readings based on the order and cycle of the liturgical year—and this translation did not include the whole of the Biblical text; the non-canonical books of the Old Testament were not translated since they are scarcely represented in Eastern lectionaries. The general supervision and execution of the work at Novgorod was officially in the hands of the bishop's archdeacon, Gerasim Popovka. The actual spiritual leader, however, was a Dominican monk named Benjamin, who, according to the words of the chronicler, was "a priest and a monk from the order of St. Dominic, by birth a Slav, by faith a Latin." We do not know much more about him. But one can hardly assume that this Dominican monk from Croatia came to Novgorod just by accident. Apparently he had brought with him some completed Biblical texts. Indeed the influence of the Vulgate is strongly felt in the Biblical Codex of Gennadii, for the Vulgate and *not* Greek manuscripts served as the model for the text. The non-canonical books were included in the Codex according to Latin usage. The Books of Paralipomenon, the third book of Ezra, the Book of Wisdom, and the first two books of Maccabees were translated in entirety from the Latin. One student of "the manuscript tradition of the Slavic Bible" [Prof. I. E. Evseev] characterizes the significance of the Codex of Gennadii as "the turning of the Slavic Bible from the Greek 'waterway' to the Latin." And one should not forget that it was precisely "the Gennadii Bible" upon which the first Slavic edition of the Ostrog Bible (1580) was based. At this opportunity the text was, to be sure, once again revised and compared (after printed editions) with the Greek—the entire historical significance of the Ostrog Bible is indeed determined by the fact that it is based on the Greek text— however, the slipping away into the Latin channel was nevertheless not fully overcome. With certain improvements the Ostrog text was reproduced in the "Elizabethan Bible" of 1751—and this is the presently used text.[4] In the "house of the archbishop" Gennadii much was translated from the Latin. During the work on the new liturgical order, the famous book by V. Durantius, *Rationale divinorum officiorum,* was (at least partially) translated, presumably for reference. Judging from the language, it seems the translator was a foreigner, i.e. not a Russian—once again it was probably the monk Benjamin. Also translated from Latin at this time was the "Short Word against Those Who Claim Possession of Holy Things, Moveable or Immoveable, from the Cathedral Churches"—a defense of Church property and of the complete independence of the clerical class, which thereby also possesses the right "to act with the aid of the secular arm." Also well-known is the significant reference of Gennadii to the "Spanish King," about whom the imperial envoys related that he "purified" his land of heretics by state executions.[5]

There is good reason to speak of a "very dominant Catholic atmosphere" surrounding Gennadii [I. E. Evseev]. Russian iconography of the 15th and 16th centuries was also penetrated by Western motives and themes, again coming from Novgorod and Pskov to Moscow where they were contested in certain circles as innovations or perversions: herein lies the historical significance of the well-known "Doubt" of D'jak I. M. Viskovatii concerning the new icons. The Church authorities, however, were in favor of these innovations, regarding them as something ancient. In any case, Western influence now asserted itself quite noticeably even in the sacred art of iconography.[6] "Western" means, in this case, Latin or Roman. And "the marriage of the Tsar in the Vatican" was the symbol of the movement toward the West. Indeed, this marriage signified Moscow's drawing nearer to the Italy of that time rather than reviving Byzantine traditions. It is characteristic that the Kremlin Cathedrals were built or rebuilt at that time by Italian craftsmen. And indeed these new Moscow buildings were, as Herberstein describes them, expressly *more italico*.[7] Even more characteristic was the fact that Maxim the Greek, summoned to Moscow from the monastery of Vatopaedi on Mt. Athos to aid in the work of translation, could find no one in all of Moscow who could speak Greek with him. "He speaks Latin and we translate it into Russian for the scribes"—the translator was Dmitrii Gerasimov, a former student and assistant of Benjamin.[8] It would indeed be totally false to interpret all these facts as proof of a Roman sympathy at Novgorod or Moscow. It was rather a half unconscious assimilation of foreign spiritual values with the naive conviction that one could still remain loyal to the native and traditional truth. Thus, simultaneously, a "Western" psychology strangely united itself with an intolerance toward the West.

II

On the other side of the Moscow border the encounter with the West was more direct and more intimate. In Lithuania and in Poland this was at first an encounter with the *Reformation* and with "Socinianism," and later on with the *Roman Church*, the Jesuit order and the "Unia." Since the circumstances surrounding the struggle for the Orthodox Church were exceedingly complicated and difficult, it was simply psychologically unavoidable to make certain accommodations with heterodox allies, associates, rivals, and even enemies. At first a Hellenistic orientation was strongly emphasized—as the ideal and goal of Slavo-Greek culture—in the Ostrog Circle and in Lemberg [Lvov] at the home of Prince Ostrozhskii himself. There were many reasons why this goal was abandoned, indeed why it had to be abandoned. Even in the Ostrog Circle the mood was unsteady and the opinions divergent.

The practical wisdom of life pushed one toward the West. In the face of the threat of "Unia," the Orthodox were the obvious, occasionally even the unwilling, "confederates" of the Protestants and "Heterodox." And many were prepared to go even beyond simple religious and practical assistance; in this respect, for example, the attitude of the Orthodox and Calvinists at the Conference and in the "Confederation" at Vilna (before 1599) is quite characteristic. Even Prince K. Ostrozhskii thought it proper to commission the Socinian Motovila to translate the Orthodox refutation of Peter Skarga's book, *On the Greek Apostasy,* a project against which Prince A. M. Kurbskii, the implacable fugitive from Moscow, protested with the greatest indignation. And the Orthodox reply to Skarga's book about the Council of Brest was actually written by a Calvinist—the well-known *"Apokrisis"* was published in 1587 under the name of Christopher Philaletes. There is good reason to presume that the pseudonym actually belonged to the well-known diplomat of that time, Martin Bronevskii, the secretary to King Stephen Batorii, who was deeply involved in the confederation of the Orthodox and the Evangelicals. In the *"Apokrisis"* itself one notices occasionally an obvious similarity with Calvin's *Institutio Christianae religionis.*[9]

There was, however, in all this no conscious betrayal of Orthodox tradition and no real inclination toward Protestantism. More important and more dangerous, however, was

the ever-increasing custom among Russian writers of discussing religious and theological questions within a Western
frame of reference. At this time, however, refuting Latinism
did not mean strengthening Orthodoxy. Especially since even
the arguments of the Reformers were employed in the
polemical discussions of that time, arguments which certainly could not always harmonize with the basic tenets of
Orthodoxy. Historically this admixture of Protestantism was
perhaps unavoidable, but under its influence the "way" of
a Slavic and Hellenic culture became dim and obscure. In
addition to this was the fact that one could no longer rely
upon the Greeks for help. In fact, at that time Greek teachers
usually came from the West where they had studied. Whether
they had studied at Venice, Padua, Rome, or even at Geneva
or Wittenberg—from none of these centers did the Greeks
bring with them the Byzantine heritage or the patristic
legacy. Rather they brought precisely Western innovations.
In the 16th century their sympathies were generally with the
Protestants; later there emerged a slightly covert Latinism.
Thus there was some truth in the malicious, ironic words of
the Uniate Metropolitan Hypatius Pociei, when he wrote to
Patriarch Meletius Pigas that Calvin has replaced Athanasius
in Alexandria, Luther rules in Constantinople, and Zwingli
in Jerusalem.[10] It is sufficient to recall the "Confession" of
Cyril Lukaris, the authenticity of which can no longer be
doubted. This unexpected presentation of Calvinism by the
Orthodox Patriarch can be partially explained as a result of
his studies at Geneva. It can also be partially explained by
the fact that he was in West Russia precisely at the time
of the common struggle against the "*Unia*." Presumably it
was there that he got the idea of a "Confederation" with
the representatives of the Swiss Confession.

The influence of the Reformation in Western Russia
was only temporary. Soon the opposite tendency prevailed—an
enthusiasm for the *Roman pattern*. The significance of this

change is illustrated by the figure of the famous Metropolitan of Kiev, Peter Mogila, whose historical influence was decisive. An entire epoch in the history of the Church and culture of West Russia is, quite rightly, denoted by his name. He and his disciples were openly and decidedly pro-Western. At its root, however, this "Westernism" was really a disguised Romanism. Although Mogila had certainly fought for the legal independence of the Kievan Church and had supported the resistance of the Orthodox Church against the *"Unia,"* there was however on many points no doctrinal difference between him and Rome. For that reason he used Latin sources quite easily and unhesitatingly, assuming that he would rediscover in them true, undistorted Orthodoxy. There was a certain inexplicable discrepancy in the image of Peter Mogila. He led the West Russian Church out of its helplessness and decay from which it had suffered so much since the Council of Brest. Thanks to Mogila, it received a legal status in the Republic of Poland. But the whole structure was at the same time reconstructed in a new and alien spirit—a Latin spirit. The struggle surrounding all Mogila's plans and projects was caused by two opposing views—the Western and the Helleno-Slavic. Peter Mogila also rendered an indubitable but ambiguous service with the establishment of the Kiev Collegium. For it was a Latin school. Not only was it a "Latinization" of language, custom, and theology but it was also a "Latinization" of the entire religious psychology: thus the very soul of the people was once again Latinized. And, oddly enough, all this occurred in the name of the most extremely national and political struggle against Rome and Poland. Because of this, internal independence was indeed lost, relations with the East were sundered; an alien, artificial and borrowed direction was adopted which often enough in the future unfortunately obstructed the pathos of creativity.

Mogila was not alone in his crypto-Romanism. He rather expressed the spirit of his time. The basic and most signifi-

cantly expressive monument of his epoch is the so-called
"Orthodox Confession." It is difficult to assert with any
certainty who the author or editor of this "Catechism" was;
generally it is thought to be Mogila himself, although it was
in fact a collective work of several assistants. It was obviously
composed originally in Latin and in this original draft one
notices a much stronger influence of Latin models than in
the definitive version which underwent a critical revision at
the conferences in Kiev (1640) and in Jassy (1642). The
instances here of borrowing and imitation are actually less
important than the fact that the *Confessio Orthodoxa* in its
entirety was merely an accommodation to, indeed an "adaptation" of Latin materials. In any case, it is more closely connected with the Roman Catholic writings of that time than
with the spiritual life of Orthodoxy or the traditions of the
Eastern Fathers. Particular Roman doctrines—for example,
the doctrine of the primacy of the Pope—are rejected here,
but the general style remains nevertheless Roman. The same
is true of Peter Mogila's *liturgical reform*. His famous *Book
of Ritual* or *Euchologion* (1646) is heavily influenced by the
Ritual of Pope Paul V, from which the introductory explanations of particular rites and ceremonies were taken almost
verbatim.[11] Mogila's *Kiev Collegium* soon became the central
base of this imitative Latinism not only for the Southern
and Western parts of Russia but also for the Muscovite
North. Kievan religious literature of the 17th century was
completely dependent on Latin sources and patterns. It is
sufficient to mention the name of *Stefan Iavorskii*, who later,
under the reign of Peter the Great, went north. His "Rock
of the Faith" [*"Kamen' Very"*] was actually only a "summary," a shortened "compilation" of various Latin works,
mainly of Bellarmine's *Disputationes de controversis christianae fidei*. His book about the coming of the Anti-
Christ is patterned after the book by the Spanish Jesuit
Malvenda.[12] The essence of this Roman pseudo-morphosis lies

in the fact that Scholasticism screened and obstructed Patristics for the Russians. It was a psychological and cultural Latinization rather than a matter of creed.

Nevertheless the scales of doctrine were also shaken. Under Peter the Great theological schools or seminaries were also established throughout Great Russia precisely according to the southern, Kievan model. These schools were thoroughly Latin and their teachers were for a long time recruited from the "institutes" of the Southwest. Even the Slavic-Greek-Latin Academy in Moscow had used Kiev as its model and pattern. This Petrine reform, however, also meant a "Ukrainianization" in the history of ecclesiastical schools. There was, as it were, a migration of South Russians to the north where they were regarded as foreigners for two reasons: their schools were "Latin" and they were themselves "foreigners." In his distinguished book on the theological schools of the 18th century Znamenskii passes the following sharp judgment (see Anm. 1, p. 216): "For the student, all these educators were in the fullest sense of the word— aliens from a foreign land—"Little Russia" was regarded at that time as a foreign land. It had its own peculiar customs and conceptions, and a strange "scholarship." Its language was difficult to understand and sounded odd to the Great Russians. In addition, these teachers never tried at all to adapt themselves to their students or to the country to which they had been called. Rather, they openly despised the Great Russians, considered them savage, and derided them. They found fault with everything which was not similar to their own "Little Russian" ways. They pushed their way of life in the foreground, forcing it on everyone as the proper style of life. This was a time when one could consecrate only "Little Russians" (Ukrainians) as bishops and archimandrites since the government was suspicious of Great Russians, presuming that they were sympathetic with pre-Petrine customs.

The people accepted the establishment of Latin schools

only reluctantly and with great distrust. And only unwillingly did the clergy entrust their children to these schools. And even the students themselves frequently ran away. All this took place not because the clerical estate was addicted to superstition or engrossed in ignorance, but because they considered these schools as something unfamiliar and foreign —as an unwanted Latin-Polish colony in the homeland, as an "institution" which, even from a purely practical point of view, could only appear useless. The "practical mind" regarded "Latin grammar" as of little use as well as the "fine manners" which were cultivated in the seminaries. For the "practical mind" there was absolutely no reason to replace the traditional manner of preparation for the priesthood—at one's own home—with new, unaccustomed and dubious ways. "It still remained to be seen who in general was better prepared for the priesthood: the psalm-reader who, from youth on, had served in the Church, learning in a practical way the readings, the hymns, and the order of services; or, the student of Latin who had merely memorized some Latin vocabulary and inflexions" (Znamenskii). In these Latin schools one began to become almost unaccustomed to Church Slavonic—even the texts of Scripture were usually quoted in Latin. Grammar, rhetoric and poetics were taught in Latin, while Russian rhetoric was taught only on the higher levels. It is understandable that parents sent their children to "these cursed schools of torture" only with mistrust. And the children preferred even the penitentiary to such schools. Indeed the depressive feeling soon developed that one could lose, if not his faith then at least his nationality, in these newly established schools. In general the establishment of the schools was obviously a positive achievement. But the extension of these Latin schools into the territory of Great Russia meant a break in the Church's mentality—a split between theological "learning" and the experience of the Church: one still prayed in Slavonic but thought in Latin.

The same Scriptural words resounded from the floor of the school in international Latin, but resounded from the floor of the Church in the maternal Slavic language. This painful split in the very spiritual mentality itself is perhaps the most tragic result of the Petrine epoch. There developed a certain "duality of faith," in any case a spiritual division, a disunity of the soul.[13] *A Western culture, indeed a Western theology was established.* It was a "school of theology" which of course had no roots in life. Established and grown on an alien foundation, it now became, as it were, a "superstructure" built over an empty spot. Instead of growing on natural foundations, it rested solely on props. *A theology on props—that is the result of the theological Westernization in 18th century Russia.*

III

Theological instruction in the schools still remained Latin in character even when the "Romish" orientation was replaced by that of the Reformation or, more correctly, by the influence of early Protestant scholasticism. And it retained its Latin character even when the influence of Aquinas in philosophy was replaced by the authority of Christian Wolff. The language of instruction remained Latin and both the "structure" of the school and its education remained Western. The Protestant trend is associated first of all with the name and influence of Theophan Prokopovich, the well-known close collaborator of Peter the Great, the latter's advisor and executor in all reforms of ecclesiastical life, and the compiler of the "Spiritual Reglament" ["*Dukhovnyi Reglament*"]. Theophan's theological lectures, given in the Kiev Academy, were published much later in Latin (in Leipzig 1782-1784), but they had circulated earlier in manuscript form and had influenced the new turn in theology. In his dogmatic lectures or "tracts" Theophan followed Western models rather closely

—he seems to depend especially upon Amandus Polanus from Polansdorf and upon the latter's *Syntagma Theologiae Christianae* (1609). He systematically used Johann Gerhard's *Loci communes*. He was, however, not just a compiler even when he followed foreign masters. Well read and knowledgeable of contemporary literature, he was thoroughly in control of his material, handling and adjusting it in his own manner. One point is in any case beyond doubt: he was not just "connected" with Protestant scholasticism of the 17th century; he simply belonged to their tradition. He was not only under the influence of Protestantism, but he was simply a Protestant himself (A. V. Kartashov). His works actually belong to the history of German theology of the Reformation. And if there was not on his books the name of a Russian bishop, it would be most natural to seek the author among the professors of some Evangelical theological faculty. Everything he wrote was permeated by the atmosphere of the Reformation, by the Western spirit. This atmosphere can be traced everywhere—in the entire manner of his thought and expressions. It is not just a man writing under Western influence, but one who is a Western man himself—a foreigner. Theophan looked at Orthodoxy as though he himself were a Westerner. He did not know or experience Orthodoxy from *within*. He was pre-occupied with Western problems and controversies, completely taking the side of the Reformation. The entire pathos of his tracts was directed against Rome and he was never able to extricate himself from the "enchanting sphere" of the polemics of Western confessional theology.[14]

In his well-known book *Stefan Iavorskii and Theophan Prokopovich,* Iurii Samarin wanted to present the clash of Romish and Reformation trends as a moment of an alleged inner *"dialectic of Russian theological thought."* One can hardly speak about any such organic process here. It was simply a confrontation of foreign influences and because of

the opposition of these influences Russian theological thought
was only narrowed. One cannot speak of any inner spontaneous dialectic. There was rather a forcible *pseudomorphosis* of Orthodox thought. The Orthodox were forced to
think in essentially alien categories and to express themselves
in foreign concepts. At most theological seminaries and
academies the instruction in the second half of the 18th
century was based on Western Protestant manuals. Since
Latin was used as the common scholarly and instructional
language, even the trouble of translation was not necessary.
Metropolitan Philaret recalled that he had studied theology
at school from the textbook by Hollatz (d. 1713). Certain
sections of the textbook were simply dictated in class. Other
parts of the course were taken from the manuals by Quenstedt
or from I. A. Turretini (d. 1737). But even manuals written
by Russians themselves did not deviate much from Western
models—this is true of the *Doctrine* written by Theophylakt
Gorskii (Leipzig 1784), the *Compendium* by Iakinth Kar-
pinskii (Leipzig 1786), the *Compendium* by Silvester
Lebedinskii (1799 and 1805), as well as Irenei Falkovskii's
manual (1802!), a manual faithfully based on Theophan
Prokopovich. One would seek in vain for any independent
thought in all these compendia and tracts. These were books
for memorization, presenting a "theology of the school," a
ballast of formal school tradition. By habit, certain Protestant
doctrines were accepted—their doctrine of Scripture and
Tradition, their definition of the Church, and their concept
of Justification.

In the second half of the 18th century the powerful
stream of *Pietism* was added to the previous influence of
Protestant Scholasticism. One only needs to mention the name
of Simeon Todorskii (1701-1754), who died as Bishop of
Pskov. Previously, however, he had been for a while a
teacher at the famous *Waisenhaus* in Halle where he
translated Johann Arndt's *Wahres Christentum* into Russian,

basing his translation on the 1735 Halle-edition. Most significant in this connection is Platon Levshin (1737-1811), the
famous Metropolitan of Moscow under Catherine II, later
described so appropriately by the historian of the Academy,
S. K. Smirnov, as "to some extent the Peter Mogila of the
Moscow Academy." Platon was more of a preacher and
catechist than a systematic theologian. But his "catechisms,"
sermons or "initial instructions in Christian doctrine,"
delivered in Moscow while he was still in his early years
(1757-1758), marked a change in the history of theology
itself. His instructional lectures given to the Grand Duke
(the future Emperor) Paul were published in 1765 under the
title *Orthodox Doctrine or Christian Theology in Summary.*
This was the first attempt at a theological system in the
Russian language. Nevertheless, this "theological book" was
also inevitably translated into Latin for the theological
schools. And it was Platon himself who insisted on this, for
he also believed that theological instruction in a language
other than Latin would be a lowering of scholarly standards.
His view was especially remarkable since it came from one
who was such a zealous fighter for the "catechization of
the people," a popularizer of Christian faith and Christian
morals. Even in his old age, before the Patriotic War of
1812, Platon was greatly excited when the plan of using
Russian as the instructional language at theological schools
was brought up. He vigorously and constantly advised against
this. In Platon's Russian writings one clearly sees the complete inadequacy of confused theological definitions and
descriptions which he took from his Latin sources. He had
much more interest in morals than in the doctrines of faith.
Throughout the entire 18th century the doctrines of the
Church, of Tradition, of the Sacraments—these remained
quite undeveloped.[15]

The Reform of Russian theological schools at the beginning of the reign of Alexander I was not a return to Byzantine

or Eastern foundations. The entire reform was concerned
more with the spirit of Pietism, of "inner Christianity"
rather than with the corporate life of the Church. As previously, instruction remained closely bound up with the
patterns of Western schools in which pietistic moralism and
a certain inclination toward mysticism was conspicuous at
that time. Innerly the schools remained Western. Yet an
opposite tendency was taking place which later overcame
the split between "school" and "life": *instruction could be
given in Russian*. The goal of the new theological "school
reform" was to awaken both society and the people, to urge
them on to higher spiritual interests, and to stimulate a
religious and moral independence. This intention was, of
course, organically connected with the entire *Zeitgeist* of
that epoch; it was rooted in the mystical inclinations of the
epoch, the epoch of the Holy Alliance and the Bible Societies.
The "Latin Captivity" could easily be replaced by a German
or English "captivity," only in the place of scholasticism
there arose the danger of vague mysticism and German
Theosophy. From that time on the shadow of German
scholarship falls over the whole of Russian theology for
quite some time—much to its detriment. Since that time it
became a standard practice in Russian theological academies
to learn German as the basic language of theology in general.

Despite this, it was a step forward, the beginning of
a creative rise. Although much was unsound in this new
pseudo-morphosis, it was nevertheless a *sickness unto life
and unto growth* and not a sickness unto death or degenera-
tion. Between the two extremes of mystical and philosophical
enthusiasm on the one hand, and mistrustful fears on the
other, the narrow and precipitous way of Church Theology was
gradually discovered. Outstanding in this epoch is the majestic
figure of Philaret, Metropolitan of Moscow (1782-1867),
perhaps the most significant Russian theologian of earlier
times. He too had studied in a Latin school and had grown

up under the gentle guidance of Metropolitan Platon in the seminary at Troitsko-Sergievskii Monastery where that mixture of pietism and scholasticism dominated at that time. In his young years he passed through the mystical movement and was also a convinced supporter of the Bible Society. One can also find certain traces of these "Protestant" and "mystical" influences in his later theological works. In general, however, his *Weltanschauung* remained ecclesial. With Philaret begins the real liberation of Russian theology not only from Western influences but from Westernization in general. It occurred in the only way which could have achieved lasting results—that is, by a creative return to Patristic foundations and sources, by a return to the Fathers of the Church—this was the true source of inspiration for Philaret and served as the criterion of his own presentation. Externally Philaret did not immediately break away from the earlier "old-Protestant" traditions of the Russian schools, from the tradition of Prokopovich. There is much in Philaret's own expressions which reflect the influence of Protestant doctrines or which simply reveal a borrowing from Protestant sources. In his *Survey of Theological Scholarship,* prepared in 1814 for the St. Petersburg Academy, he himself refers the reader to Protestant works. That characteristic imprecision or defectiveness of conceptual definitions in his early writings, often pointed out by Philaret's enemies, originated from these Protestant sources—especially striking was his omission of Holy Tradition as an authoritative doctrinal guide, which was not mentioned at all in the first edition of his *Catechism.* However, this omission does not in fact indicate so much an error or inaccuracy of thought, but rather it was a matter of the common habit of that time.

Psychologically the reversion to Scholasticism and to Romanizing moods is thoroughly understandable and explainable in connection with the reforms of the Chief Prokurator of the Holy Synod under Nicholas I, Count Pratasov.

Yet this return to the Romanizing formulations of the 17th
and 18th centuries, to the *Orthodox Confession* of Peter
Mogila, to the works of St. Dmitrii of Rostov, or to Stefan
Iavorskii's *Rock of Faith* proved fruitless because it offered
no creative exit from the historical difficulties of Russian
theology. The inclination to Protestantism could only be
overcome by a return to the historical sources of Eastern
Orthodoxy, by a creative restoration of that once existing
organic continuity and cultural tradition and not by hasty
and scholastic assessments of ready-made "solutions" of
Western thought. In this sense Philaret accomplished in-
comparably more of the actual *"Churchification"* *["Verkirch-
lichung"]* of Russian "school theology" than did Pratasov
and his advisors. The *Dogmatics* by Makarii Bulgakov, an
eminent historian of the Russian Church and later the Metropolitan of Moscow, remained—despite all its merits—a dead
book, a memorial to lifeless scholarship, uninspired by the
true spirit of the Church: once again precisely a Western
book. The return to a truly genuine and living Christianity
was possible only by the *historical path,* not by the path of
scholasticism. It is possible only by the living, albeit sometimes contradictory, experience of the history of the Church
which contains embryonically the sought-for synthesis, and
not by a hasty "systematization" based on alien sources. This
"historical method" was the path of Russian theology at the
end of the previous century. This method (see, for example,
the *Dogmatic Theology* of Bishop Silvester) was the most
important achievement of the Russian theological heritage.[16]

IV

In the history of Western Theology of the previous
centuries the influence of *German idealistic philosophy* was
one of the most significant phenomena, not only in Evangelical circles but also—suffice it to mention the Roman

Catholic school at Tübingen—to a very significant extent in the works of Roman Catholic theology and scholarship, especially in Germany. This influence of German *Idealism* was strong in the Russian theological schools, although here it was more of a philosophical, than theological, concern. The influence of philosophical idealism was almost not at all apparent in the genuine theological literature, genuine in the strictest sense of the term. This is partially explained by the strictness of censorship. We know from the memoirs of contemporaries that many of the Academy professors were inclined to a philosophical interpretation of the *data* of Revelation rather than to a strictly theological interpretation.

The psychological influence of Romanticism and Realism was, in any case, strong. Schelling and Baader, as well as Romantic psychologists such as G. H. Schubert (d. 1860), were very popular among the students of the Academies. Even in the works of Theophan the Recluse, the authoritative interpreter of patristic asceticism, we find certain traces of Schubert's *History of the Soul* [*Geschichte der Seele;* 1830, 4th edition, 1850]. Schubert's book was used as a textbook in the Kiev Academy when Theophan was a student. In any case, the philosophical awakening in Russia began precisely in the theological schools and all the early disciples of philosophical idealism came from theological Academies or Seminaries: Vellanskii from the Kiev Academy, Nadezhdin from Moscow, Galich from the seminary at Sevsk, and Pavlov from the Voronezh Seminary. Later, university professors of philosophy also came from the theological Academies: Sidonskii and M. I. Vladislavlev in St. Petersburg, P. D. Iurkevich and M. M. Troitskii in Moscow (both from the Kiev Academy), Archimandrite Theophan Avsenev, O. Novitskii, S. S. Gogotskii in Kiev, and I. Mikhnevich in the Richelieu Lyceum of Odessa. Professors of philosophy at the Academies were: Th. Golubinskii and V. D. Kudriavtsev at the Moscow Academy, V. N. Karpov, the well-known translator of Plato, and M. I. Karinskii in St. Petersburg. Thus a specific internal tradition of religio-philosophical idealism was created in the Academies. It kept alive a philosophical thirst for knowledge and directed attention to problems of faith. It was precisely from the theological schools that the Russian "love for wisdom" began and Russian theological knowledge was exposed to a speculative testing. One of the *conservative* professors of the Theological Academy outlined at the beginning of this century the task of philosophical Dogmatics: behind every dogma one must search spiritually for that question to which the dogma responds. "This is the analytics of the natural demands of the spirit in relation to various truths." First, one must establish the positive witness of the Church from Scripture and Tradition, "and here a mosaic of texts is never sufficient but only an organic growth of knowledge." Then dogma comes alive and discloses itself in its entire speculative depth— as a divine answer to human questions, as a divine Amen and as a witness of the Church. It appears as a "genuine self-understanding" which is spiritually unthinkable to contradict. Dogmatic theology, when it confronts the questions of the present, must constantly re-create dogmas afresh so that the dark coals of traditional formulas are transformed into the illuminating jewels of true faith."[17] In such a presentation of the speculative problems of theology the philosophical and historical methods go hand in hand. The historical method, for its part, leads back to the speculative confession of the faith of the Holy Fathers.

The influence of philosophy is especially clear in the systematic construction of Russian "secular theologians"— the Slavophiles and Khomiakov, but especially Vladimir Solov'ev and his followers. The close connection between the religio-philosophical *Weltanschauung* and quest of Vladimir Solov'ev with German idealistic philosophy, especially with Schelling, partly with Baader, Schopenhauer, and Ed. von

Hartmann is completely obvious. Solov'ev's system, however, was an attempt to re-shape afresh the dogmas of Christian belief and Tradition in the categories of modern philosophy, a task which had already concerned Khomiakov. From Solov'ev this tradition, taken up by his spiritual followers and successors, passed into the contemporary religio-philosophical tradition. To such an understanding of theological tasks one should oppose another: the task of theology lies not so much in translating the Tradition of faith into contemporary language, into the terms of the most recent philosophy, but lies rather in discovering in the ancient patristic tradition the perennial principles of Christian philosophy; this task lies not in controlling dogma by means of contemporary philosophy but rather in re-shaping philosophy on the experience of faith itself so that the experience of faith would become the source and measure of philosophical views. The weakest side of Solov'ev and his school was precisely this misuse of the speculative process which can enchain, and often even deform, Tradition and the experience of faith. The influence of German philosophy, in any case, organically penetrated Russian theological consciousness.

V

From the foregoing brief and fleeting survey of Western influences in Russian theology the following disquieting and hopeless conclusion seems inevitable: was not and is not Russian theology, in its development—as one critic sharply stated—always a *"wandering theology"*? Was it not peculiarly moveable, changeable, inconsistent and incomprehensible? Such is quite often the conclusion of foreign—especially of Roman Catholic—theologians, who usually get the impression from reading Russian theological works of something uncertain, something indefinable. Impressions and conclusions

of this type are in fact the results of a very dangerous misunderstanding, a kind of optical illusion. Something very
tragic, however, stands behind such an interpretation—a
disastrous schism, a split in Orthodox consciousness, traceable
in the history of Russian theology as a certain *creative confusion,* as a lack of clarity about the road to be followed.
Saddest of all was that this peculiar split was between piety
and theology, between theological erudition and spirituality,
between theological schools and Church life.

This new theological *scholarship* came to Russia from
the West. It remained an alien accretion in Russia much too
long. It continued to use a special language, foreign to the
people, a language which was neither that of common life
nor of prayer. It remained an alien body in the structure of
the Church, developing into artificial and totally estranged
forms. It was and it remained "school scholarship." As such
it transformed itself into a text for instruction and all too
often ceased seeking the truth and the profession of the
faith. Theological thought gradually digressed from hearing
the rhythm of the Church's heart and thereby lost the "way"
to this heart. It did not understand the necessity of awakening
attention as participation in the wider circles of the Church
community and of the people. It looked at them rather with
distrust, jealousy, and enmity. There were, in fact, reasons
for this. They lay in the prejudice against an imported and
self-sufficient scholarship which was not even rooted in the
reality of religious experience or in life, a prejudice against
a theology which had ceased to express and bear witness to
the faith of the Church. To this extent it can be justly
characterized as a "wandering theology." Herein lies the
entire problem of Russian religious existence: in the depths
and the intimacy of Church experience the *Faith* is kept
and preserved undistorted. In the quiet acquiescence to God,
in the style of prayer, in its monasticism the Russian soul
preserved the old, strict, patristic style; it lived in a fully

undisturbed and undivided fulness of *Sobornost'* and Tradition. In this spirituality and depth of prayer the ancient Faith still remained "the apostolic, patristic Faith,"—the faith of ancient, Eastern, and Byzantine Orthodoxy. But *"thought"* had separated itself, had torn itself away from these spiritual depths, returning only too late to the realization of its unholy deviation. The wanderings of *thought,* however, could not and did not destroy the authenticity of faith: Orthodoxy remained, nevertheless, unchanged. One serious danger exists, however, in that theological pseudo-morphosis, when natural language is lost and theology becomes alien and strange. Most dangerous was the fact that theological problematics lost their proximity to life and that the Truth of God became a school exercise limited to specialists and professionals. N. P. Gillarov-Platonov gives a very characteristic example of such an alienation of school from life in his extraordinarily captivating memoirs:

> The semi-Protestant interpretation of Tradition was then quite common in the schools. Even the catechism of Philaret had no section on Tradition. The Theology of Ternovskii did not discuss it either. The handwritten text from which I taught, when I was already forty, was also silent on this subject. The age of Prokopovich still lingered on . . . This situation was not just restricted to the subject of Tradition . . . The doctrine of Justification was also presented in conformity with Latin books . . . While Moscow more or less wandered in the footsteps of Prokopovich, a reaction took place in St. Petersburg, the result of the theology of A. N. Murav'ev . . . It is particularly noteworthy that professional theologians remained quite indifferent to the innovations in the obviously important dogma of Tradition (Tradition as a second and independent source of Faith). They began to write and teach in the

new manner as if they had always done so . . . The
reader may think this is an unusual lack of faith
on the part of these religious persons. But what
appears at first glance a peculiar indifference was
really no lack of faith. It rather indicated that the
formulae of Western theology had no "living" content for the Eastern Church. In the West these
questions belong to the essence of various confes-
sions and are burning issues. In the East, however,
these questions were in general not raised at all.
Informative in this regard is the exchange of letters
in the 16th century between Patriarch Jeremiah
of Constantinople and the Tübingen theologians.
The latter asked him for his views on the issues
which constituted the essence of the strife between
Rome and Luther—for example, the issue of faith
and works. The Patriarch, however, answered
casually and superficially; he could not understand
the full context of these questions precisely because
these questions had arisen from the religious speculations in the Western Church, the latter being involved in these problems because of a peculiarity
of its own historical development."

In these observations there is much truth, especially from
a psychological point of view. The danger lay not so much
in the errors as in the separation of theological thought and
its scholarship from the people.

*Western influences in Russian theology must be over-
come.* This concerns, first of all, the inorganic *"Western
style."* This process actually began long ago in the Russian
schools—precisely at the time of Philaret and in connection
with the revival of asceticism in Russian monasteries. It is
sufficient to recall the school of *Staretz* Paisii Velichkovskii
and especially the hermitage of Optino. Orthodox theology
can ultimately restore the independence from Western

influences only through a *spiritual return to patristic sources* and foundations. To return to the Fathers does not mean to retreat from the present or from history; it is not a retreat from modernity or from the field of battle. It means much more—it is not only a preservation and protection of patristic experience but also the very discovery of this experience and the bringing of this experience into life. On the other hand, independence from the West must not degenerate into an alienation which becomes simply opposed to the West. For a complete break with the West does not give a true and authentic liberation. Presently Orthodoxy can and must no longer circumvent or hush up the issue. This, however, means that Orthodoxy must encounter the West creatively and spiritually. The dependence and imitation of the past cannot be considered *an encounter.* An *encounter* only really occurs in the freedom and equality of love. It is not sufficient merely to repeat Western answers, to play one Western answer off against another. But rather we must precisely recognize, experience, and penetrate these Western questions, we must familiarize ourselves with the entire dramatic problematic of Western religious thought.

VI

Orthodox Theology's path of overcoming the Western "scandal" does not lie in rejecting or even overthrowing Western results. The path, rather, lies in overcoming and surmounting them in a *new creative activity.* Only a creative return to the unique and ancient depths will serve Orthodox thought as the authentic "antidote" against the open and hidden—or even yet unknown—aspects of "Western poisoning." Orthodox Theology is summoned to answer Western questions from the depths of the unbroken Orthodox ex-

perience and to confront the movements of Western thought
with the unchanged *truth* of *patristic Orthodoxy.*

Translated from the German by
THOMAS BIRD and RICHARD HAUGH

The Ways of Russian Theology

I

THE HISTORY of Russian culture is marked throughout with crises, intermittent occurrences, fits of disillusionment or enthusiasms, betrayals or ruptures. It shuns a continuous and integral coherence. Its fabric is entangled, rumpled, frayed. "Most characteristic of Russian history are its scissions and breaks of continuity" (Nicolas Berdyaev). It displays foreign influences rather than its own creativity. There are many more contradictions and incompatibilities in the soul of the Russian people than the Slavophiles or the Populists [*narodniki*] were ready to admit. The traditional *mores* keep strange company with a revolutionary spirit. P. Kireevski has rightly observed that the very *being* of Russia evolved on several levels. This is also true of the intimate being, the inner, subtle structure of the popular soul. The latter has ever been living simultaneously in several eras or different ages. In it, psychic forms which cannot be measured, hailing from diverse epochs, combine and inter-

Translated from "Les Voies de la Theologie Russe," in *Dieu Vivant,* 13 (Paris, 1949), 39-62. Translated from the French by Georges A. Barrois. Printed by permission of the author.

penetrate. This does not mean that they constitute a synthesis. In fact, a synthesis did not succeed. This complexity of the popular soul is caused by the weakness of an excessive impressionability and an exaggerated sensitiveness. The Russian soul has a dangerous tendency, a treacherous inclination toward those transformations or those cultural metempsychoses of which Dostoevski spoke in his discourse on Pushkin. Or in the words of Alexander Blok:

> We perceive every thing,
> The sharp mind of France,
> And the somber genius of the Germans
> > [*The Scythians*]

This gift of being a sonorous and universal echo is, all in all, fatal and ambiguous, since sensitiveness and lively reactions make the concentration of the spirit very difficult. By roaming freely through ages and cultures, man runs the risk of not finding himself. The soul is unsettled and becomes lost under wave after wave of impressions and historical experiences. The soul seems to have lost the capacity for returning into itself, attracted and distracted as it is by too many things, which detain it elsewhere. Thus it acquires nomadic habits, it gets used to living in ruins or in encampments. The Russian soul is oblivious of its ancestry. It is customary to quote its propensity for dreaming, its feminine suppleness. Now this is not false. But the trouble does not derive from the fact that the fundamental element, plastic and highly fusible, of the Russian people, was not reinforced nor armored with "logoi," that it did not crystallize into cultural action. There is no way of measuring or exhaustively explaining the Russian *temptation* merely by naturalistically contrasting "nature" with "culture." This temptation arises from within the culture itself. Generally speaking, the "popular soul" is less a biological quantity than a historical, created value. It is made and it grows through history. The

Russian "element" is by no means an "innate reaction to its being," the natural, inborn "original chaos," which does not bear any fruit yet, which the light of the spirit has not yet brightened and enlightened. It is rather the new secondary chaos, that of sin and disintegration, of the fall, the revolt, the hardening of a darkened and blinded soul. The Russian soul is not stricken by original sin only, it is not poisoned only by an inherent Dionysiac strain. More than that, it bears the burden of its historic sins, whether conscious or unconscious: "A dismal swamp of shameful thoughts wells up within me. . . ." The true cause of this evil lies not in the fluidity of the primordial element of the people, but rather in the infidelity and the fickleness of its love. Only love is the true *fora* for synthesis and unity, and the Russian soul has not been steady and devoted in this ultimate love. Too often was it swayed through mystical unstableness. Russians have become far too much used to suffer at fatal crossroads or at the parting of ways, "not daring to carry the scepter of the Beast nor the light burden of Christ. . ." The Russian soul feels even passionately drawn toward such crossings. It does not have the steadfastness necessary for choice, nor the willpower for taking responsibilities. It appears, in some undefinable way, too "artistic," too loose-jointed. It expands, it extends, it languishes, lets itself be overcome as ensnared by a charm. But being under a spell is not synonymous with being in love, not any more than amorous friendship or infatuation are synonymous with love. Only sacrificial love, voluntary love, makes one strong, not the fits of passion, nor the mediumnistic attraction of a secret affinity. Now the Russian soul lacked precisely that spirit of sacrifice and self-denial in the presence of Truth, of the ultimate humility in loving. It divides itself and meanders through its attachments. *Logical conscience,* being sincerity and responsibility in the act of knowing, wakes up late in the Russian soul.

Two temptations keep it spellbound; on the one hand,

the temptation of the holy life: it is the temptation of Old Russia, of the "Old Believers," the optimism of a Christian order established on the historic soil, followed, as if it were by a shadow, with the apocalyptic negation in the schism [*raskol*]. On the other hand, the temptation of pietistic consolation, which is the temptation of the new "intelligentsia," whether the occidentalist or the populist. It is also a temptation *sui generis* of the spiritual life, the charm of a spiritual *Gemütlichkeit*. History is not assumed in a creative way, as superior high feat, as pilgrimage, as impersonal forces, even unconscious and elemental, on "organic processes," on the "power of the earth," as though history would evolve, as if it would *just happen,* rather than being *self-creative.* "Historicism" is no defense against "pietism," for it remains a point of view of the intellect. The category of responsibility is missing, in spite of historical sensitiveness, receptivity, and keenness of observation. This irresponsibility of the national spirit is most conspicuous in the evolution of Russian thought. And here is the essence of our cultural tragedy. It is a Christian, not an *antique,* tragedy; the tragedy of voluntary sin, of a freedom which ceases to be clear-sighted; it is not the tragedy of a blind fate, nor of the primordial darkness; it is the tragedy of divided love, of mystical infidelity, that of spiritual servitude and of demoniac possession. Therefore it reaches its dénouement in a paroxysm of red madness, of God's denial, of war against God, of fall. And it is impossible to tear oneself loose from this whirl of passion except by penitence, vigil, concentration, spirituality, and the return of the soul. The way out is not found in culture, in society, but in asceticism, beyond the "internal desert" of the spirit which returns.

II

One perceives a certain embarrassment of the creative

spirit in the history of Russian theology. The main neuralgic point is the strange divorce between theology and piety, between erudition and meditative prayer, between the school and Church life; a separation and a schism between the "intelligentsia" and the "people," in the very bosom of the Church. Let it suffice to recall at this point that this estrangement has been harmful to both parties. The Athonite disturbances (1912-1913), caused by controversies about the Divine Name and the "Prayer of Jesus," are a typical illustration.

Theological scholarship was borrowed from the West. Too long did it remain foreign with us. It even persisted in using a particular language (which was neither that of everyday life, nor of prayer). Theology remained an enclave within the organism of the Church. As it developed in an artificial milieu and in isolation, it became and remained a school discipline, more and more a matter that is taught, less and less a quest for truth or a profession of faith. Theological thought gradually lost its faculty to apply itself to the live pulsations of the Church. It could not any more find the way to its heart. It attracted neither the attention nor the sympathy of large social and popular circles of the Church. Theology, in the best circumstances, seemed useless. But often incomprehension worsened into umbrageous mistrust, even ill-will. Consequently numerous believers acquired the unfortunate habit of doing without theology altogether, and replaced it, some with canons, some others with prayers, with ancient traditions, with ritual, with the lyricism of the soul. This gave rise to an obscure sort of abstinence, to a refusal of knowledge, we might say to theological *aphasia,* to uncalled for "a-dogmatism" or even to agnosticism under pretence of piety; in a word, to a renewal of the heresy of the "antisophoi," "gnosimachoi."

The sin consisted not only in the fact that spiritual riches remained buried and deliberately unused; this "gnosimachia,"

threatened even the soundness of the spirit. In the practice
of devotion, private as well as liturgical, there always lurks
the danger of "psychological subjectivism," the temptation
to receive or to offer the psychic for the spiritual. It can
take the appearance of ritual or canonical formalism, or else
of an enticing sensibility. It is nonetheless a temptation. The
theological spirit alone—humble, straightforward, vigilant,
experience—may preserve us from such temptations. Neither
the traditional rites nor the canons are a sufficient safeguard.
The soul lets itself be carried away by the lure and the
appeal of its own plight. In such a psychological climate,
the mistrust with regard to theology became doubly harmful.
Research lacked ground. Without a theological criterion, the
Russian soul was so unstable, so exposed to temptations!....
Since Peter I, "piety" had been, so to speak, driven back
toward the lower strata of the society. The break between
the "intelligentsia" and the "people" had occurred precisely
at the level of faith! The higher strata were soon con-
taminated with unbelief and rationalistic libertarianism. Faith
had been preserved in the lower classes most of the time in a
superstitious and "popular" context. Orthodoxy was reduced
to being the confession of "simple folks," of the merchants,
of the peasants. Many began to think that they could not
possibly rally to the Church unless they would make themselves simple, unless they would blend with the people, dig
as deep as the national, historical foundations, and return to
the land. And they confused too often rallying to the Church
with going back to the people. Shortsighted zealots, such as
repentant intellectuals, the rudes and the snobs, concurred in
spreading dangerous prejudices. The Slavophiles carried their
share of responsibility. According to them, the life of the
people itself was a kind of natural catholicity. The com-
mune, the "*mir*," was an embryo of the Church. Even today
there are too many who regard a certain "populism" as the
necessary mode of true Orthodoxy. The *foi du charbonnier*,
the faith of the old nanny, or of the illiterate churchgoer,

was considered as the model and the most authentic type. It seemed proper and safer to enquire concerning the essence of Orthodoxy from the "people" rather than from the "Fathers." Theology, therefore, was not included in the structure of "Russian Orthodoxy." In the name of "simple piety," it is generally acceptable, even today, to use a made up language, falsely popular, bearing the stamp of compunction and piety. This is the most dangerous form of obscurantism and often the appanage of repentant intellectuals. In such a context, orthodoxy often turns into some sort of moralizing folklore. "What would Tsar Alexis Mikhailovich have said, if he had been told that true orthodoxy, outside of monastic enclosures, was preserved only among peasants, that it had been dispelled from among the boyars, the nobles, the prominent merchants of the capital, the officials, and a great many representatives of the small bourgeoisie? In its time, the Church was founded upon the better people of the land, not upon the obscure masses of the countryside, which retains to this day so many uncertain beliefs, pagan survivals, and among which the schism had soon grown deep roots." (S. Trubetskoy)

The entire falsity of religious "populism" is clearly shown by the fact that contrition can never be an "organic" process, although it restores or initiates the spiritual integrity of the soul. For repentance is always a *crisis,* that is to say, a judgment. The only means for truly rallying to the Church is a severe asceticism, and not a return to the people, to the rudiments, and to the simple unity of the origins. Not the folklore, the popular traditions of daily life, but fasting and penitence. There is no reverting to native primitivism, but one has to enter into history, by the assimilation of ecumenical and catholic traditions. "Christianity in Russia, like everywhere else, has ceased to be a popular religion in essence. The people, the simple folk, for the most part, ebb toward half-intellectualism, materialism, socialism; they experience a first-taste infatuation for Marxism, Darwinism, etc. On the contrary, the intellectuals, from the upper, cultured strata of society return to Christian faith. The old-style Orthodoxy, folklore and peasantish, has come to an end; it cannot be brought back to life. We make infinitely higher demands on Christianity, be it ever so mediocre. The Christianity of the humble peasant woman is today a myth; she has become nihilistic and atheist. The believer of today is the philosopher, the man of culture" (Nicolas Berdiaev).

There is in the Russian spirit a fatal *schizothymia*. On the one hand, a craving for knowledge, an intellectual restlessness, an Aristotelian spirit of inquiry. On the other hand a dry and cold passion for simplification. Two wills oppose each other; more exactly, the will is split asunder in twain. We hear often about Russian obscurantism. Now, rare are those who perceive its truly tragic depth. The movement is extremely complex; I say "movement," for it should not be confused with numbness or drowsiness of the rational will; we have to deal with a most active attitude, a positive stand, by no means a passivity. Most diverse elements concur in tying a desperate knot. In the last analysis, what is called "obscurantism" is a *mistrust with regard to culture*. The *stubborn suspicion* of many toward theological science is only a particular case of whatever poisons the Russian genius. Historically, this "obscurantism" was born as a restlessness and vigilance in the presence of a borrowed science, allegedly self-sufficient, yet without roots in the reality of religious experience and life. It was above all a protest and a defense against a lifeless erudition. Such a protest was liable to turn easily into the flattest utilitarianism, as it often happened, and still happens. However, erudition or intellectualism are not yet real knowledge, and the distrust was not without motives or without grounds. The ultimate reason for distrust was that theology had ceased to express, and to witness to, the faith of the Church. And not without cause did one hold theology as being mistaken. In this lies the essential paradox of our religious history. In the depths and recesses of ecclesiastical experience, faith remained intact. Through its contemplation, prayer, and practice of devotion, the Russian soul keeps the style, ancient and rigorous, of the Fathers, it lives in a total communion. But thought has detached itself from it; too often did the soul retreat from the depths and find itself, quite late, aware of this fatal uprooting. "Obscurantism" was the dialectical warning of this loss of ground. Creative theological thought alone will be able to overcome these adverse circumstances, when theology shall return to the depths of the Church and lighten them from within, when reason shall find its center in the heart, and when the heart shall mature through rational meditation. Only then shall there be an entrance into the understanding of truth.

III

Our crisis of breaking away from Byzantinism in the 16th century was an abandonment of Patristic tradition as well. There was no rupture within spiritual experience; on the contrary Russian piety, if we look back, appears even archaic. But theology had lost the Patristic style and methods. The works of the Fathers became archives, lifeless documents. It is not enough to be acquainted with the texts and to know how to draw from them quotes and arguments. One must possess the theology of the Fathers from within. Intuition is perhaps more important for this than erudition, for intuition alone revives their writings and makes them a *witness*. It is only from within that we can perceive and distinguish what (actually) is a catholic testimony from what would be merely theological opinion, hypothesis, interpretation, or theory. "The Fathers are," Newman observed keenly, "our teachers, but not our confessors or casuists; they are the prophets of great things, not the spiritual directors of individuals" (*Essays,* 11, 371). Reviving the Patristic style is the very premise of theological renaissance. This does not mean a restoration, a return to the past, nor a repetition. "Returning to the Fathers" means, for all intents, to advance, not to go backwards. What we need is to be faithful to the spirit, not to the letter of the Fathers, to let ourselves be kindled at the flame of their fiery inspiration, not to gather specimens for a herbarium.

There are two types of consciousness; individual and catholic. "Catholic consciousness" is not collective consciousness, not a kind of "consciousness in general." The ego does not disappear, nor is it dissolved in the "we." On the contrary, personal consciousness reaches its completion and its accomplishment in the catholic transfiguration, liberates itself from its reclusion and alienation, and inhales the integrality of the other individuals. According to a suggestive formula of Prince S. Trubetskoy, "it holds in itself the communion with all." This is why it acquires the capacity and the strength to assimilate and to express the consciousness and the life of the all. Only in the integral communion of the Church is this "catholic transfiguration" of consciousness truly possible. Those who, by reason of their humility in the presence of the Truth, have received the gift to express this *catholic consciousness* of the Church, we call them Fathers and Doctors, since what they make us hear is not only their thought or their personal conviction, but moreover the very *witness* of the Church, for they speak from the depth of its catholic fullness. Their theology evolves on the plane of catholicity, of universal communion. And this is the first thing we must learn. Through asceticism and concentration, the theologian must learn to find his bearings *in* the Church: *Cor nostrum sit semper in Ecclesia:* We must mature and rise up to the catholic level, go beyond our narrow subjectivism and out of our particular retreat. In other words, we must be engrafted in the Church, in order to grow in it and live in that mysterious tradition, integral and trans-temporal, which embraces the sum of all revelations and visions. There, and there only, is the guaranty of creative work, and not in the seductive affirmation of a prophetic freedom. We need less to worry about freedom than about Truth. Only truth makes free. To believe that "a thought without roots, a schismatic truth, is always freer" would be a dangerous illusion.

Freedom is neither in being rooted in the natural soil, nor in being uprooted; it is found in Truth and in the life of Truth, in the illumination of the Spirit. The Church alone possesses the strength and power of the true, catholic synthesis. In this consists its *potestas magisterii,* the gift and unction of infallibility.

The consciousness of knowing must expand, embrace the fullness of the past, and, at the same time, the continuity of growth into the future. Theological consciousness must become historical. Only on account of its historicity can it possibly be catholic. Indifference for history always leads to a sectarian dryness, to a doctrinaire attitude. Historical sensitiveness is indispensable to the theologian, it is the necessary condition for being in the Church. Whoever is insensitive to history would hardly be a good Christian. Not by mere chance did the decline of ecclesial awareness during the Reformation coincide with a mystical blind spot with regard to history. It is true that the Protestants, in their polemic with Rome on papal innovations, were in fact the creators of "Church history" as a particular discipline, and they contributed more than any others to this ecclesiastical science. Nevertheless the historical phenomenon as such had, in their eyes, lost its religious value and virtue; what they saw in history was merely the genesis of a decadence (it was their purpose to prove this), the object of their research being rather "primitive" Christianity, to wit, something which antecedes the history of the Church. Such is the very point of "modernism." It implies a kind of unbelief toward history; it hails back to positivism and humanism; one begins by thinking that Christian truth cannot be established from history as a starting point, and that it can be affirmed only by "faith." History knows only Jesus of Nazareth; faith alone confesses in Him the Christ. This historical scepticism is overcome in the Church through the catholicity of its experience, far beneath the surface, on which a humanist's glance strays and skids. The Church recognizes and proclaims dogmatic events as facts of history. Theandry is such a fact, and not merely a postulate of the faith. In the Church, history must be for the theologian a perspective that is *real*. To do the task of a theologian in the Church is to work in the element of history. For "ecclesiality" is tradition. The theologian must discover history as a *theanthropic process*, a pass-over from time to the eternity of grace, the becoming and the building of the Body of Christ. Only in history is it possible to know this growth of the Mystical Body, to be convinced of the mystical reality of the Church, and to rid oneself from the temptation which consists in dehydrating Christianity in order to reduce it to an abstract Doctrine or a system of morals. Christianity is whole in history, it concerns history. It is not a revelation in history, but rather an appeal to history, to *historical action and creation*. Everything in the Church is dynamic, everything is in action and in motion since Pentecost until the Great Day. Now such a movement is not a movement away from the past. On the contrary, it is much more to be regarded as its continuous bearing of fruit. Tradition lives and quickens within creation. *Accomplishment* is the fundamental category of history. Theological endeavor is justified only within the perspective of history, in as much as it is a creative ecclesiastical datum.

The historical sensitiveness of Russian thought, the testing of its meditations and of its experiences, are the best token of its expected theological renewal. To be sure, the road of historical reminiscence was travelled too fast, and only on the plane of contemplation. It would not be correct to say that Russian theology, in its creative development, has perceived and assimilated completely or deeply enough the

Fathers and Byzantium. This, it must still do. It must pass through the austere schooling of Christian Hellenism. Hellenism, so to speak, assumed a perpetual character in the Church; it has incorporated itself in the very fabric of the Church as the *eternal category* of Christian existence. Of course what is meant here is not that ethnical Hellenism of modern Hellas or of the Levant, nor Greek phyletism, which is obsolete and without justification. We are dealing with Christian antiquity, with the Hellenism of dogma, of the liturgy, of the icon. In the liturgy, the Hellenic style of the "piety of the mysteries" enter into the rhythm of the liturgical *mystagogy* without passing through some sort of mystical "re-hellenization." Could anyone who is in the Church be foolish enough to deliberately "de-hellenize" the services and transpose them into a more "modern" style? Moreover, Hellenism is something more than a passing stage—in the Church. Whenever a theologian begins to think that the "Greek categories" are outmoded, this simply means that he has stepped out of the rhythm of communion. Theology cannot possibly be catholic except within Hellenism. Now, Hellenism is ambiguous. An anti-Christian element was predominant in the ancient mind. Till now, there are many who take refuge themselves in Hellenism for the express purpose to rise and fight against Christianity (simply think of Nietzsche!) But Hellenism was integrated into the Church; such is the historic meaning of Patristic theology. This "integration of Hellenism" involved a merciless rupture, the criterion of which had been the preaching the Gospel, the historical manifestation of the Incarnate Word. Christian Hellenism, transfigured as it was, is wholly historical. Patristic theology is always a "theology of facts," it confronts us with events, the events of sacred history. All the errors and temptations of a Hellenization forwarded indiscretely—they happened repeatedly in the course of history—cannot possibly weaken the significance of this fundamental fact: the "good news" and Christian theology, once and for all, were expressed from the start in Hellenistic categories. Patristic and catholicity, historicity and Hellenism are the joint aspects of a unique and indivisible datum.

This plea for Hellenism will stir up foreseeable objections. These were formulated more than once, and from several sides. The attempt of A. Ritschl and his school is well known. It aimed at emptying Christian doctrine of all its historical elements, in order to return to a purely "Biblical" foundation. Whenever this process is carried to its logical conclusion, the result is that the whole of Christianity disintegrates into humanitarian morals, in effect a travesty; such a return to the Bible is an illusion. Equally insufficient would be any interpretation of Revelation based exclusively on "semitic" categories, namely the "Law" and the "Prophets."

This approach has seduced many scholars; it is particularly evident in "dialectical theology," in K. Barth, E. Brunner, and others. The New Testament is interpreted in the framework of the Old, at the level of Prophecy, but Prophecy without a consummation, as if the prophecies had not been fulfilled. History is underrated, and the emphasis is placed on the Last Judgment, with the effect of narrowing the full span of Revealed Truth. But Biblical prophecy finds precisely its true realization in Christian Hellenism: *Vetus testamentum in Novo patet.* The New Testament and the Church of the New Testament embrace Jew and Greek in the unity of a new life. The categories of sacred Hebraism have lost their independent meaning. Every attempt at disengaging them or extracting them from the Christian synthesis leads to a relapse into Judaism. The truth of "Hebraism" is included in the Hellenic synthesis. Hellenism was integrated into the Church precisely through the Biblical engrafting. It is impossible, even from a historical point of view, to justify the opposition between "Semitism" and "Hellenism." When German idealism conquered the hearts, some scholars devised to transpose all the dogmatics and even the dogmas from the allegedly obsolete language of Hellenism into the idioms, more intelligible and actual, of the new idealism, in the manner of Hegel, Schelling, Baader, and their like (Khomiakov himself had thought to do that). Similar attempts went on to our days. Could the man of Faustian culture be satisfied with the static code of an ancient Hellenism? All these antiquated words, have they not lost their flavor? The soul itself, was it not so altered, as to lose its faculty of being impressed by all those terms "hopelessly and fatally obsolete?" But why, shall we ask straightway? Would it not be that our contemporaries fail to remember their lineage, and are therefore unable to understand, within themselves, their own past which they have rejected? After all, "modern philosophy and psychology" must first be submitted to a test and a justification, the criterion of which is rooted in the depths of ecclesiastical experience. And there is no common measure between the latter and the methods of Hegel or Kant. Or are we supposed to evaluate the fullness of the Church according to a Kantian standard, or to re-measure it with the yardstick of Lotze or Bergson, even perhaps of Schelling? The very idea is somewhat tragi-comic.

No, what is wanted, is not to translate the old dogmatic formulas into a modern language, but, on the contrary, to return creatively to the "ancient" experience, to re-live it in the depth of our being, and to incorporate our thought in the continuous fabric of ecclesial fullness. All those tentative transpositions or translations have never been anything else but betrayals, that is to say, new interpretations in terms thoroughly *inappropriate.* Their terms always suffered from an incurable particularism. They satisfied less the needs of contemporaries than the fads of the day. Turning away from Christian Hellenism is by no means moving ahead, but backwards, toward the dead ends and the perplexities of the other Hellenism, the one that had not been transfigured, and from which there was no escape but through Patristic integration. German idealism itself was nothing else but a backsliding into pre-Christian idealism. Whoever is unwilling to abide by the Fathers, who fears to be left trailing after "Patristic scholasticism," who strives after progress and presses onward on the secular plane, in vain, is fatally thrown back by the very logic of things and finds himself again in the company of Plato and Aristotle, Plotinus and Philo, that is to say, before Christ. His journey is a futile, outmoded excursion from Jerusalem to Athens.

Other objections against the "plea for Hellenism" come from the opposite side, not from Western philosophy, but form the spirit of the Russian people itself. Would it not be proper to transcribe orthodoxy in the Slavic key, in conformity with the style of this "Slavic soul" recently gained for Christ? A few Slavophiles (for example Orest-Miller), and after them some Populists, conceived of such endeavors. Whatever was Greek was suspected of intellectualism and consequently pronounced superfluous and alien to the exigencies of the Russian heart. "Not by chance did our people assimilate Christianity by starting, not from the Gospel, but from the Prologue; was catechized, not by predication, but by the liturgy, not by theology, but by worship, adoration and reverence for the sacred things." Tareiev has recently questioned Greek "tradition" or influence more frankly than anyone else. Quite logically, he extends to Patristic tradition his rejection of all kinds of Hellenism. "Patristic doctrine is from end to end a gnosticism," he believed. It is proper therefore that theology should proceed along its own track in order to obviate "Byzantine gnosticism." It is necessary to create a "philosophy of the heart." If such a philosophy does not replace dogmatic theology, which is a typical product of Greek intellectualism, it might at least disguise it. Tareiev declaimed with pathos against Greek oppression, against the Byzantine yoke: "Greek gnosticism had fettered religious thought, checked our theological creativity; it hindered the growth of our philosophy of the heart, it caused its root to dry up, it burned its shoots." In fact Tareiev is simply inserting surreptitiously an illusory foundation beneath that sweet and widespread kind of obscurantism which appears whenever one seeks in the ardor of piety as in the "philosophy of the heart" a refuge from all the tribulations of the spirit. We cannot help wondering how a man can so naively withdraw himself from history and from the Christian heritage, with the candor and indifference of those who have forgotten their origins. Russian theology did not suffer from Greek oppression. It suffered, on the contrary, for its imprudence and lightheartedness in breaking up the continuity of the Hellenic and Byzantine traditions. The fact of excluding itself from this succession has cast a lasting spell on the Russian soul and made it barren, for creation is impossible without living traditions. Renouncing the Greek patrimony is actually tantamount to ecclesiastical suicide.

IV

In the order of imitation, our theology went through the principal stages of religious thought in modern Europe, namely: the theology of the Council of Trent, the period of the Baroque, Protestant scholasticism and Protestant orthodoxy, pietism and freemasonry, German idealism and romanticism, the social-christian fermentation in the wake of the French revolution, the decomposition of the Hegelian school, the new critical and historical science, Tübingen and Ritschl, neo-romanticism and symbolism; all these came and left their imprint on the Russian cultural experience. Dependence and imitation, however, did not yet mean an intimate meeting. The latter is achieved only in the freedom and equality of love. It is not sufficient to repeat the ready-made answers of the West; we must rather analyze them and personally experience them, penetrate and appropriate to ourselves all the problematics and the drama of Western religious thought, follow and interpret the most difficult and winding course travelled since the Schism. One cannot possibly enter into a life as it is being created, except through the channel of its problematics, and one must feel and perceive it precisely in its problematic aspect as a quest and as an unrelenting search. Orthodox theology shall not be able to establish its independence from western influences unless it reverts to the Patristic sources and foundations. This does not mean forsaking our time, withdrawing from history, deserting the battlefield. We must not only retain the experience of the Fathers, but moreover develop it while discovering it, and use it in order to create a living work. Likewise, independence with regard to the heterodox West must not degenerate into alienation. Breaking away from the West does not bring about any true liberation. Orthodox thought has to feel the Western difficulties or temptations and bear with them; it may not usurp the right to bypass or brazenly to ignore them. We must, through creative thinking, resume and transmute all this experience of the West, its pangs and its doubts; we must take upon ourselves, as Dostoevsky used to say, "the European anguish," accumulated through centuries of creative history. It is only through such sympathy, such active compassion, that the divided Christian world may possibly find the way to union, welcome the separated brethren and witness their return to unity. We must not merely refute and reject Western pronouncements and errors, but rather overcome them through a new creative activity. This will constitute for Orthodox thought the best possible antidote against the hidden or unknown poisons which affect it. Orthodoxy is called upon to answer the questions of the heterodox from the utmost depth of its continuous catholic experience, and to offer to Western heterodoxy less a refutation than a testimony, even the truth of Orthodoxy.

There has been much concern among us Russians concerning the meaning of the Western evolution. Several found Europe truly a "second fatherland." Could one nevertheless affirm that we really knew the West? There was much more dialectical arbitrariness than correct vision in the current schemes which were applied to the Western process. The picture of an imaginary Europe, as we wished to see it, hid too often the real Europe. The soul of the West manifested itself principally through the arts, chiefly since the end of the nineteenth century, following the renewal of esthetics. The heart had been moved, and sensibility had increased. But *"Einfühlung"* never leads to the core of things, it even precludes feeling all the acuity of religious distress and anxiety. The attitude of "esthetism," generally speaking, does not favor much problem raising; it satisfies itself too easily with an inactive contemplation. More and earlier than any others, the Slavophiles, since Gogol and Dostoevsky, perceived the Christian strain and restlessness of the West. Soloviev was less familiar with the West, less aware of its inconsistencies and contradictions, obsessed as he was with "Christian politics." In fact, he knew very little of the West, besides ultramontanism and German idealism (one should add perhaps Fourier, Swedenborg, the spiritualists and, among the ancient masters, Dante). But Soloviev believed overmuch in the steadiness of the West. He was unaware of the romantic thirst and of the anguish from which Christian souls suffered; this he realized only toward the end of his life. The categories of the "old" Slavophiles were also very narrow. Yet they had some sort of intimate acquaintance with the most secret themes of the West. Moreover still, they were conscious of the kinship and responsibility of the Christians, they had an instinct of brotherly compassion, and an awareness or a premonition of the Orthodox calling in Europe. Soloviev dealt with the nation's calling, the theocratic mission of the Russian Empire, rather than with the mission of Orthodoxy. The "old" Slavophiles disengaged the Russian problems from the European exigencies, from the unsolved or insoluble questions raised by the other half of the one Christian world. The feeling of Christian responsibility did constitute the high truth and great moral strength of the early Slavophiles.

Orthodoxy is called to witnessing. Today more than ever,

the Christian West stands before open prospects, as a living question addressed also to the Orthodox world. In this lies the entire significance of the so-called ecumenical movement. Orthodox theology is called upon to demonstrate that the ecumenical problem cannot possibly be solved unless the Church reaches its fulfilment in the fullness of the catholic tradition, intact and immaculate, yet renewed and always growing. Again, it is impossible to "return" save through a crisis, for the way to Christian restoration is *critical,* not *irenic.* The old "polemic" theology has for a long time lost all internal relation to reality. It was nothing more than a school discipline, edified by means of similar western "manuals." *New theology,* in order to refute errors, must be informed by a *historiosophic exegesis* of the religious tragedy of the West. However, such an exegesis must be tested; we must make it our own, and show that it can undergo *catharsis* in the fullness of ecclesial experience and of Patristic tradition. In the new Orthodox synthesis, the centuries old experience of the West must be taken into consideration and studied with more attention and sympathy than our theologians ever did thus far. This does not mean that we should borrow nor adopt Roman doctrines, and indulge in romanizing mimesis. What I try to say is that Orthodox thought shall, at any rate, find a better source of creative inspiration in the great systems of higher scholasticism, in the experience of the western mystics and in the theology of modern Catholicism, than in German idealism, in the Protestant critique of the past centuries or of the present, or even in contemporary "dialectical theology." The rebirth of the Orthodox world is the necessary condition for the solution of the "ecumenical problem."

The *"encounter"* with the West has also another aspect. During the Middle Ages, the West had given birth to a theological tradition characterized by an extreme complexity and intensity, science, culture, research, action, and controversies. Such a tradition continued, to some extent, even

in the epoch of the quarrels and most violent antagonisms of
the Reformation. The solidarity in knowledge was not completely lost in the later free-thinking and libertarian age. In
a sense, western theology remained one up to our day, being
gathered through a feeling of mutual responsibility in the
presence of similar weaknesses and errors. Western tradition
presided to the birth of Russian theology with regard to its
method and contents. We should therefore participate in this
same tradition, with freedom, with responsibility, with conscience, openly, and we should by no means abandon it.
The Orthodox theologian must not and dares not disengage
himself from the universal tide of religious research. It
happens that, after the fall of Byzantium, the West alone
continued in the theological endeavor. The latter constitutes
essentially an ecumenical, catholic problem, but the solution
of this problem was sought only in the schism. Here is the
fundamental paradox of the history of Christian culture. The
West works, while the East keeps silent, or else, and this
is worse; the East repeats bits of sentences spoken by the
West, but without passing them through the sieve of criticism.
The Orthodox theologian is still depending too much on
Western support for his own work. Orthodox theology
borrows its sources from the West; it reads the Fathers and the
acts of the Councils in Western editions, often merely for
the sake of example, and it learns the methods and the
technique of utilization of sources at the school of the West.
We know the past of our Church above all thanks to the
efforts of many generations of Western scholars, as far as
both the facts and their interpretation are concerned. The
fact that the conscience of the West is constantly attentive to
the ecclesial reality of history, that it assumes a responsible
and heedful attitude toward it, that it never desists from
reflecting and meditating on the Christian sources, this fact
already is important. Western thought continues to live in that
past, thereby compensating, so to speak, the weaknesses of its
mystical memory with the liveliness of its recollections. To

the western world, the orthodox theologian himself must bring its witness, the witness of the intimate memory of the Church, in order to have it coincide with the results of historical research. It is only that intimate memory of the Church which vitalizes fully the silent witness of the texts.

V

Prophetizing is not the historian's task. Yet the historian must perceive the rhythm and the meaning of events. And eventually events do prophetize. In such cases, the historian must be aware of his own mission in the presence of their entanglements. Who could possibly doubt this? A new aeon has recently begun in the history of the Christian world. It can be labelled as apocalyptical. I do not mean that our task is to decipher with temerity unknown or forbidden terms. But the *apocalyptic theme* appears far too evident in the entire evolution of actual events. For the first time in history, so it seems, the revolt against God and without God is unleashed with unheard of violence. All Russia is aflame with this anti-God fire and exposed to this fatal precipitation. Generation after generation is dragged into this deadly temptation. There is nothing left neutral in the world, no more dealing with ordinary, homely things; everything now is denied, debated, split asunder, and must be wrestled out of the hand of Antichrist, since his claim is universal; he aims at leaving his imprint on all things; all men are faced with the choice: faith *or* unbelief, and this *or* has become a burning issue. "He that is not with me is against me, and he that gathers not..., scatters abroad." The Revolution has revealed a hard and terrifying truth concerning the Russian soul, to wit an abyss of ancient faithlessness and denial, of demoniac possession and of deterioration. This soul is poisoned, subverted, torn to pieces. Being possessed and seduced, beset by doubt and lure, it cannot possibly be healed and recover its strength except through intense catechizing, through the light of Christian reason, through the language of sincerity and truth, through the voice of the Spirit and through its power. The time is come already when the debate concerning the souls of men appears in plain daylight. Now is the time when every question about knowledge and life must truly find and receive its Christian answer, when it must be integrated in the synthesis and plenitude of confession. Now is the time when theology ceases to be a "private affair," to which everyone may freely attend or show no regard, in proportion of his aptitudes, tendencies, or moods. In this time of temptation and judgment, theology becomes again a public thing, a universal catholic mission. It behooves all to take to spiritual arms. Now is already the time when theological silence, uncertainty, inarticulate witness, are tantamount to treason and flight before the enemy. Silence can cause trouble as much as a hasty or elusive answer. Moreover, unto him who keeps silent, his mutism can be poison and mean his downfall, and he becomes an accomplice, as though faith were "a fragile thing, and not so certain."

A "new theological epoch" has begun. Our time is called upon to resume the task of theology. Some may find this affirmation presumptuous, excessive and arbitrary. Was our epoch not placed under the sign of "social Christianity" ever since Lamennais and Morris, perhaps since Saint Simon? In our troubled age, should not Christianity be called to "social endeavors" for the edification of the New City? Is it still in order today to re-direct religious consciousness toward the intellectual problems of theology and to divert it from the actual "social theme" which an irreversible course of events has brought to the fore? To do this seems rather incongruous in view of the conditions which prevail today in Russia. Is not Russia marked for action, rather than contemplation? Are we justified in weakening the militant "activism" through an appeal to reflection and concentration of the soul? "Doing some theology" in our days appears to many among us

almost a treason or an escapism. Such objections or doubts
manifest a fatal blindness. This is certainly not the time to
withdraw from the "social question" precisely when the
"scarlet star" of socialism is risen to the firmament of
history. However, is not the "social question" first and foremost a spiritual question, a question of conscience and wisdom? Is not the social revolution above all a psychic, confused reversal of the tide? Is not the Russian Revolution a
spiritual catastrophe, a collapse of souls, a passionate out-
burst? Should it not be explained in spiritual terms? The
secret of Russia's future lies far less in her social structure
or technique, than in the *new man* that they try over there
to grow and develop, without God, without faith, without
love. As for the question of faith itself, is it not brought
back to the fore by an irretrievable course of events, in its
rigor, and its ultimate, apocalyptical evidence? Does not
all the intimate problematics of the absence of faith, of the
struggle against God, impose itself today with extreme acuity?
"The spirit, not the flesh, has grown corrupt today, and
man knows a hopeless anguish." (Tyutchev)

It is precisely because we are already engaged in the
apocalyptic struggle that we are called upon to do work as
theologians. Our task is to oppose a responsible and conscious
profession of Christian truth to the atheistic and anti-God
attitude which surrounds us like a viscosity. There cannot be,
there is not, a "neutral" science of God and of Christianity,
indifference and abstention are no longer "neutral" also;
unbelieving knowledge of Christianity is not objective knowledge, but rather some kind of "anti-theology." There is in it so
much passion, at times blind, often obscure and malignant.
There is also restlessness and unexpected glimmers; it would
be only an "anti-theology." Here again theology is called not
only to judge, but also to heal. It is necessary to enter into this
world of doubt, illusion and lies, in order to answer doubt as
well as reproach. But we must enter into this world with the
sign of the Cross in our heart and the name of Jesus in our

spirit, because this is a world of mystical wanderings, where everything is fragmentized, decomposed and refracted as if through a set of mirrors. And here again the theologian must bear witness. This situation is not unlike that of the early centuries, when the seeds had been sown and sprouted in a soil not yet transfigured, but which this first sowing sanctified for the first time. By then, those who announced the Good News had to address themselves most of the time to hearts not enlightened, to the obscure and sinful conscience of the "nations" to which they had been sent, and which were sitting in darkness and in the shadow of death. Our contemporary world, atheistic and ridden with unbelief, is it not comparable in a sense with that pre-Christian world, renewed with all the same interweaving of false religious trends, sceptical and anti-God? In the face of such a world, theology must all the more become again a witness. The theological system cannot be a mere product of erudition, it cannot be born of philosophical reflection alone. It needs also the experience of prayer, spiritual concentration, pastoral solicitude. In theology, the good news, the *kerygma,* must be proclaimed. The theologian must speak to living beings, address himself to living hearts, he must be full of attention and love, conscious of his immediate responsibility for the soul of his brother, and particularly for the soul that is still in the dark. In knowledge in general there is and there must be an element, not merely dialectic, but *dia-logical.* He who knows bears witness for the benefit of those who together with him have the knowledge of the truth; he calls upon them to bow and be humble before it, and he should humble himself as well. Humility is particularly necessary to the theologian. He cannot possibly solve today the problems of souls and consciences arising daily in the pastoral-pedagogical domain, but should not brush them aside either. He must answer from within a complete system of thought, by a theological confession. He must experience in himself, as through an intimate suffering, the entire problematic of the soul which believes not and seeks not, the problematic of voluntary ignorance and of ignorance not desired. The time is come when the refusal of theological knowledge becomes a deadly sin, the stigma of self-conceit and lovelessness, of cowardice and maliciousness. Affected plainness seems a demoniac maneuver; distrusting the reason that seeks must be condemned as satanic mischief. "They are stricken with fear, where there is no fear..." It may be appropriate to recall the sharp words of Metropolitan Philaret of Moscow, here, spoken long ago in a time of trial and of evasive attitudes. "It is very true that the gift and the duty to teach are not everybody's lot, and rare are those whom the Church has honored with the name of Theologian. However, it is not permissible to anyone in Christianity to know nothing at all and to remain ignorant. Was not the Lord himself called Master and did he not call his followers disciples? Christians, before they assumed this title, bore the name of disciples. Would these terms be vain or meaningless? And why did the Lord send apostles into the world? It was first and foremost to teach all nations... If you refuse to teach or to learn within Christianity, you are not disciples of Christ and you do not follow Him; the apostles were not sent for you; you are not what all Christians were from the very beginning of Christianity. I do not know what you are, nor what shall become of you." (*Sermons and Discourses,* IV, pp. 151-2; sermon preached in 1841, on the feast of St. Alexis).

VI

The future reveals itself to us under the sign of duty more surely and with greater depth than it would under the sign of expectation and foreboding. The future is not merely something we are looking and waiting for, but rather something we must create. Our vocation has its source precisely in the responsibility of duty. Even though we are not expecting, yet we find in obedience itself the strength to create and the power to beget. The arbitrariness of the will, on the contrary, is a principle of dispersion. Integration in the Church is through prayer, apocalyptic faithfulness, return to the Fathers, a free *encounter* with the West: these, and other similar factors compose the *creative postulate* of Russian theology within the contemporary framework. Here also is the legacy of the past, and our responsibilities, our obligation toward it. Past errors and failures should not disturb us. We have not reached the term of our course, the history of the Church is not over yet, Russia is not yet at the end of the road. The way ahead is still open, even though it is difficult. The rigorous verdict of history must be transformed into a creative appeal, in order that we may achieve what remains to be done. "Through many pains does it behoove one to enter into God's kingdom." Orthodoxy is not a tradition only; it is also a task; not the unknown *x,* but the data of the problem, which we must forthwith work out. It is a germ of life, a seed that sprouts, our duty and our mission.

The Russian way shall be for a long time a double one. For those who have remained, there is the mysterious way of asceticism, of the secret, silent work of acquiring the Spirit. As for those who have left, there is also a way they must travel, since freedom was left to us and also the power for the spiritual activity of witnessing and preaching. It is only through such effort that the past, filled as it is with forebodings and premonitions, shall be justified, in spite of its weaknesses and errors. True historical synthesis consists not merely in interpreting the past, but also in shaping the future by a creative act.

> "Erat ante in operibus fratrum candida, nunc facta est in matyrum cruore purpurea. Floribus ejus nec lilia, nec rosae desunt."
>
> *St. Cyprian*

Translated from the French by
GEORGES A. BARROIS

III
NINETEENTH CENTURY ECUMENISM

[PUBLISHER'S NOTE: The following article is the *full* text, including notes, of Fr. Florovsky's survey of "Orthodox Ecumenism in the Nineteenth Century." An *"abridged"* form of this article appeared as a *part* of an over-all historical survey of the Orthodox Church's relations with other Christian communions in Volume II of *The Collected Works of Georges Florovsky— Christianity and Culture.*]

Orthodox Ecumenism
in the Nineteenth Century

I

THE EARLY DECADES of the XIXth century were marked by an unusual spiritual unrest in Europe. It was a period of great historical shifts and tensions, catastrophes and commotions. The memories of the French Revolution were still quite fresh. Napoleonic wars turned the whole of Europe into an armed camp, and even a battlefield. The very rhythm of events was feverish. Apocalyptic forebodings and apprehensions were widespread. Napoleon's defeat in Russia was interpreted by not a few as "the Judgment of God on the icy fields," or simply as an eschatological victory over the Beast. There was a growing urge for spiritual unity. Theocratic utopianism was just in the air. In the turbulent atmosphere of those stormy years many were led to the conviction that the whole political and social life of nations had to be radically rebuilt on a strictly Christian

"Orthodox Ecumenism in the Nineteenth Century" originally appeared in *St. Vladimir's Seminary Quarterly*, Vol. IV, Nos. 3 and 4 (1956), 2-53. Reprinted by permission of the author.

foundation. Many utopian plans were laid at that time, of which the most conspicuous was the famous *Holy Alliance* (1815). Contracted by three monarchs—one a Roman Catholic (Austria), another a Lutheran (Prussia), and the third an Eastern Orthodox (Russia)—it was an act of an utopian ecumenism, in which political scheming and apocalyptic dreams were ominously mingled. It was an attempt to re-enact the unity of Christendom. There was but one Christian Nation, of which the nations are the branches; and the true Sovereign of all Christian people was Jesus Christ himself, "no other than He to Whom belongeth might." The Kingdom of God has already been inaugurated, God himself ruling through His anointed. The idea of Divine Providence assumed at that time a rather magical glow. "And then the true New Year will come." As a political venture, the *Holy Alliance* was a complete failure, a dreamy fiction, even a humbug. Yet, it was a symptomatic venture. It was a scheme of Christian unity. But it was to be a "Unity without Union," and not a "Re-union of Churches," but rather a federation of all Christians into one "holy nation" across the denominational boundaries, regardless of all confessional allegiances. Confessional divergences were simply disregarded or ignored, or else disavowed as irrelevant. History became, as it were, transparent, and one could, by faith and hope, discern the signs of the approaching Eschatological Age. The Kingdom of the Spirit will soon be manifested.

Initiative of the *Holy Alliance* was taken by the Russian Emperor, Alexander I, but inspiration came to him from the German pietistic and mystical circles (Jung Stilling, Franz Baader, Mme. Krudener). The Emperor himself was quite convinced of his theocratic vocation. He felt himself called upon to assume religious leadership in his country and to bring together all denominations. Alexander was well read in the mystical and pietistic literature of the West and had personal links with various mystical and revivalist groups. He was especially attracted by the doctrine of the Inner

Light. He wanted to propagate the pure and "Inner Christianity" in his country. A special ministry was created in 1817, the "Ministry of Spiritual Affairs and National Instruction," and, under the leadership of Prince Alexander N. Galitzin, it immediately became the central office of utopian propaganda. Another center of this utopian ecumenism was the Russian Bible Society, inaugurated by an imperial rescript in December, 1812, immediately after Napolean's retreat from Russia, and finally reorganized on a national scale in 1814. Many local branches were established throughout the Empire. Prince Galitzin was the president, and prelates of different Churches were invited to act as vice-presidents or directors: Eastern Orthodox, Armenian, and even the Roman Catholic and Uniate Metropolitans. All had to co-operate in the propagation of the Bible as the only source and only authority of true Christianity. The Russian society was in standing cooperation with the *British and Foreign Bible Society,* and some representatives of the latter were always on the Russian committee. The main purpose of the Bible Society was, as in Britain, "to bring into greater use" the Word of God, so that everyone could experience its saving impact and meet God, "as His Holy Scriptures reveal Him." The unbreakable rule of the Society was to publish the Sacred Books "without any notes or explanations," in order not to contaminate the Divine Word by human opinions and not to compromise by partial interpretations its universal significance. Behind this rule was the theory of "mute signs" and "the living Teacher, dwelling in the hearts."

The immediate objective of the Society was to publish and to distribute Bible translations in all languages spoken in the Russian Empire, including Modern Russian. In the first ten years over 700,000 copies were distributed, in 43 languages or dialects. Along with the distribution of the Scriptures, a mystical ideology was also propagated, an ecumenism of the heart. The positive results of this endeavor should not be overlooked; especially important was the initiative of the translation of the Bible into Modern Russian, taken by the Society with the formal consent of the Holy Synod. Unfortunately, the new ideology was often enforced upon believers by administrative pressure, and no criticism of the doctrines of "Inner Christianity" was permitted. This policy could not fail to provoke a vigorous resistance in the wider circles. Many felt that the Bible Society was propagating, as it were, a "new faith" and tended to become a "new Church," above and across the existing ones. "Non-theological factors" of the resistance cannot be denied. Yet, essentially it was an instinctive self-defense on the part of the historic Churches against the sweeping enthusiasm of the "spirituals." Ultimately, the Bible Society was disbanded by order of the Government in 1826 and its activities cancelled. The Russian translation of the Bible was to be completed only fifty years later, and this time by the authority of the Church itself.

The whole episode was an important essay in ecumenism. It was an encounter of people of various backgrounds. They had to face the problem of division. Unfortunately, the problem was badly presented. The emphasis was shifted from doctrine to "piety." Instead of facing the existing differences and discussing the controversial points, people were invited to disregard them altogether and to seek communion instantly in mystical exercises. Doctrinal problems were simply disregarded or silenced. There was an obvious "awakening of the heart" at that time, but no "awakening of the mind." *Pectus est quod facit theologum:* this was the motto of the time. In any case, it was a narrow approach. One did not have to be a rationalist to feel compelled to vindicate the rights and claims of reason in theology. In any case, doctrinal problems existed. "Inner Christianity" was a doctrine itself, and a very particular doctrine indeed. It must be added that the whole process was closely watched by a competent Roman Catholic observer, who happened to be on the spot. He was the famous Joseph De Maistre, at that time Sardinian Royal ambassador at St. Petersburg. His *Soirées de St. Petersburg*

are, in fact, based on his Russian impressions and on conversations he had with the Russians. His interpretation is
especially interesting because he was originally initiated in a
similar mystical experience and never abandoned the basic
presuppositions of his "theosophic" youth. His ultramontane
solution of the ecumenical problem was, in fact, a duplicate
of the utopian ecumenism of the "spirituals." Both left their
stamp on the further development of ecumenical thinking
in Russia.[1]

II

In the *Conversation of a seeker and a believer concerning
the truth of the Eastern Greco-Russian Church,* by Philaret,
Metropolitan of Moscow, we find a considered opinion on
the basic ecumenical question by one who had been through
the experiences of the "revivalist" age, and yet was deeply
rooted in the catholic tradition. The immediate purpose of
this "dialogue" was to give guidance to those Russians who
were, at that time, troubled by Roman Catholic propaganda
(the work was first published in 1832). But Philaret sets
forth the problem of Church unity in all its width. He
begins with the definition of the Church as the Body of
Christ. The full measure and inner composition of the Body
is known to Christ alone, who is its Head, its principle of
life and ruling wisdom. The "visible Church," the Church in
history, is but an external manifestation of the glorious
"Church invisible," which cannot be "seen" distinctly, but
only discerned and apprehended by faith. The visible Church
includes the "infirm" members, also. The main criterion here
is that of the Christological belief. "Mark you, I do not
presume to call false any church, believing that *Jesus is Christ.*
The Christian Church can only be either *purely true,* con-
fessing the true and saving Divine teaching without the false
admixture and pernicious opinions of men, *or not purely true,*

mixing with the true and saving teaching of faith in Christ the false and pernicious opinions of men." Christendom is visibly divided. The Church of Rome deviated from the teaching of the early Church Universal; yet it is still united with the rest of Christendom in its Christological faith. Authority in the Church belongs to the common consent of the Church Universal, based on the Word of God. Ultimately, separated from the Church are only those who do not confess that Jesus is Son of God, God Incarnate, and Redeemer. The Eastern Church has ever been faithful to the original deposit of faith; it has kept the pure doctrine. In this sense, it is the only true Church.

But Philaret would not "judge" or condemn the other Christian bodies (he had in view, first of all, the "Western Church," i.e., Rome). Even the "impure" churches somehow belong to the mystery of Christian Unity. The ultimate judgment belongs to the Head of the Church. The destiny of Christendom is one, and in the history of schisms and divisions one may recognize the secret action of Divine Providence, which heals the wounds and chastizes the deviations, that ultimately it may bring the glorious Body of Christ to unity and perfection. "You expect now that I should give judgment concerning the other half of the present Christianity, but I just simply look upon them; in part I see how the Head and Lord of the Church heals many deep wounds of the old serpent in all the parts and limbs of this body, applying now gentle, now strong remedies, even fire and iron, in order to soften hardness, to draw out poison, to clean the wounds, to separate our malignant growths, to restore spirit and life in the half-dead and numbed structures. In such wise I attest my faith that in the end the power of God patently will triumph over human weakness, good over evil, unity over division, life over death." Obviously, Philaret was much ahead of his time, not only in the East; and yet to some extent his ideas served as a basis for the reunion of the Uniates in Western Russia (1839).

On the other hand, Philaret's outline was clearly incomplete. He spoke of one aspect of unity only, namely of unity in doctrine. He did not say much of the Church order. And probably Vladimir Soloviev was right in his critical remarks: "The breath and conciliatory nature of this view cannot conceal its essential defects. The principle of unity and universality in the Church only extends, it would seem, to the common ground of Christian faith, namely the dogma of the Incarnation . . . The Universal Church is reduced to a logical concept. Its parts are real, but the whole is nothing but a subjective abstraction." This is, of course, an exaggeration. The Church Universal was for Philaret not "a logical concept," but a mystery, the Body of Christ in its historical manifestation. What is true, however, is that the "sacramental aspect" of the Church was not sufficiently emphasized; and for that reason, the relationship between the "invisible" unity of the Church and its historical state at present, "the Church in its divided and fragmentary condition," was not clearly explained.

Philaret was probably the greatest theologian of the Russian Church in modern times, and his influence on the life and theological thinking in Russia was enormous. He was a great scholar, Biblical and Patristic, and a man of a sensitive heart, warm piety and mystical insight. In addition he was a master of speech, a great preacher. Yet, Philaret did his studying at a time when Russian theological schools were dominated by Protestant textbooks and the influence of Protestant phraseology can easily be detected in his writings. He was well read in the mystical literature of all ages and of different denominations, and was invariably impressed by "warm piety" wherever he might find it. All these influences enlarged his theological vision, and he was fully aware of the unity of Christendom, and of Christian destiny. With all this he was truly traditional, and the real masters of his thoughts were the Holy Fathers of the Church. Philaret had a strong anti-Roman bias and was an avowed enemy of "scholasticism." In later years, he had several occasions to express himself on certain particular ecumenical topics (mainly in connection with Anglican-Orthodox relations; see below). He was regarded as the chief theological expert in the Russian Church of his day. He was a living link between several generations: Born in 1782, he died in 1867, and was Metropolitan of Moscow for 47 years (from 1821), active and fresh until the day of his death.[2]

III

The second quarter of the XIXth century was a time of theological revival in many countries. Interest was centered precisely on ecclesiology. It was, in a certain sense, a true *rediscovery of the Church,* as being an organic and concrete reality, with special stress on her historic continuity, perpetuity, and essential unity. The famous book by John Adam Moehler (1796-1838), Professor of Church History on the Catholic Faculty of Tubingen (and later at Munich), *Die Einheit in der Kirche, oder das Prinzip des Katholicismus* (1825), must be mentioned first of all in this connection. It was a great ecumenical book, although its ecumenical implications were not obvious at first glance, and its immediate sequel, Moehler's *Symbolik* (1832), led the author into a vigorous polemics with the Protestants. In any case, Moehler's conception of Church Unity meant a move from a "static" to a "dynamic," or even "prophetic," interpretation. The Church was shown to be more than an "institution," rather a living organism, and its institutional aspect was described as a spontaneous manifestation of its inner being. Tradition itself was interpreted as a factor of growth and life, and Moehler's appeal to Christian Antiquity was by no means just an archeological concern. The "past" was still alive, as the vital power and spiritual leaven—as "the depth of the present."[3] It may be argued whether Moehler's conception had any direct influence on the formation of the Tractarian theology of the Church. Yet, a "palpable convergence of views" between the Early Tractarians and the Catholic School of Tübingen cannot be denied, even if it can be explained by a parallel development of the same fundamental presuppositions.[4]

About the same time, Alexis S. Khomiakov (1804-1860) in Russia was very close to Moehler in his treatment of ecclesiological doctrine, and probably was well acquainted with his writings, even if he arrived at his conclusions by an independent study of the Fathers.[5] In all these cases there was a renewed interest in Christian antiquity, but it was regarded as a source of inspiration, rather than as an established pattern to be reinforced. What actually was rediscovered was the vision of an organic continuity in the Church, both structural and dynamic. Or perhaps one should say it was a rediscovery of the *sacred character* of the historical process in the Church. The identity of Christian belief had to be warranted by a universal consent through the ages. But it was no longer just a formal identity of doctrine, regarded in itself as a set of propositions, but rather a perpetuity of the living Church, which professes beliefs and teaches doctrines out of its unchangeable vision and experience. The Church itself now becomes the main subject of theological study. The most spectacular episode in this ecclesiological revival was, no doubt, the Oxford Movement in the Church of England (and its ramifications in the other branches of the Anglican Communion). Its main concern was the vindication of the "Catholic" character of the Anglican Church. The Church of England had to be regarded as the "Catholic Church in England." Then, it was inevitable to ask an "ecumenical" question: what was the relation of this local or territorial "Catholic" Church to all other "Catholic Churches" in various parts of the world? The answer currently given to this question is commonly known as "the branch theory" of the Church. It is very difficult to find

out by whom this imagery of the "branches" was first used
in this connection,[6] but it does not particularly matter. There
was already a suggestion behind the famous phrase of
Lancelot Andrewes: *Pro Ecclesia Catholica: Orientali, Oc-
cidentali, Brittanica.* Apparently Newman used it in the same
sense at an early date: "We are the English Catholics; abroad
are the Roman Catholics, some of whom are also among
ourselves; elsewhere are the Greek Catholics."[7]

Much later, many years after his "conversion," Newman
interpreted "the formal teaching of Anglicanism" ("this is
what we held and professed in Oxford forty years ago")
in the following way (written in 1882): at present, the
Church existed in three branches, "or rather in a triple presence,"—the Latin, the Greek, and the Anglican—"these
three being one and the same Church," except for some
secondary, fortuitous and local variations, even if they are
rather important. "And, whereas the whole Church in its
fullness was at once and severally Anglican, Greek and Latin,
so in turn each one of those three was the whole Church;
whence it followed that, whenever any one of the three was
present, the other two, by the nature of the case, were absent,
and therefore the three could not have direct relations with
each other, as if they were three substantive bodies, there
being no real difference between them except the external
accident of place. Moreover, since, as has been said, on a
given territory, there could be no more than one of the three,
it followed that Christians generally, wherever they were,
were bound to recognize, and had a claim to be recognized
by, that one, ceasing to belong to the Anglican Church, as
Anglican, when they were in Rome, and ignoring Rome as
Rome, when they found themselves in Moscow. Lastly, not to
acknowledge this inevitable outcome of the initial idea of
the Church, viz., that it was both everywhere and one, was
bad logic, and to act in opposition to it was nothing short
of setting up altar against altar, that is, the hideous sin of
schism, and sacrilege."[8] This theory amounted to the conten-

tion that, strictly speaking, the Church *was not divided* at all, and only *visible* communication (or "communion") had been broken, and therefore the problem of "re-union" consisted in the restoration of the suspended "inter-communion," or in the mutual recognition of the separated branches of the Catholic Church. This point of view was held, strongly and persistently, by William Palmer, of Worcester College, Oxford, in his book, which can be regarded as the first systematic presentation of Tractarian ecclesiology: *A Treatise on the Church of Christ: designed chiefly for the use of students of Theology* (first published in 1838; 2nd ed. 1839; 3rd ed. 1842; 2 vols.). In the author's opinion, "external communion" did not belong to the essence of the Church, and consequently the Church was still One, although the visible unity of the body had been lost.

It should not be forgotten that this theory was concerned with the "Catholic Churches" only, and all non-Episcopal denominations were not regarded as "churches" in any proper sense of the term. It should be noted again that, according to this theory or interpretation, a very wide variety, and even a serious divergence, of doctrinal views and practices was compatible with essential unity. In other words, the main emphasis was on the reality of the Church, and not so much on the Doctrine as such.[9] Practically, this interpretation of Church unity has remained, ever since, the basic presupposition, on the Anglican side, of all negotiations between the Anglican Communion and the Orthodox Churches of the East. And it was precisely at this point that a major misunderstanding between the Churches was bound to arise, even if the Orthodox would not on all occasions openly and formally question the initial assumption of the Anglicans. In any case, the former would always insist upon an identity of doctrine and make the "reality" of the Church itself dependent upon the purity and completeness of the Faith. It may even be argued that the basic obstacle for the *rapprochement* between the Anglicans and the Churches of the East lay in the field of Ecclesiology. Eastern theologians would repeatedly insist that the Orthodox Church is the *only* true Church, and all other Christian bodies are but "schisms," i.e. that the unity of Christendom had been essentially broken. This claim of the Orthodox could be variously phrased and qualified, but, in one form or another, it would unfailingly be made on all occasions.

IV

The Early Tractarians were not especially interested in the contemporary Churches of the East. Of course, all of them, and especially Newman and Pusey, were deeply interested in the Greek Fathers, as authoritative witnesses and interpreters of the Apostolic and Catholic Faith. The "Tracts for the Times" were full of Patristic references and quotations, and the *Library of Fathers of the Holy Catholic Church, anterior to the division of the East and West* was one of the main enterprises of the Tractarians. Yet, the Early Tractarians would not identify the "Church of the Fathers" with the contemporary "Churches of the East." In spite of theoretical recognition, the Christian East was not yet recognized as an integral part of Christendom in practice. It was still felt to comprise rather a "strange world." The prevailing impression in the Anglican circles was that the Churches in the East were decadent, backward, ignorant or somnolent, and "corrupt"; even the Tractarians were not free from this prejudice. "Some Early Tractarian writings suggest complete indifference (to the Eastern Church), and seem content to take into account only Rome and the Church of England. And besides poverty of allusion, there are instances of insufficient familiarity with the subject" (P. E. Shaw).[10] More information became available in the 'forties, but interest was growing rather slowly.

It was disappointment in the West, i.e. Rome, which

diverted attention to the East. As early as 1840, Pusey raised the question.

> It will come as a painful question to many, and to some be a difficulty as to our Church (as they come to see the perfect unity of Antiquity), why are we in communion with no other Church except our own sisters or daughters?—We cannot have communion with Rome; why should we not with the *Orthodox* Greek Church? Would they reject us, or must we keep aloof? Certainly one should have thought that those who have not conformed with Rome would, practically, be glad to be strengthened by intercourse with us, and countenanced by us. One should have hoped that they would have been glad to be re-united with a large Christian Church exterior to themselves, provided we need not insist upon their adopting the *Filioque*.[11]

In the following year, Pusey repeated the same question in his "Open Letter" to Dr. Jelf: "Why should we...direct our eyes to the Western Church alone, which, even if united in itself would yet remain sadly maimed, and sadly short of the Oneness she had in her best days, if she continued severed from the Eastern?"[12]

Pusey was probably impressed by contacts recently established with the Greek Church (to which he was alluding, also, in his "Letter" to the Archbishop of Canterbury), in connection with the proposal of erecting an Anglican bishopric in Jerusalem (jointly with the Church of Prussia).[13] In the fall of 1839, the Rev. George Tomlinson, at that time Secretary of S.P.C.K. (and later first Bishop of Gibraltar), was sent to the East, primarily in order to ascertain the needs of the Greek Church in the field of religious literature. He was given commendatory letters, addressed to "the Bishops of the Holy Eastern Church," by the Archbishop of Canter-

bury and Bishop of London, and written in ancient Greek.
He called on the Patriarch of Constantinople and explained
to him the character of the English Church, stressing its
Catholic character and its friendly disposition "toward the
Mother Church of the East." He wanted to stress especially
that the Anglican Church, as such, had no missionary objective in the Levant, but was interested only in fraternal
intercourse with the Eastern Church.[14] The same attitude was
taken by the American Episcopalian representative at Constantinople, The Rev. Horatio Southgate (later Bishop),
acting head of the "Mission" of the Protestant Episcopal
Church to the East. He was following closely the official
instruction given him by the Presiding Bishop, Alexander V.
Griswold: "Our great desire is to commence and to promote
a friendly intercourse between the two branches of the One
Catholic and Apostolic Church." Bishop Griswold himself
was a man of strong "evangelical" convictions, but his
directives were colored by another conception of Ecumenical
relationship.[15]

Pusey seemed to be justified in his conclusion. "This
reopened intercourse with the East," he wrote to the Archbishop, "*is a crisis in the history of our Church. It is a wave
which may carry us onward, or, if we miss it, it may bruise
us sorely and fall on us, instead of landing us on the shore.
The union or disunion of the Church for centuries may
depend upon the wisdom with which this providential open-
ing is employed."[16] The question of the Eastern Church, in
any case, had been brought to the fore. In this perspective,
"the Palmer episode," i.e. William Palmer's (of Magdalen
College, Oxford) visits to Russia in 1840 and 1841, and
his protracted conversations (oral and epistolary) with the
Orthodox authorities and scholars, appears to be much more
than an eccentric personal venture or just a detached "episode," as much as it has been colored by the individual
character of the man and his private convictions and manners. One should not forget that Palmer vigorously inter-

vened in the debate about the Jerusalem Bishopric and took an anti-Protestant position.[17] His visit to Russia was, as it were, an experimental test of the ecumenical validity of the general Tractarian conception of the Church Universal.

V

William Palmer (1811-1879) has been described by one of his friends as an "ecclesiastical Don Quixote" (Canon F. Meyrick). He was also called the Ulysses of the Tractarian Movement. He was an an ecumenical traveller indeed. Palmer was a man of unusual abilities: he had wide and profound learning, a powerful intellect—though rather inflexibe and obstinate—steadfastness of purpose, unbending sincerity and strong will. His main weakness was precisely his organic inability to compromise, or to adjust himself to the circumstances—"his inability to reconcile himself to the conditions of imperfect humanity and human institutions," as Canon Meyrick put it—which made him ultimately a champion of forlorn hopes. He had a very solid classical background—having commenced Greek at the age of six (and Latin at five), and he was already using the Greek Testament as a boy of nine. It provided an early preparation for his later study of the Christian East. A graduate of Eton and Magdalen College, Oxford, where he obtained first class in Classics, Palmer was for some years classical tutor at Durham, subsequently returning to Oxford, as a Fellow of his own college.

His interest in the East was probably first aroused by his contact with a Nestorian Christian, who happened to be on a visit to England (in 1837). In 1839, during the visit of the Russian Heir Apparent to Oxford, Palmer presented him a memorandum (approved by the old Dr. Routh), suggesting that a Russian ecclesiastic should be sent to Oxford (to reside at Magdalen) in order to examine the doctrines

of the Anglican Church, and asking for protection in the
case of his own visit to Russia with a similar purpose. He
actually went to Russia in the following year and was given
a letter of introduction by the President of Magdalen, in
spite of the strong objection raised by certain Fellows of
the college "against this Society's giving any encouragement
to the idea of intercommunion with the *idolatrous* Greek
Church." Curiously enough, the man who raised the objection
went over to Rome in the next year (R. W. Sibthorp).[18] The
letter was in Latin, on parchment, and sealed. It was stated
that Palmer was going to Russia in order to study doctrines
and rites of the Church, and to learn Russian. Then followed
an unexpected clause. "Further, I ask, and even adjure in the
name of Christ, all the most holy Archbishops and Bishops,
and especially the Synod itself, that they examine him as to
the orthodoxy of his faith with a charitable mind, and, if
they find in him all that is necessary to the integrity of the
true and saving faith, then that they will also admit him to
communion in the Sacraments."

Palmer was instructed to conform with all injunctions
of the Russian bishops, while in Russia, provided he would
not contradict the faith and teaching of the British Church.
The document was probably composed by Palmer himself,
but Dr. Routh consented to issue it in his own name, although he anticipated that Palmer's request could not be
granted: "for a separation there unhappily is." Archbishop
Howley of Canterbury declined to be implicated in the venture
in any way, although he was rather interested in its prospects.
As should have been expected, Palmer's hope was frustrated.
His claim to be a member of the Catholic Church was met
with astonishment. Was not the Church of England, after all,
a "Protestant" body? As Newman put it at that time, "the
Russians will not believe him against the evidence of all
the English they ever saw before."[19] In 1838 and 1839, Palmer
wrote (in Latin) an Introduction to the Thirty-Nine Articles,
in which he endeavored to interpret them in a Catholic

sense, anticipating in a certain sense what Newman was going to do in his famous Tract XC (published in February 1841), although Newman himself read Palmer's essay only after his own had been published. Palmer's "Introduction" was printed privately and apparently was not widely circulated. Now, he offered it to the Russian authorities as a basis for doctrinal discussion. He felt, himself, that he could agree with the Eastern doctrine on all essential issues, except the teaching about the procession of the Holy Spirit, on which he was still holding the Western view. Not everything in Palmer's explanations was satisfactory to the Russians. They were insistent on a complete conformity in all doctrines, and would not consent to confine the "agreement" to those doctrines which were formally stated in the period before the separation of the East and West. The main interlocutor of Palmer was the Archpriest Basil Koutnevich, the Chaplain General of the Army and Navy, and Member of the Holy Synod. He was ready to admit that doctrinal differences between the Orthodox and Anglican Churches, if properly interpreted, were rather slight. Nevertheless, in his opinion, the Anglican Church was a separate communion. His conception of the Church was, more or less, the same as that of Metropolitan Philaret. The Eastern Church was the only true and orthodox Church; all other communions have deviated from the truth. Yet, "Christ is the center of all," and Christian life was possible in the separated bodies also.

For Palmer it was *"amabilis sane sententia, sed perniciosissima doctrina,"* which could only encourage relativism, indifference, and even unbelief. For him, no real "sanctity" was possible in heretical or sectarian bodies. Moreover, he could not equate the Eastern Church with the Church Universal. In any case, she did not act as a Universal Body, and was too tolerant. Russians, on the other hand, were staggered, as Palmer himself stated, "at the idea of one visible Church being made up of three communions, differing in doctrine and rites, and two of them at least condemning and anathematizing the others." In Palmer's opinion, Russian theologians and prelates were not clear at all on the definition of the visible Catholic Church, "but were either vaguely liberal, or narrowly Greek." One should keep in mind that when Palmer visited Russia it was during a time of theological transition, or of a "Struggle for Theology." A great variety of opinions could be found among theologians. They were in search of a new theological synthesis. This was probably a common feature of the epoch, a revival of search after the decline of the Enlightment.[20]

It was recently stated by a competent Roman Catholic scholar that in the 'forties there was no Catholic theology, but only some edifying Apologetics.[21] It does not mean, however, that there was doctrinal confusion. In his *"Notes,"* Palmer gives an interesting picture of the Russian Church. He met there many people with whom he could discuss problems as he could have at home, at Oxford or elsewhere, although his errand seemed to his Russian friends rather bizarre. Finally, he had an interview with Metropolitan Philaret. The latter could not accept Palmer's initial assumption that unity of the Church could be preserved when there was no longer unity in doctrine. "The Church should be perfectly one in belief," Philaret contended. Distinction between essential "dogmas" and secondary "opinions" was for him precarious and difficult to draw. In fact, the invocation of saints, prayer for the departed, the use of ikons, etc. were as essential for the Orthodox as they were a stumbling-block, at that time, even for the Anglo-Catholics. "Your language," Philaret told Palmer, "suits well enough for the fourth century, but is out of place in the present state of the world . . . now at any rate there is division." It was almost the same as what Palmer was told at Oxford by Dr. Routh: "a separation there unhappily is." And therefore it was impossible to act as if there were no division or separation. Moreover, it was impossible to act in a particular case before the question of relationship between the two Churches, the Anglican and Orthodox, had been settled in a general form. Again, it was by no means clear to what extent Palmer could be regarded as an authentic interpreter of the official teaching and position of the Anglican Church. In fact, he was speaking only for one particular trend in the Church. Palmer failed to obtain an official letter of introduction from the Archbishop of Canterbury, because the latter would not associate himself with that interpretation of the Thirty-Nine Articles which Palmer elaborated in his Latin thesis.

In brief, Russian authorities refused to regard Palmer's membership in the Church of England as a sufficient reason for claiming a communicant status in the Orthodox Church, and could not negotiate reunion with a private individual, who had no credentials from his own Church. Yet, there was full willingness, on the Russian side, to inaugurate some sort of negotiations. Palmer visited Russia again in 1842, and this time he was supplied with an episcopal recommendation, which he obtained from Bishop M. H. T. Luscombe, residing in Paris as supervisor of the Anglican chaplancies on the Continent. He had no title and could not be regarded as a diocesan bishop. He was consecrated by the Scottish bishops, but even the Episcopal Church in Scotland would not regard him as a regular member of the Scottish episcopate. There was another, though accidental, complication. Palmer was very much upset by the fact that one Russian lady had been received in the Church of England. It contradicted his theory. Anglicans should not "convert" the Orthodox, but could admit them to communion—precisely on the basis of their being Orthodox. It was a situation similar to Palmer's own, but in reversal. Palmer succeeded in imposing this interpretation on Bishop Luscombe, but failed to convince the lady. Finally he decided to refer the whole case to the Bishops of the Scottish Episcopal Church. The Russian Synod once more refused to negotiate on Palmer's terms, but welcomed the desire to enter into communion with the Orthodox Church. Identity of belief was stressed

as an indispensible pre-requisite of communion, and a reference was made to the answer given by the Eastern Patriarchs
to the Non-Jurors in 1723. Palmer persisted and presented
a new petition to the Synod, asking that a confessor should
be appointed to examine his beliefs and show his errors.
Fr. Koutnevitch was appointed and made it clear that, in his
opinion, certain of the Thirty-Nine Articles were obviously
not in agreement with the Orthodox doctrine. Palmer, on the
other hand, offered his own reconciliatory explanation of
the articles in question. Koutnevitch replied that even Bishop
Luscombe, under whose sponsorship Palmer came to Russia
this time, was interpreting them in a quite unorthodox way
in his recently published book: *The Church of Rome Compared with the Bible, the Fathers of the Church, and the
Church of England* (1839).

Palmer still wondered when the Church of England separated from the Eastern Church. The answer was—in 1054.
Palmer was prepared to anathematize most of the points
indicated by Fr. Koutnevitch, but persisted in denying that
they could be found explicitly or implicitly in the Articles.
Now, he had to prove that this contention of his would be
endorsed by the Church. The first thing Palmer did was to
gather evidence "from Scottish and Anglican authorities,"
exhibiting conformity with Orthodox doctrine. For that
purpose Palmer republished, in 1846, Blackmore's translation of the "longer Russian Catechism" (by Philaret; English
translation first published in 1845, Aberdeen, under the title
The Doctrine of the Russian Church, with a valuable introduction), with an Appendix of his own: "consisting of notes
to the foregoing Catechism, with extracts from public documents of the Scottish and Anglican Churches, and from the
writings of some of their most celebrated Divines; designed
to show that there is in the Anglican Communion generally,
and more particularly and preeminently in the Scottish Church,
an element of Orthodoxy, capable, by a synodal act, of
declaring unity and identity with the Eastern Catholic

Church." The title of the book was: *A Harmony of Anglican Doctrine with the Doctrine of the Catholic and Apostolic Church of the East...* (Aberdeen, A. Brown & Co., 1846; the name of the author was not given). A Greek version of the book was published by Palmer in Athens in 1851. The dedication of the book was phrased: "To the Most Reverend the Primus, and to the Bishops, Clergy and Laity generally, of the Scottish Church...as to the only existing representative of that Catholic remnant which in the reign of Peter the First held a correspondence with the Eastern Patriarchs, and with the Russian Synod"—this phrasing was significant. It was a betrayal of the author's diffidence in the Church of England. It also betrayed his indebtedness to the Non-Jurors.

Palmer still had hopes. There was always in the Anglican Church "a Catholic school" or party, along with the Puritan one. Was it impossible to hope that this school should prevail and succeed in purging out "the remaining leaven of Calvinism?" Then "the communion with the East" would be re-opened to Anglicans. In Palmer's opinion, the Scottish Church was exceptionally qualified for leadership in this endeavor. It had never descended to the level of the English Church, which had been overruled by the civil authority. If there was no "actual agreement" between the Anglican and Eastern doctrines, it was possible to prove that on every point "an Anglican doctrine similar to the Eastern" really did exist. It might ultimately become the "formal doctrine" of the Church. Palmer then commended the "Russian Catechism" to the consideration of the Scottish Church as a document, which could "be read and used not merely as an Eastern or Russian document, but equally as our own." If only this sound doctrine, which, as Palmer contended, was held by many leading teachers of the Anglican (especially Scottish) Church, could be "synodically asserted" in the name of the whole Church, communion with the East would be secured. It was on the basis of this conviction that Palmer made his formal "Appeal" to the Scottish Church, first to "the

Presbyters of the united Dioceses of St. Andrews, Dunkell and Dumblane," and finally to the Episcopal Synod.

His "appeal" included two points: the right of "passive communion" in other Catholic bodies and the "orthodox" interpretation of the Articles. Of course, it was quite unrealistic to expect that Scottish bishops could accept Palmer's proposal, which would amount to a disavowal of the current Anglican trend of thought and might split the Anglican Communion. It is significant, however, that Palmer's "appeal" was favorably received in the Diocese of St. Andrewes and could be published with an "advertisement" by Bishop P. Torry (*quoad* the importance of the subject). There was a considerable body of agreement behind Palmer's appeal. His book was warmly appraised by people like J. M. Neale. In the latter's opinion, it was a "very remarkable book," and he regretted that it was not given much more attention. "It will probably stand, in the future history of our Churches, as the most remarkable event that has occurred since the disruption of the Non-Jurors."[22] Palmer's "appeal" was declined by the bishops. It came as a shock to him. He was disoriented for a time, and then decided to seek admission in the Orthodox Church, as he became quite certain by that time that she kept and was faithfully keeping the pure Apostolic doctrine. He still had certain scruples. In this connection his new book was of importance: *Dissertations on subjects relating to the "Orthodox" or "Eastern-Catholic" Communion* (London, 1853; cf. the Greek version, Athens, 1852). An unexpected difficulty confused his plans. His baptism had been contested by the Greeks, whereas in Russia it was formally recognized as valid. He could not reconcile himself with such a flagrant dissension within the same Communion on a matter of primary importance. On the other hand, he could not continue outside of the visible communion of the Catholic Church. Finally, he joined the Church of Rome. He made it clear, however, that it was but an act of obedience, and, as to his private judgment, he was assenting to Greek

rather than to Latin Theology, even on the points controversial between Rome and the East, including the doctrine
of the Church itself. Even after his "conversion," he was
deeply interested in the Orthodox Church. He spent years
working on a monumental book on Patriarch Nikon, which
was finally published in six volumes: *The Patriarch and The
Tsar* (London, 1871-1876). He was wrestling here with a
general problem, which had already been suggested by his
Anglican experience: the relationship between the Church
and the State. He was a strong defendent of Church supremacy
and independence.[23]

VI

In his conversations with the Russian ecclesiastical authorities Palmer was concerned mainly with those particular
points of doctrine on which disagreement was alleged to
exist between the two Churches. It was chiefly these points
which he covered once more in his *Dissertations.* He had,
however, an opportunity to discuss the basic doctrine of the
Church and its impact on the problem of Christian unity
with a man who had no official position in the Russian
Church, but, in the years to come, was to exercise an enormous
influence on the ways of Russian theology: A. S. Khomiakov,
who was a layman. Khomiakov wanted to re-state the
Orthodox tradition in a new idiom, which would be at the
same time modern and traditional, i.e. in conformity with the
teaching of the Fathers and with the continuous experience
of the living Church. He wanted to liberate Russian theology,
first of all, from the bondage of Western Scholasticism,
which had been cultivated for a long time in the schools.
He began, accordingly, with the doctrine of the Church itself.
It was only on this point that he succeeded in formulating
his belief, in a brief but almost "catechetical" pamphlet:
"The Church Is One."[24] He gives no definitions, but rather

describes the mystery. The Church is for him just "a unity of the grace of God, living in a multitude of rational creatures, submitting themselves willingly to grace." Yet, the mystery is fully expressed in the "visible," i.e., the historical, Church. The "One Church" for Khomiakov was essentially identical with the Orthodox Church. It was not just one of the many existing "communions," but precisely *the* Church. "Western Communions," in his view, did not belong to the Church, being in fact the "schisms." Communion had actually been broken. There was a division not only on an historical plane, but also in the very ontology of Christian life. Some links obviously still existed, but they were of such a nature that no theological analysis could adequately grasp them: that is, in relation to the "One Church," other communions were "united to her by ties which God has not willed to reveal to her." Theologians could wrestle only with the problem of schism: *the* Church and the [separated] "communions"[25] whose ties "God has not willed to reveal to her."

The Church on earth cannot pass an ultimate judgment on those who do not belong to its fold. It is impossible to state to what extent errors may deprive individuals of salvation. The real question is, however, in regard to the identity of the Church itself. What is essential here is, first of all, "a complete harmony, or a perfect unity of Doctrine." For Khomiakov, it was not just an agreement, but rather an inner unanimity, a "common life" in the Catholic Truth. "Unions" are impossible in the Orthodox Church; there can be only "Unity." This "Unity" has been broken: the West separated itself from the unity, i.e., acted as a self-contained entity. It was a violation of Christian love, a substitution of the particular for the universal. Unity can be restored only by the return of those who went their own way, instead of abiding in it originally. This was just the opposite of what Palmer contended. Thus, discussion was brought sharply to focus on this issue. "The Church cannot be a harmony of discords; it

cannot be a numerical sum of Orthodox, Latins, and Protestants. It is nothing if it is not perfect inward harmony of
creed and outward harmony of expression." Khomiakov
believed that "Sacraments were performed only in the bosom
of the true Church," and could not be separated from that
"Unity" in faith and grace, which was, by his interpretation,
the very being of the Church. It did not matter in which
way the Orthodox Church received those who would decide
to join it. The rites may vary, but in any case some "renovation" of the rites conferred outside of the Orthodox Church
"was virtually contained in the rite or fact of reconciliation."

This was written before Palmer had to face the fact of
divergent practice in the matter of reconciliation in his own
case. When it happened, Khomiakov expressed his disagreement with the Greek practice, but would not exaggerate the
importance of the difference. For him, in any case, there had
to be some act of first incorporation into the Church. At this
point he obviously diverged not only from the current practice,
but also from the teaching of the Russian Church, and was
nearer to the modern Greek interpretation, although he did
not mention the concept of *"oeconomia."* Probably he wanted
to dissociate himself from the current Roman doctrine (which
goes back to St. Augustine), which would allow, under
certain conditions, the existence of "valid" Sacraments also
outside the visible and canonical boundaries of the (Roman)
Church. From his point of view, it was a sheer legalism.
For Khomiakov, the Church was real precisely as an actual
communion in the Truth and in Grace, both inseparably
belonging together. Those who do not share in this communion are not in the Church. The reality of the Church is
indivisible. It was at this point that the first editor of
Khomiakov's letters to Palmer (in Russian), Fr. Alexander
M. Ivantzov-Platonov (Professor of Church History at the
University of Moscow), found it necessary to add a critical
footnote. On the whole, he shared Khomiakov's interpreta-

tion of the Church, but he was not prepared to deny the presence of Sacramental grace in separated communions. Ivantzov did his studying at the Moscow Academy, and was probably influenced by the ideas of Philaret. There was an obvious difference between the two interpretations: Philaret's conception was wider and more comprehensive; Khomiakov's was more cautious and reserved. Both interpretations still co-exist in the Orthodox Church, with resulting differences of approach to the main Ecumenical problem.[26]

VII

Palmer's approach to the Russian Church was a private and personal move. Yet it did not fail to arouse an interest in the Anglican Church among the Russians. At his first departure from Russia in 1842, he was told by the Chief Procurator of the Holy Synod, Count Pratassov, that a new chaplain was to be appointed to the Russian Church in London, who might be able to learn the language and study Anglican divinity. It was precisely what Palmer wanted at that time. Accordingly, the Rev. Eugene Popoff, a graduate of St. Petersburg Theological Academy, was transferred in the next year from Copenhagen to London, where he was to serve for many years, until his death in 1875. Fr. Popoff used to send periodic reports to the Holy Synod concerning ecclesiastical affairs in England, and he established close links with the leading churchmen in the country, including Pusey and Newman. Unfortunately, these reports were published only in part, many years after the author's death, and only in Russian. Fr. Popoff had hopes in the beginning, but changed his attitude in the later years.[27]

Certain links were established between Oxford and Moscow, and theological professors and students in Moscow used to collate Greek manuscripts of the Fathers for the *Library of the Fathers*. Nor were the books on Anglicanism which Palmer brought to Russia and presented to the Academy in St. Petersburg left without use. One of the students was advised to write his Master's thesis on Anglicanism compared with Orthodoxy, apparently on the basis of materials supplied by Palmer.[28] In both countries, Russia and Great Britain, there were groups earnestly interested in the *rapprochement* of the respective Churches. John Mason Neale, by his historical studies and translations of the Eastern liturgical texts, did more than anyone for furthering this idea.

In 1851, under the impression of the famous Gorham case, there was an attempt to approach the Church of Russia in order to secure recognition of a group of Anglicans considering secession from the Established Church. A number of pamphlets were circulated for this purpose, and subscriptions were invited to a "Memorial" to be presented to the Holy Synod of Russia. The initiative seems to have been taken by somebody in Scotland. Although it was not an "ecumenical move" in a proper sense, some points in the project were of importance. The basis of reunion should include recognition of the Seven Ecumenical Councils, the Russian Catechism as an outline of doctrine, and repudiation of Lutheran or Calvinist leanings. Connection with the Russian Church was expected to be only temporary. Rites and devotional forms had to be kept, and the English language used. The Synod was asked to investigate the problem of Anglican Orders and, in the case of a positive decision (which was expected), to confirm the respective clergy in their pastoral commissions. It is difficult to identify the promoters of the scheme. There were obviously only a few. But it was an attempt, on the side of those whose confidence in the established Church had been shaken by the decision of the Gorham case, to find a solution to their conscientious objection in a manner less radical than just "secession" to Roman obedience. The scheme failed, and it is not clear whether the "Memorial" was presented at all. In any event, this was proof of increasing concern, in certain quarters, for a more intimate connection with the Orthodox East.[29]

The "Association for the Promotion of the Unity of Christendom" was founded in 1857, with the intention of uniting "in a bond of intercessory prayer" Roman Catholics, Greeks, and Anglicans. The membership was impressive, and some Orthodox were included in it. But the whole scheme collapsed in 1869, after the formal prohibition of participation by Rome. An Orthodox essay, "by a Priest of the Archdiocese of Constantinople," was included in the volume published in connection with this venture, by the Rev. F. G. Lee, D.C.L., with an introduction by Pusey.[30] Russia's defeat in the Crimean war could not fail to cool its ecclesiastical intercourse with the Anglicans. Yet, the "Eastern Church Association" was created in 1863, by the initiative of John Mason Neale, and two Orthodox priests were on the list of its standing committee from the beginning: Fr. Popov and the Greek Archimandrite, Constantine Stratoulias. The leading Anglican members were: Neale, George Williams, and H. P. Liddon. Pusey, as Liddon says, "took great interest in the foundation of the E. C. Association."[31] Williams was keenly interested in the venture. He spent several years in Jerusalem, as chaplain to the Anglican bishop there. His well-known book on the Non-Jurors in their relations with the East, in which all documents concerning this important episode of ecumenical relations were published (in English) for the first time, was undoubtedly related to the new ecumenical endeavor.[32] Neale never had an opportunity to visit the Eastern countries. But Liddon went to Russia in 1867 (together with C.L. Dodgson, i.e., "Lewis Caroll"), had an interview with Philaret (shortly before the latter's death in the same year), and was deeply impressed by all he saw in Russia. A "sense of God's presence—of the supernatural—seems to me to penetrate Russian life more completely than that of any of the Western nations."[33] The Primus of the Episcopal Church in Scotland, Robert Eden, Bishop of Moray, Ross and Caithness, visited Russia in 1866 and had a talk with Metropolitan Philaret, also. His concern was solely with "Intercommunion," as distinguished from, or even opposed to, "Reunion." It was the old idea that the One Church still continues in the divided "communions." There should be a restoration of that "Intercommunion" which existed "between members of independent Churches in the early days of Christianity." Prejudices should be removed, and some mutual understanding between bishops of the different Churches established. Nothing else was envisaged.[34] It should be emphasized that interest in the East was clearly connected with a defensive position regarding Rome, which was quite natural in the days when the Roman Church, only recently re-established in England, was making steady progress. The first stimulus for this renewed and revived interest in the East, however, came from the United States. Initiative in the negotiations was taken by some members of the Protestant Episcopal Church in the U.S.A.

VIII

Purchase of Alaska and the Aleutian Islands from Russia by the United States and the transfer of the Russian episcopal see from Sitka to San Francisco (in 1861) brought the Anglican Church in the United States into direct contact with the Church of Russia. It is curious to find that when, in the middle of the century, in connection with the gold rush in California, a considerable number of Anglicans established themselves there, the question was raised whether they might not appeal to the Russian bishop on the spot, rather than to the remote Anglican bishops in the Eastern States, for aid and authority, and call themselves the Church of California. However, it seems to have been just a passing idea of a few clergymen, and no action was taken in this direction. A regular Anglican diocese was established in 1857.[35] On the other hand, some others viewed the new situation with apprehension. At the General Convention of the Episcopal Church in 1862, one of the deputies, Dr. Thrall, raised this question. Russians in the West had no organized bishopric at that time. The prospective establishment of an Orthodox bishopric might bring the two Churches into conflict, in respect to jurisdiction. It seemed desirable to nominate a special committee of inquiry and correspondence, to present to Orthodox authorities the Protestant Episcopal Church's claim to be a part of the Church Catholic, and therefore qualified to assume care of the Russians in the Pacific area. While the House of Deputies was prepared to adopt the proposed phrasing, the House of Bishops changed the terms of reference. A commission was appointed with a limited authority: "to consider the expediency of communication with the Russo-Greek Church, to collect information on the subject," and to report to the next General Convention. A resolution to this effect was passed by a majority vote (11 against 8). Obviously, there was some uncertainty as to the timeliness of the venture.[36] This commission was known as a "Russo-Greek Committee."

The decision of the American Convention was almost immediately followed by some steps in England. It seems that the main promoters of the cause were the Rev. Dr. John Freeman Young in America (later Bishop of Florida) and George Williams in England. The formation of the "Eastern Church Association" was probably connected with the American initiative too. In any case, in 1863 a petition was presented to the Upper House of the Convocation of Canterbury, requesting the Archbishop to appoint a committee which might communicate with the "Russo-Greek Committee" in America concerning the question of intercommunion. The petition was presented to the House by the Bishop of Oxford (Samuel Wilberforce), and a corresponding motion adopted. The English committee was not authorized to enter into direct intercourse with the authorities of the Eastern Church but merely kept in touch with the Americans. American delegates stopped in England on their way to the East (Dr. Young and the Hon. Mr. Ruggles) and conferred with the British. Some special consultations were held with the Russian experts, Fr. Popov and Fr. Joseph Vassiliev (the Russian chaplain in Paris, who was invited especially for this purpose). The problem under discussion was that of intercommunion, i.e., mutual recognition of both Churches, including the recognition of Anglican Orders by the Orthodox. The general feeling was that the Anglican Church in America was better equipped for the purpose; there was more inner agreement (probably it was an exaggerated estimate, as the Church was involved in an inner debate on "tractarian" principles), more flexibility, and less inhibition by historical commitments. Therefore it could more easily make those adjustments (or "concessions") which might be required by the Orthodox. The situation in England was rather tense and bishops had to exercise extreme caution. It was clear that the Eastern Church would be unable to enter into any formal communion with the Anglicans unless certain changes were made in Anglican formularies, etc. The Church of England was hardly in the position to do so. Americans were expected to go ahead and create a precedent.[37] Dr. Young visited Russia in 1864 and was received by the Metropolitans of St. Petersburg (Isidor) and Moscow. He also visited the Moscow Ecclesiastical Academy (in the Monastery of St. Sergius), having there a theological discussion on the problem of reunion. He brought with him commendatory letters from several bishops in America. The Russian Synod was not prepared, however, to take any formal steps, but recommended further study of a rather informal nature. Philaret was favorably disposed, but anticipated misunderstandings among the laity; bishops and the more learned members would understand the problem, but (as Young recorded his words) "the difficulty will be with the people." It was a pertinent remark: in Philaret's opinion, obviously, "Reunion," or *rap-proachment,* could not be enacted simply by an act of hier-archy, but presupposed also the participation of the body of believers. He had some difficulty concerning the validity of Anglican orders (Parker's consecration, etc.). Finally, he suggested five points for further study. They were as follows: (1) The Thirty-Nine Articles and their doctrinal position; (2) the *Filioque* clause and its place in the Creed; (3) Apostolic Succession; (4) Holy Tradition; and (5) the Doctrine of Sacraments, especially the Eucharistic doctrine.

It was decided that an interchange of theological *memo-randa* should be arranged between the Russian and Anglican commissions. Dr. Stubbs was invited to present a statement on the problem of succession, John M. Neale on the *Filioque* clause, etc. At the same time, the common interests of Russia and America in the Pacific area were stressed, including the missionary endeavors of both nations. At this point American delegates favored a plan to establish a Russian bishopric at San Francisco and also a Russian parish in New York (the latter was opened in 1870, but closed in 1883). A long report on these negotiations was presented by the Russo-Greek Committee to the General Convention in 1865. It was decided to extend the Commission and empower it to correspond with the authorities of all Eastern Churches, and to secure further information. It was clearly asserted, however, that the Church was not prepared for any other type of negotiations.[38]

The problem was brought to the fore once more in 1868. Several diocesan conventions suggested a revision of the Nicene Creed, i.e., in fact, the removal of the *Filioque* clause from the Creed. Action to this effect was found inexpedient and was indefinitely postponed. It should be mentioned at this point that the problem of the *Filioque* clause was seriously discussed in the Anglican theological press in the 'sixties. An unsigned article appeared on "The *Filioque* Controversy" in *The Christian Remembrancer,* in October, 1864. As it coincides almost completely, as far as the evidence and comments are concerned, with the "dissertation" on the same subject in J. M. Neale's *History of the Holy Eastern Church* (Part I, General Introduction, v. 2, London, 1850, p. 1095-1168), one may plausibly guess that it was also written by Neale. The main conclusion of both the article and the earlier "dissertation" was that the clause was undoubtedly an "accretion." Three practical attitudes were envisaged: (a) to strike the clause out; (b) to retain it, but express regret at its addition, suggesting that it should be interpreted as concerning the *temporal* mission only; or (c) to offer a suitable commentary on the doctrine concerned. The first solution seemed to be practically (first of all, psychologically) impossible; in America, perhaps, it might have been much easier, especially because the Athanasian Creed was not yet commonly used in this branch of the Anglican Communion. But the choice had to be between the second and third solutions. Bishop Pearson was quoted in the conclusion: "The schism between the Greek and Latin Churches was begun and continued: never to be ended, till those words, the *Filioque,* be taken out of the Creed."[39] Even Pusey, who was, himself, in full agreement with the clause and by no means prepared to "strike it out" (see the following section), felt himself compelled to emphasize that the English Church "had no share" in the addition and therefore was in a position to ask that it be allowed "to continue to use the formula, which, without any act of our own, has been the expression of our faith immemorially."[40]

A comprehensive report on the negotiations was presented to the General Convention. The prospect seemed to be rather bright, and no insuperable barriers were discovered. The main problem was that of Orders. It was suggested that the Russian Synod might be willing to send delegates to investigate the problem. Intercommunion had to be interpreted, as stated by the theological commission of the Canterbury Convocation

in 1867, as "mutual acknowledgement that all Churches
which are one in the possesion of a true episcopate, one in
sacraments, and one in their creed, and are, by this union
in their common Lord, bound to receive one another to full
communion in prayers and sacraments as members of the
same household of Faith." The authority of the Russo-Greek
Committee was then extended to a new period.⁴¹ In the
meantime, the Archbishop of Canterbury approached the
Ecumenical Patriarch requesting him, in compliance with the
recommendation of the Committee on Intercommunion of
the Convocation, to allow Anglicans dying in the East to be
buried in the Orthodox cemeteries and to be given religious
funerals by the Orthodox clergy. A copy of the *Common
Prayer Book* in Greek translation was appended to the letter.
The Archbishop's request was granted by the Patriarch
(Gregory VI), but at the same time he raised certain difficulties about the Thirty-Nine Articles.⁴²

   The most interesting episode in the story of the negotiations at that time was connected with the visits of the
Archbishop of Cyclades, Alexander Lycurgos, to England
in 1869 and 1870. A few years later he was to play a
prominent role at the Reunion Conferences at Bonn. In 1869,
he came to England to consecrate the new Greek Church
at Liverpool, and was congenially entertained by the English
prelates, as well as by some distinguished laymen, such as
Gladstone and others. George Williams acted as his guide
and interpreter. Archbishop Lycurgos' personal theological
position was rather comprehensive (his scholarly background
being German), and in his early years, as Professor at the
University of Athens, he had some difficulties because of his
broad opinions. During his stay in England, a conference
was organized at Ely, at which all points of agreement and
disagreement between the two Communions were systematically surveyed, the Bishop of Ely being the main Anglican
speaker (assisted by Williams and Canon F. Meyrick). The
only point at which no reconciliation between the two posi-

tions could be reached was precisely the *Filioque* clause. The Archbishop insisted on its unconditional removal.

Then followed some other controversial topics: the number and form of the Sacraments, the doctrine of the Eucharist, the position of the priesthood and the second marriage of the bishops, invocation of the saints, prayers for the departed, the use of ikons and the connected question of the authority of the Seventh Ecumenical Council. A certain measure of understanding was reached, but the Archbishop staunchly defended the Orthodox point of view. He concluded, however, that, in his opinion, the English Church was "a sound Catholic Church, very like our own," and that "by friendly discussion, union between the two Churches may be brought about." There was no discussion of Doctrine or Orders, and no attempt was made to clarify the conception of the prospective "union," or mutual recognition. The Archbishop favorably reported on his visit and negotiations to the Synod of Greece.[43] The American General Convention in 1871 took cognizance of these new developments and decided to continue the activities of the Russo-Greek Committee.[44] For the last time, the problem of Intercommunion with the Eastern Church came before the American Convention in 1874. By that time some contacts were established, also, with lesser Eastern Churches, the Armenian and Coptic. The general feeling was that further negotiations should be conducted directly by the hierarchy of the two Churches, and therefore the Russo-Greek Committee was discontinued.[45] The 1873 Convocation of Canterbury was presented with several suggestions concerning the interpretation of the *Filioque* clause, with reference to the proposal of the Royal Commissioners of 1689. No action was taken by the Convocation, either in 1873 or later.[46] At that time, the question of the "Old Catholics" came to the fore in ecumenical discussions and the negotiations between the Anglican communion and the Eastern Churches temporarily lost their importance. Political troubles in the East in the late 'seventies also contributed to this decrease in activity.

IX

The secession of a substantial "Old Catholic" group from Rome, after the Vatican Council (1870), challenged the Orthodox Church to form an opinion as to the nature and ecclesiastical status of the new body and as to the attitude it should take with regard to this "non-conforming" Catholic minority in the West. The Vatican Council was preceded by a long period of inner struggle and conflict within the Roman Church, between the "Ultramontane" and more moderate or "liberal" sections or trends. The non-Roman Christians in various countries watched this struggle with keen interest, anxiety and apprehension, sympathy and expectation. The "non-theological factors" played a prominent role in the development of the ecclesiastical conflict. Ecclesiological attitudes had an immediate impact on the ordering of civil society. The prospective proclamation of Papal infallibility was felt to be a threat both to the sovereignty of the national states and to the general cause of freedom. The actual promulgation of the "new dogma" led to the desperate and protracted political *Kulturkampf* in Germany, which had its reflections in other European countries as well. Already in an earlier period the new growth of Papal absolutism had compelled some more liberal Catholics in Germany (and elsewhere) to look in the direction of the Orthodox East. In this connection the name of Franz Baader must be mentioned once more. His interest in the Eastern Church dates from early years. In the 'thirties he had to reconsider the whole problem afresh, in the context of a growing resistance to the Ultramontane trend of thought and practice. "Catholicism" had been disrupted since the split between the East and the West, and it was in the East that the true Catholic position had been retained and continued. The Eastern Church therefore had much to contribute to the prospective reintegration of Christian existence. Baader summarized his ideas in the book: *Der Morgenländische und der Abendländische Katholizismus mehr in seinem innern wesentlichen als in sienem äusserlichen Verhältnisse dargestellt* (Stuttgart, 1841; written in 1840). This book has been recently described as "the greatest ecumenical writing of the XIXth century" (E. Benz). It would be difficult, however, to determine to what extent it actually exercised direct influence on wider circles.[47]

In the years immediately preceding the Vatican Council there was an increasing unrest among the Roman clergy, especially in France. In 1861, a learned French priest, Abbé Guettée, whose *History of the Church in France* was put on the *Index*, joined the Orthodox Church in Paris and was attached to the Russian Embassy chapel. In cooperation with the Russian chaplain, Fr. Joseph Vassiliev, who was himself engaged in the literary struggle with the French Ultramontanes, Guettée founded a magazine dedicated to the cause of Reform and Reunion, *Union Chrétienne,* which for many years had quite a wide circulation in the West. It was, in fact, one of the earliest Ecumenical publications. In the beginning, Guettée was interested in Anglican cooperation, but later became bitterly hostile to them. He regarded the "return" to the faith and practice of the Early Church and reunion with the East as the only way out of the Roman impasse. In a sense, it was an anticipation of the later "Old Catholic" movement. Eugene Michaud, later editor of the famous *Revue Internationale de Théologie* (still continued as the *Internazionale Kirchliche Zeitschrift*), was for a time associated with Guettée, and it was probably from him that he inherited his sympathy for the Eastern Church.[48]

Another name must be mentioned in this connection. That is, Dr. Joseph J. Overbeck who published in the 'sixties a number of booklets and pamphlets, in German, Latin, and

English, advocating not only a "return" to Orthodoxy, but also a re-establishment of the Orthodox Church in the West. Overbeck (1821-1905) was originally a Roman Catholic priest and for a time Privat Dozent on the Theological Faculty at Bonn. During that period he had some connections with Döllinger. He left the Church and migrated to England, where he stayed the rest of his life. In 1865, he joined the Russian community in London, as a layman. But he had a larger plan in his mind. He anticipated the secession of a considerable number of clergy and laymen from the Roman authority in the near future, and was eagerly concerned with the problem of restoring "Orthodox Catholicism" in the West. He regarded reunion with the East as the only practical solution, yet wanted to preserve the Western rite and all those Western habits and traditions which might be compatible with the faith and canons of the Orthodox East. In fact, it was an ambitious project of "Orthodoxy of the Western Rite," somewhat parallel to the "Catholicism of the Eastern Rite."

A formal appeal was presented to the Russian Synod (and probably to the Ecumenical Patriarchate) in 1869; and in 1870 and 1871 Overbeck visited Russia. A provisional draft of the proposed rite was prepared by Overbeck, based mainly on the Roman Missal, with certain insertions from the Mozarabic rite. Fr. Eugene Popov heartily commended the project to the Russian Synod. In principle, the Holy Synod was prepared to approve the plan, but a final decision was postponed in connection with the further development of the Old Catholic movement. The Synod was anxious to ascertain whether there were a sufficient number of people in the West to join the project in question. The scheme was forwarded to the Ecumenical Patriarch in the same year (or in 1872), but it was only in 1881 (and after Overbeck's personal visit to the Phanar) that action was taken. A committee was appointed to examine the project. It reported favorably in 1882 and the Patriarch gave his provisional approval, provided that the other Churches would concur. It seems that a protest was made by the Synod of the Church of Greece. The whole project came to nothing and was formally abandoned by the Russian Synod in 1884, upon the advice of the new Russian chaplain in London, Fr. Eugene Smirnov. There was an obvious utopian element in the scheme, and it failed to attract any appreciable number of adherents. And yet it was not just a fantastic dream. The question raised by Overbeck was pertinent, even if his own answer to it was confusedly conceived. And probably the vision of Overbeck was greater than his personal interpretation. It was a vision of an *Urkatholizismus,* restored in the West with the help of, and in communion with, the Catholic Orthodox Church of the East, which had never been involved in the variations of the West. Overbeck differed from the main Old Catholic movement chiefly in his emphatic stress on the need for a restored communion with the East in order to make the return to a pre-Roman Catholicism real. It was unrealistic to disregard the fact of an age-long separation. This was the main contention of his brief Latin tract: *Libellus Invitatorius ad Clerum Laicosque Romano-Catholicos qui antiquam Occidentis Ecclesiam ad pristinam puritatem et gloriam restauratam videre cupiunt* (Halle, 1871). His magazine, *The Orthodox Catholic Review,* begun in 1867, cannot be ignored by historians of the idea of "Catholic Reunion." Overbeck's project was utterly resented by the Anglican partisans of intercommunion with the East. It was denounced (by the Chairman of the Intercommunion Committee of the Convocation of Canterbury, Dr. Frazer) as "a schismatic proceeding, and a mere copying of the uncatholic and uncanonical aggressions of the Church of Rome." It was described as an attempt to set up "a new Church," with the express object of proselytizing "within the jurisdiction of the Anglican Episcopate." On the other hand, Overbeck was suspected by those who could not separate Catholic Orthodoxy from the *Eastern* rite. This was the case with a group of English converts to Orthodoxy,

led by Fr. Timothy Hatherly, who was received in the Orthodox Church in London in 1856—by (*re*)-baptism and or-
dained to the Orthodox priesthood at Constantinople in 1871.
He had a small community at Woolverhampton. His missionary zeal was denounced to the Patriarch of Constantinople and he was formally prohibited by the Patriarchate
"to prozelytize a single member of the Anglican Church," as
it would undermine the wider scheme of ecclesiastical reunion.
It was a result of the formal intervention of the Archbishop
of Canterbury at the Phanar. It seems that this disavowal of
Hatherly's intentions was the cause of his joining the Russian
Church. He had no sympathy for Overbeck's plan. He wanted
just an Eastern Orthodoxy, only probably with the use of
English. In Russia, Overbeck's project was heartily supported
by the Chief Procurator of the Holy Synod, Count Dmitry
A. Tolstoy, a staunch opponent of all Roman Claims and the
author of a book on *Roman Catholicism in Russia* (English
edition, with preface by the Bishop of Moray, etc., 2 vols.,
London, 1874). Tolstoy's interest and sympathy were probably determined by rather "non-theological" considerations.
So also, was the support of the Old Catholic Church in
Germany by the Governments of Prussia and some other
lands. The whole scheme can be fully understood only in
the context of the intricate historical situation in Europe in
the years preceding and following the Vatican Council. The
ecclesiastical question could not be separated from the political, and the "Vatican dogma" itself had obvious "political"
implications."

X

The hope of Reunion was clearly expressed in the Munich
Whitsunday Manifesto of the German "Old Catholic" group
(in the process of formation), June, 1871, and reunion with
the "Greek-Oriental and Russian Church" was mentioned in

the program of the (first) Catholic Congress, held at Munich in September of the same year (para. 3). The purpose, and the guiding principle, of the new movement was to "reform" the Church in the spirit of the Early Church. An Orthodox visitor was present at the Congress, Professor J. Ossinin, of the Theological Academy at St. Petersburg, who was to play a prominent role in the later negotiations between the Orthodox and Old Catholics. The following Orthodox visitors also attended the Congresses at Cologne (1872), Konstantz (1873), and Freiburg i/Br. (1874): Fr. John Janysheff, at that time Rector of the Theological Academy at Petersburg; Colonel (later General) Alexander Kireev; and some others from Greece, including Professor Zikos Rhossis of Athens, as a "semi-official" representative of the Holy Synod of the Hellenic Church. A special Commission on Reunion had been set up by the Second Catholic Congress at Cologne, which was empowered to establish contacts with existing agencies for reunion and to study the situation in the Churches. It included leading theologians of the Old Catholic group: von Döllinger, Friedrich, Langen, Michaud, von Schulte. In his lectures on Reunion, delivered at Munich in January and February of 1872, von Döllinger laid special stress on the patristic and traditional character of the Eastern Church. "In general, the Eastern Church has remained where it was when the two halves of Christendom were still in communion." Even in the XIIth century the sense of unity was not yet lost. Separation was stiffened when the West advanced in its independent development, culminating in the Counter-Reformation. (The Döllinger "Lectures" were published first in a German periodical, *Die Allgemeine Zeitung,* and immediately translated into English by H. N. Oxenham, *Lectures on the Reunion of the Churches,* London and New York, 1872; separate German edition only in 1888, Nordlingen). Anglicans, both in England and in the United States, were keenly interested in the new movement on the Continent from the very beginning, the "Anglo-Continental Society" being the main agency of study and contact (Edward Harold Browne, Bishop of Ely, President, and Canon F. Meyrick, Secretary).

In Russia the cause of the Old Catholics was sponsored and promoted by a group of clergy and intellectuals, united in the "Society of the Friends of Religious Instruction," St. Petersburg Branch, under the presidency of the Grand Duke Constantine (brother of the Emperor, Alexander II). Russian visitors at the Old Catholic conferences were members and delegates of this Society, and not official representatives of the Church. A special commission to carry on negotiations with the Orthodox was appointed at the Third Old Catholic Congress at Konstanz, under the chairmanship of Professor J. Langen. This commission established at once a very close contact with the Russian group. The main problem under discussion was that of a doctrinal agreement. An "Exposition of the principal differences in the dogmas and liturgy which distinguish the Western Church from the Eastern Orthodox" was prepared by the Russian Society and submitted to the Old Catholic Commission, early in 1874. It was vividly discussed by correspondence. Finally, a Reunion Conference was convened at Bonn, in September 1874. It was an informal Conference of theologians, not a formal meeting of official delegates. The historical significance of this Conference was that for the first time theologians of the two traditions met for a frank and impartial conference on the basic tenets of the Catholic faith. An historical method was adopted, and the "canon" of Vincent of Lérins was used as a criterion: *Quod semper, quod ubique, quod ab omnibus creditum est.*

There was some ambiguity about that criterion. Anglican representatives insisted that conversation should be restricted to the doctrine and practice of the Church of the first six centuries, "and no documents of later date be taken into consideration," as Canon Meyrick put it in one of his letters to Döllinger. Did not this contention imply an essentially static conception of the Church and Tradition? Should "universal" be reduced to "ancient"? Was not the "living voice" of the Church left out, and an academic research substituted for a spiritual search for truth? Was the truth to be found just in the ancient texts, and not in the living experience of the Church? The first point of divergence was once more the *Filioque* clause. After a long debate it was agreed that the clause was inserted unlawfully and that it was highly desirable to find a way in which the original form of the Creed could be restored, without compromising the essential truth expressed in the article (the final draft was suggested by the Bishop of Winchester, Dr. Browne, formerly of Ely). Discussion of the doctrine itself was postponed, and a special theological commission appointed to prepare a report.

On the whole, the findings of the Bonn Conference were received with satisfaction and hope. The Second Conference met, at Bonn again, in 1875, and the membership was much larger. There were about 65 Anglican representatives. The Orthodox group, also, was much larger and more representative, including delegates officially appointed by the Ecumenical Patriarch, the Church of Roumania, the Church of Greece, the Metropolitan of Belgrade, et. al. The main problem was that of reconciliation between the Western and the Eastern doctrines of the Holy Spirit. After a protracted and rather strained debate, the Conference finally agreed on a common statement, based on the teaching of St. John of Damascus, which could be regarded as a fair summary of the doctrine commonly held by the East and the West in the age of the Ecumenical Councils. St. John was always regarded as an authority in the West, while at the same time he was an exponent of the Greek tradition. Some other questions were raised and discussed, but no decisions taken. Orthodox delegates hesitated to commit themselves to any statement on the validity of the Anglican Orders. On the other hand, they could not agree that invocation of the saints should be regarded as an optional practice and left to the private discretion of individual believers or communities.

Anglicans, however, were most apprehensive at this point. The general feeling was that the Conference succeeded in providing a basis for agreement on the doctrine of the Holy Spirit. Unfortunately, it proved to be an unwarranted optimism. It is true that Old Catholics were fully satisfied by the Bonn theses on this topic. Professor Langen summarized once more the whole discussion in his book *Die Trinitarische Lehrdifferenz zwischen der abendländischen und der morgenländischen Kirche* (Bonn, 1876). On the Russian side, similar statements were made by S. Kokhomsky (*The Teaching of the Early Church on the Procession of the Holy Ghost,* St. Petersburg, 1875; and N. M. Bogorodsky *The Teaching of St. John of Damascus on the Procession of the Holy Ghost,* St. Petersburg, 1879; in Russian).

There was agreement between the Orthodox and Old Catholics. But among Anglicans there was a sharp division. Some Anglican delegates at Bonn were quite prepared to omit the *Filioque* clause from the Creed, and it was stated that in America an action to this effect was formally requested by 56 dioceses of the Protestant Episcopal Church. Some others, however, were staunchly in favor of retaining it, and were unable to go further than some kind of explanation concerning the insertion of the clause, etc. After the Conference the latter position was forcefully defended by Pusey. In general, he had his own misgivings with regard to the Old Catholic move, and he was at that time especially disappointed by what he felt to be the "impracticable attitude of the Russian Church" (as Liddon puts it). As early as 1872, he wrote to Williams: "I think that we are doing mischief to our own people by accustoming them to the idea of abandoning the *Filioque,* and to the Russians by inflating them." He wanted to keep the Western position intact and even impose it upon the East. Just before Second Conference at Bonn, he instructed Liddon: "I do not see any occasion for any formula in which the Greeks and we should agree. We are content to let them alone. . . We ask nothing of them, in case of reunion, but to go on as we are." When he learned that the Eastern Church Association was petitioning the Convocation to take the Bonn resolution in consideration, he immediately intervened with a letter to the *Times* containing a warning about "the aggressive line" taken by Russian ecclesiastics and an argument against communion with the Eastern Church, "not knowing what consequences it would involve as to ourselves."

The House of Bishops of the Convocation of Canterbury approved the Bonn statement, as did the Committee of the Lower House. It was expected that the Lambeth Conference of 1878 might remove the clause. For Pusey it was an imminent disaster. He summarized his objections in a long tract: *On the clause, "And the Son," in regard to the Eastern Church and the Bonn Conference. A letter to the Rev. H. P. Liddon, D.D.* (Oxford, 1876). "The loss of the 'and the Son' would to our untheological English mind involve the loss of the doctrine of the Trinity," he contended. He contested the authority of St. John of Damascus, "a writer who was, I conclude, unacquainted with the early Greek Fathers, whose language he rejects, and who certainly knew nothing of our Latin Fathers." One gets the impression that Pusey was afraid of anything which could be interpreted as a "concession" to the East. Or, as Canon Meyrick, one of the Bonn delegates, put it, he was too much interested in the links with Rome (he corresponded with Newman on the topic), and wanted to avoid anything that could widen the chasm between England and Rome. Under these circumstances the Old Catholics felt it would be unwise to hold a new Conference, which had been provisionally scheduled for 1876.

The other unfavorable factor was that Dr. Overbeck (who was at Bonn himself) succeeded in creating some embarrassment among the Orthodox. He contended that there was no real unity among the Old Catholics and no leaning toward Orthodoxy (see his book: *Die Bonner Unionskonferenzen, oder Altkatholizismus und Anglicanismus in ihrem*

Verhältnis zur Orthodoxie. Ein Appellation an die Patriarchen und heiligen Synoden der Orthodoxen Katholischen Kirche (Halle, 1876). Overbeck was still much concerned with his own scheme of an "Orthodoxy of the Western rite" and did not sympathize with any other proposed manner of Catholic reconciliation. An important point was involved here. Some Orthodox favored an immediate recognition of, and inter-communion with, the Old Catholics, as an ecclesiastical body which had preserved the Apostolic Succession and professed *de facto* the Orthodox doctrine on all essential points, and therefore was already (*de facto*) a unit of the Orthodox Church, i.e., as it were, a faithful Orthodox "remnant" in the West, even if it had been temporarily involved in the Roman schism. There was, then, no need for any special act of reunion. All that was needed was that the existing unity should be acknowledged and attested. This point of view was represented, among the Russians, by A. A. Kireev, Fr. Janyshev, and Professor Ossinin. On the other side, it could be argued that, even after their secession from Vatican Rome, the Old Catholics were still in schism, simply because Rome had been in schism for centuries, and separation from Rome in the XIXth century did not mean necessarily a true "return" to the undivided Church of the early centuries. Accordingly, more guarantee was needed and a special act of reconciliation was inevitable. Unfortunately, the doctrine of the Church was never discussed at this period of the negotiations, and the meaning of "reunion" was not properly clarified. Political complications in the late 'seventies (the growing tension between England and Russia centered precisely around the "Eastern question") made theological cooperation between the Anglicans and Orthodox impossible for a time. Contacts between the Orthodox and Old Catholics were also lost.[50] They were renewed only after a long interval, after the formation of the Old Catholic Union (1889) and the Second International Old Catholic Congress in Lucern (1892). A new link between the Orthodox and Old Catholic theologians was established by cooperation in the newly created periodical: *Revue International de Théologie* (since 1893).

The Russian Synod appointed, in 1892, a special committee under the chairmanship of Anthony (Vadkovsky), at that time Archbishop of Finland (later Metropolitan of St. Petersburg and Presiding Member of the Synod). By the end of the year this committee was ready with a report, which was approved by the Synod and communicated to the Eastern Patriarchs. Conclusions were generally in favor of recognition. This was also the tenor of the book on *Old Catholicism* by V. Kerensky, later Professor at the Theological Academy of Kazan (in Russian, Kazan, 1894). In Greece there was a sharp division of opinion: Archbishop Nicephoros Kalogeras of Patras and Professor Diomedes Kyriakos, of the University of Athens, defended the Old Catholic cause, whereas two other Professors, Zikos Rhossis and Mesoloras, opposed it violently. Patriarch Anthimos of Constantinople, replying to the Reunion Encyclical of Leo XIII, *Praeclara gratulationis,* in 1895, cited Old Catholics as defenders of the true faith in the West. In the meantime, the Third International Congress of Old Catholics at Rotterdam, in 1894, appointed its own commission to examine the Russian report. Three points were singled out for further study: the *Filioque* clause; the doctrine of transubstantiation; and the validity of Dutch orders. This time there was division among the Russian theologians: two Kazan Professors, Gusew and Kerensky, found the Old Catholic interpretation of the points under discussion evasive and discordant with the Orthodox position; Janyshev and Kireev, on the contrary, were perfectly satisfied with them. A vigorous polemic ensued.

The most important contribution to the discussion was an essay by Professor V. V. Bolotov, eminent professor of Church History at the Academy of St. Petersburg: "Thesen über das *Filioque*" (published in German translation, by Kireev, without the name of the author, in the *Revue Internationale,* in 1898). Bolotov suggested a strict distinction between (1) dogmas, (2) *"Theologoumena,"* and (3) theological opinions. He described *"Theologoumenon"* as a theological opinion held by those ancient teachers who had recognized authority in the undivided Church and are regarded as "Doctors of the Church." All *"Theologoumena"* should be regarded as permissible, as long as no binding dogmatic authority is claimed for them. Consequently, *Filioque,* for which the authority of St. Augustine can be quoted, is a permissible theological opinion, provided it is not regarded as a *credendum de fide.* On the other hand, Bolotov contended that *Filioque* was not the main reason for the split between the East and the West. He concluded, that *Filioque,* as a private theological opinion, should not be regarded as an *impedimentum dirimens* to the restoration of intercommunion between the Orthodox and Old Catholic Churches. It should be added that the Credal clause was omitted by the Old Catholics in Holland and Switzerland (and put in parentheses in the liturgical books in Germany and Austria, to be ultimately omitted also). That is to say that it was excluded from the formal profession of faith.

At this point in the negotiations the doctrine of the Church was mentioned for the first time, to the effect that "Old Catholic" should be regarded as a schism and could be received into communion with the Orthodox Church only on the basis of a formal acceptance of the full theological system of the contemporary Church. This thesis was first substantiated by Fr. Alexis Maltzev, the Russian chaplain at Berlin and a distinguished liturgiologist, in 1898, and then developed by Bishop Sergius (Stragorodsky), at that time Rector of the Theological Academy of St. Petersburg (later the second Patriarch of Moscow, after the Russian Revolution). This contention was strongly opposed by another Russian theologian, Fr. Paul Svetlov, Professor of Religion in the University of Kiev. Probably, he went too far. His definition of the Church was too vague and all-inclusive. In his opinion, the Church was "an invisible or spiritual unity of believers, scattered in all Christian Churches," ultimately embracing all who would describe themselves as Christians. After all, all Christian denominations coincide in the essential. Differences are not essential and are usually exaggerated. The Orthodox Church is no more than a part of the Church Universal, of which the Old Catholic Church, in its own right, is another part. This radicalism could not commend itself to the ecclesiastical authorities. Nevertheless, theological conversation was continued, until the outbreak of World War I, and Orthodox visitors and observers attended all Old Catholic Congresses. But no actions were taken.[51]

XI

Friendly contacts between Anglican and Eastern Orthodox hierarchs and individuals, especially in the East, were quite numerous in the 'seventies and 'nineties. They were openly motivated by certain "non-theological" considerations, and did not perceptibly promote the cause of reunion or *rapprochement*. In 1888, the Third Lambeth Conference adopted an important resolution (17): "This Conference, rejoicing in the friendly communications which have passed between the Archbishops of Canterbury, and other Anglican Bishops, and the Patriarchs of Constantinople and other Eastern Patriarchs and Bishops, desires to express its hope that the barriers to fuller communion may be, in course of time, removed by further intercourse and extended enlightenment." It seems, however, that the "barriers" were felt to be formidable, if not insuperable. The Sub-Committee of the Conference had to mention once again not only the *Filioque* clause, but the Eastern insistence on trine immersion at Baptism, and an inadequate rite of Confirmation. "It would be difficult for us to enter into more intimate relations with that Church so long as it retains the use of icons, the invocation of the Saints, and the cultus of the Blessed Virgin," even if the Greeks disclaim the sin of idolatry.[52]

In the same year, in connection with the celebration of the Nine Hundredth Anniversary of the Conversion of Russia, Archbishop Edward Benson of Canterbury decided to send an official letter of congratulations and good wishes to the Metropolitan of Kiev. In the letter he referred to common foes of the Russian and Anglican Churches, obviously meaning Rome, and to the unity in the Faith of the Gospel, as expounded by the Ecumenical Councils of the Undivided Church. This move was suggested to the Archbishop by a group of churchmen interested in Oriental Christendom, and probably the East's antagonism against Roman claims commended its Church to the Archbishop. In his reply, Metropolitan Platon unexpectedly raised the question of a formal reunion. "If you also, as appears from your letter, desire that we may be one with you in the bonds of the Gospel, I beg you to communicate to me distinctly and definitely upon what conditions you consider the union of your and our Churches would be possible." The aged Metropolitan wrote on his own behalf, and yet it is improbable that he would have raised such an important problem, without the advice of people in authority. It is true, however, that Metropolitan Platon had a rather broad view of the Church's unity and on one occasion publicly stated that "the walls of partition did not reach Heaven." Archbishop Benson replied in the name of the Bishops of England and made two points. "First and above all, the drawing together of the hearts of the individuals composing the two Churches which would fain 'be at one together'. Secondly, a more or less formal acceptance of each other's position with toleration for any point of difference: non-interference with each other upon any such point." The first point amounted to the authorization of intercommunion, and in the second recognition of the Anglican Orders was implied. No action was taken by the Russian Church on this proposal. From the Orthodox point of view, of course, the real problem was not that of mutual "toleration" or "non-interference," but that of *agreement*.[53]

Nevertheless, in the next decade official contacts between the Church of England and the Church of Russia were strengthened and multiplied. Bishop Creighton of Peterborough (later of London) attended the Coronation of Emperor Nicolas II in 1896, as an official envoy of the Church of England, and Archbishop Maclagan of York visited Russia in the following year. Both prelates were accompanied by Mr. W. J. Birkbeck, a layman of wide erudition and profound piety, very well acquainted with Russian history and life. The English bishops were given a hearty welcome by the Church authorities, but no official negotiations were initiated and there was no discussion on Faith and Order. In 1898, Archbishop Anthony (Vadkovsky) of Finland went to England to represent the Russian Church at the Diamond Jubilee of Queen Victoria. These visits belong rather to the history of attempts to promote "the friendship between nations through Churches" than to the history of Christian Reunion. Queen Victoria is reported to have said that the drawing together of the two Churches was "the only sure way" for bringing together the two nations. One should not forget, however, that the official policy of Great Britain at that time was not in favor of Russia, and therefore all these ecclesiastical overtures surely were not directly inspired by politicians.

There was, however, one feature in the general situation which could not fail to bring the Church of England a bit closer together precisely at this very moment. Discussion of the Anglican Orders in Rome in the middle 'nineties and the final repudiation of their validity by the Pope in 1896 (the Bull *"Apostolicae curae"*) were followed in Russia with keen interest, and the *"Responsio"* of the English Archbishops was accepted with satisfaction. Copies of this "Response" were officially communicated to all Russian bishops (and

probably to all Orthodox bishops in various countries of the
East). It is interesting to observe that the reply of Roman-
Catholic bishops in England to the epistle of the Anglican
Archbishops was also forwarded officially to all Orthodox
bishops by Cardinal Vaughan, with a covering letter, in which
the Cardinal expressed his awareness that the Orthodox were
as solicitous in guarding the true doctrine of Priesthood and
Sacraments as the Church of Rome. One gets an impression
that both partners in the dispute were seriously interested in
the stand which the Orthodox Church would take in the
controversy. In any case, she did not join Rome in its blunt
rejection of Anglican Orders as "utterly null and void," indi-
cating thereby that a favorable solution of the problem, from
the Orthodox point of view, was not excluded. It was quite
natural that at this very moment an inquiry into the Validity
of Anglican Orders should be initiated in Russia, if in an
unofficial way. "An Enquiry into the Hierarchy of the
Anglican Episcopal Church" was published (in Russian) by
Professor V. A. Sokolov, of Moscow Theological Academy.
It included a critical analysis of the Papal Bull, and the
author concluded with the suggestion that Anglican Orders
could be recognized by the Orthodox. Professor Sokolov was
awarded a D.D. degree for his thesis and was confirmed by
the Holy Synod, though the Synod made it clear that an
approval of a theological thesis did not necessarily imply an
endorsement of the author's conclusions. Another Russian
scholar, Professor Athanasius Bulgakov, of Kiev Theological
Academy, reached the same conclusions. Both tracts were
translated into English and published by the Church Historical
Society (presided over at that time by Bishop Creighton).

By the end of the century, the Church of England was
once more involved in a controversy over "Ritualism," and
the time was not favorable for negotiations with the East.[54]
Nevertheless, the Fourth Lambeth Conference (1897) recon-
firmed the desire to establish closer relations with the
Churches of the East, and empowered the two English Arch-

bishops together with the Bishop of London to act as a Committee for that purpose, with the right of cooption. It was desirable to ascertain to what extent the interest in and desire for a *rapprochement* with the Anglican Communion, expressed by not a few individuals among the Orthodox Prelates, was actually shared by the ruling authorities of the Orthodox Churches themselves.[55] In 1898, Bishop John Wordsworth of Salisbury went to the East and visited the Ecumenical Patriarch (Constantine V). "Friendly relationship" [*epikoinenia*] between the two Communions was initiated, and a direct correspondence between the Phanar and Lambeth Palace established. A special commission was created at Constantinople in order to survey the doctrinal position of the Anglican Church, and an Anglican representative, Archdeacon Dowling, was invited to participate. An explanatory pamphlet was published by Bishop Wordsworth, with the approval of the Archbishop of Canterbury in 1900, and immediately translated into Russian and Greek: *Some points in the Teaching of the Church of England, set forth for the information of Orthodox Christians of the East in the form of an answer to questions* (S.P.C.K., London, 1900; 2nd edition, in Greek and English, 1901). It was a semi-official statement.[56]

In 1902, the new Ecumenical Patriarch, Joachim III, formally invited all autocephalous Orthodox Churches to express their opinions on relations with other Christian bodies. The Russian Synod replied with an elaborate epistle. The Synod was inclined to consider the baptism conferred outside of the Orthodox Church as valid, respecting the sincerity of belief in the Holy Trinity, and to consider the Apostolic Succession in the Latin Church as preserved. With regard to the Anglican Church, the Synod felt that, first of all, "it was indispensable that the desire for union with the Eastern Orthodox Church should become the sincere desire not only of a certain fraction of Anglicanism, but of the whole Anglican community, that the other purely Calvinistic current which in essence rejects the Church, as we understand her, and whose attitude towards Orthodoxy is one of particular intolerance, should be absorbed in the above-mentioned pure current, and should lose its perceptible, if we may not say exclusive, influence upon the Church policy and in general upon the whole Church life of this Confession which, in the main, is exempt from enmity towards us." All charity should be extended to the Anglicans "but at the same time a firm profession of the truth of our Ecumenical Church as the one guardian of the inheritance of Christ and the one saving ark of Divine grace" should also be included. The language was rather stern and harsh, but, as Birkbeck (who translated the "Epistle" for *The Guardian*) commented, sufficiently justified by what the Orthodox could infer from events which took place in England in the years immediately preceding.[57] In the same year, obviously at the invitation of the Ecumenical Patriarchate, Chrestos Androutsos, the distinguished Professor of Dogmatics in the University of Athens, published his great essay on "The Validity of English Ordinations, from an Orthodox-Catholic point of view" (1903; English translation, 1909).

He made two preliminary points. First, Intercommunion cannot be separated from Dogmatic Union. Secondly, it was impossible to discuss the Validity of Orders of any body separated from the true Church, and no statement can be made on them. Consequently, the only question that could be profitably discussed by Orthodox theologians was a practical one: what attitude should the Orthodox Church adopt in the case of reception of individual Anglican clerics in the Church? The external, i.e. ritual, aspect of the Anglican Ordinations could be regarded as adequate. There was, however, some uncertainty as to the purpose of these rites, as the Anglican doctrine of Ministry seemed to be rather ambiguous, if judged by Orthodox standards. Yet, on the condition that this ambiguity be removed by a formal declaration of the Church, there was a possibility of accepting the

Orders of those Anglican priests who were ready to join the Orthodox Church as valid. The prerequisite of such an action was that the Church of England should accept, in a formal way, the doctrine of the ancient Church "as a sure foundation and as an unquestionable principle," and make it clear that "Articles of faith" have authority and should be held only insofar as they actually agree with the ancient doctrines. No doubt, it was a document of momentous importance. As a matter of fact, it has been ever since, and still is, the basis of the ecumenical policy of the Greek Church. There are good reasons to believe that "Professor Androutsos was speaking as the mouthpiece of the then Ecumenical Patriarch," and his essay was a kind of invitation extended to the Anglican Church.[58] The underlying idea was in no sense new. It had already been expressed, in a more theological manner, by Khomiakov. There was no question of reunion in any proper sense of the word. There was no invitation to a corporate "healing of the schism" either. The problem was shifted from the plane of theology to that of canon law, or pastoral discretion. What was new was the use of a new terminology. For the first time, the conception of "economy" was applied to ecumenical relations. This conception has never been properly defined, nor elaborated. Its meaning was nevertheless quite clear: instead of a principal solution some occasional practical arrangements were substituted.

The theological problem was left unsolved, or rather its existence was simply denied. It was assumed that the Orthodox Church simply could not say anything about the ecclesiastical status of the separated bodies, as they had none. At this point there was an obvious difference between the Greek approach and that of the Russian Church. It has been suggested that "Russian theologians retained more traces of the influences of those scholastic methods which infiltrated the Eastern-Orthodox Churches in the seventeenth century," and moved "in a world apart from the main tradition."[59] It should not be forgotten, however, that "infiltrations" are found precisely in the Greek documents (such as *"Confessio Dosithei"* or the *"Orthodox Confession"* of Peter Mogila, which was carefully edited by Greek theologians), and Russian theology of the XIXth century strongly resisted these "scholastic methods"—in any case so did Metropolitan Philaret. But Russian theologians would not dispense with the theological, i.e. ecclesiological, problem as such, as difficult and, in the last resort, "antinomical" as it might be. The problem of Unity was for them essentially a theological, and not primarily a canonical problem. No action was taken in the Anglican Church at the time with regard to the Androutsos "invitation." "The chill which fell on the few workers for reunion, left after the Bonn blunder and fiasco, was still prevalent."[60] A petition to remove the *Filioque* clause from the Creed was presented through Bishop Wordsworth to the Convocation of Canterbury in 1902, and the Nicene Churchmen Union requested the same in 1904.[61] The Fifth Lambeth Conference (1908) requested the Archbishop of Canterbury to appoint a permanent Committee to deal with the relations of the Anglican Communion and the Orthodox East (which was actually done) and suggested that certain forms of Intercommunion could be enacted at once (e.g., in the cases of emergency).[62] No action was taken. A new stimulus was given from the United States, where the Orthodox Church (at that time under the jurisdiction of the Russian Synod) had been for a considerable time in friendly touch with the Episcopal Church.

Bishop Grafton, of Fond du Lac, Wisconsin, U.S.A., decided to visit Russia and to raise with the Holy Synod some basic theological questions concerning reunion and recognition. Bishop Grafton (1830-1912) was a staunch "high-churchman" and a "ritualist." In his early years he spent five years in England, was closely associated with Dr. Pusey and Fr. Benson, and for a time worked at St. Peter's, London Docks, and at Shoreditch Hospital. He was one of the first members of the Community at Cowley (S.S.J.E.), and was active in the organization of the American branch of this Society. Grafton's visit to Russia was his personal move; he had no formal commission from his Church, though he was given an official letter of introduction by the Presiding Bishop (Dr. Th. M. Clark, Bishop of Rhode Island). Bishop Grafton was accompanied on his trip by Mr. Birkbeck. He presented to Metropolitan Anthony (Vadkovsky), the Presiding Member of the Synod at the time, a memorandum explaining the Catholic character of Anglican beliefs and orders, and had several conversations with theologians, including the great Fr. John of Kronstadt and General Kireev. It was on the basis of materials presented by Bishop Grafton that some years later Professor Kerensky could state a far-reaching agreement in doctrine between the Anglican and the Orthodox Churches.[63]

In 1904, Archbishop Tikhon of North America, later the first Patriarch of Moscow after the restoration of the Russian Patriarchate in 1917, formally requested the Holy Synod to make an official statement on the procedure to be used in the case of reception of Anglican clerics in the Orthodox Church (a question similar to that discussed by Androutsos). In particular, he wanted to know whether it was permissible to allow them to continue the use of the Common Prayer Book for services. A special Commission was appointed by the Holy Synod which presented a detailed Report, analyzing the offices of the C.P.B. The conclusion was that the offices were rather "colorless and indefinite" with regard to their doctrinal content, and therefore, in case they should be used "in Orthodox parishes, composed of former Anglicans," certain corrections and additions must be made in the text, in order to bring it into agreement with Orthodox doctrine. This adaptation, however, was left to the local authorities of the Church in America. Concerning the reception of Anglican clergy, the Commission recommended, "pending a final judgment" of the Church, "a new conditional ordination."[64] In spite of the obvious failure of these official and semi-

official negotiations, friendly intercourse between the
Churches continued. "The Eastern Church Association" in
England was reorganized in 1893 and was quite active in
the late nineties. Dr. A. C. Headlam, the future Bishop of
Gloucester and prominent leader in the later "Faith and
Order Movement," Dr. Popham Blyth, Bishop in Jerusalem,
and a group of distinguished laymen, such as W. J. Birkbeck,
Athelstan Riley, et. al. were at that time promoters of the
cause of *rapprochement.*

In 1906, a new Society was inaugurated, by joint initiative
of Orthodox and Anglican groups, "The Anglican and
Eastern-Orthodox Churches Union," and its American Branch
was organized in 1908. The Union had its own periodical,
Eirene (1908-1914). For a short period before the outbreak
of World War I the new "Union" was very active in various
fields. A special Committee was created, under the chairmanship of Bishop Blyth, to organize the training of Orthodox
clergy for work in the English-speaking colonies in Anglican
theological schools. The project was preliminarily approved
by the Ecumenical Patriarch and Metropolitan of Athens.
Some links were established with the Orthodox Mission in
Japan. In Russia the new venture was supported by Archbishop Agathangel, at that time of Riga, later of Jaroslavl.
The American Branch was also very active. Once more the
problem of a partial Intercommunion had been raised, i.e.,
of Anglican ministration to the Orthodox in the absence of
the Orthodox clergy, and *vice versa.* Some local Orthodox
bishops were willing to agree to that proposal, and it was
done, e.g., by Bishop Raphael of Brooklyn, N. Y., the Syrian
suffragan of the (Russian) Archbishop of North America, in
1910; he repudiated his own action in 1911 and withdrew
from the "Union."[65] In 1912 a Russian "Society of the Friends
of the Anglican Church" was inaugurated in St. Petersburg.
The first President was Eulogius, at that time Archbishop
of Volynia and Member of the Governamental Duma, and
later Metropolitan of the Russian Church in Western Europe

and Exarch of the Ecumenical Patriarch. He was succeeded by Sergius, Archbishop of Finland, and later Patriarch of Moscow. The Statutes of the Society were approved by the Holy Synod. A Branch of the Society was organized in the U.S.A.

By invitation of this Society, a group of Anglican bishops and clergy joined the Parliamentary delegation of Great Britain to Russia (the "Speaker's delegation") in 1912. Four bishops participated (Eden of Wakefield, Robertson of Exeter, Williams of Bangor, and Bernard of Ossory). Two series of lectures (on the "Life of the Anglican Church") were organized, at St. Petersburg and Moscow, delivered by Dr. Walter H. Frere, C.R., the future Bishop of Truro and the first President of the Fellowship of St. Sergius and St. Alban, and by Fr. F. W. Puller, S.S.J.E. Fr. Puller's lectures were published (in English and Russian)—*The Continuity of the Church of England* (Longmans, 1912). It was an impressive vindication of the Catholic claims of the Anglican Communion. During his visit, Fr. Puller had several theological conversations with the Orthodox, of which he speaks in the Preface to his book. The question of the *Filioque* had been surveyed once more, with the result that on this point there was in principle no disagreement between the two Churches. Puller attributed this "change of attitude" on the Russian side "to the influence of the great Russian theologian, Bolotov." The World War interrupted the work of the Society. It should be mentioned that in 1914 two British organizations, "The Eastern Church Association" and "The Anglican and Eastern-Orthodox Churches Union," were fused together, under the name of "The Anglican and Eastern Churches Association" (which still continues). Even on the eve of the Revolution the Russian Society was meeting, and at the last meeting, in 1917, Archbishop Sergius "delivered a most beautiful address on the similarity and differences in the course of history, between the Eastern and Anglican Churches, and on the promising aspects of the Anglican

Church." It must be added that the great All-Russian Church Council of 1917-1918, in its very last meeting (September 20, 1918), passed the following resolution, upon the proposal of the Section on the Union of the Christian Churches (Archbishop Eudokim, of North America, chairman): "The Sacred Council of the Orthodox Russian Church, gladly seeing the sincere efforts of the Old Catholics and Anglicans towards union with the Orthodox Church on the foundation of the doctrine and tradition of the Ancient Catholic Church, bestows its benediction on the labors and efforts of those who are seeking the way towards union with the above-named friendly Churches. The Council authorizes the Sacred Synod to organize a Permanent Commission with departments in Russia and abroad for the further study of Old Catholic and Anglican obstacles in the way of union, and for the furtherance, as much as possible, of the speedy attainment of the final aim." No Commission could be organized in Russia at that time, but the work of Russian theologians in Western Europe in the ecumenical field was in line with the desire and commendation of the Council.[66]

XII

Negotiations with the Old Catholics and Anglicans revealed a serious divergence of opinions among the Orthodox theologians themselves, and these internal polemics were sometimes very heated. On the other hand, discussions were often confined to one form or another of ecclesiastical agreement. There was no deeper experience of unity, and both sides were mainly engaged in the defence of their respective historical traditions, Western or Eastern, in spite of all persistent references to the "Undivided Church." The spiritual and psychological barriers between the East and the West were not yet broken, and for that reason very few indeed were prepared to go beyond mere schemes and projects.

Christian unity implies two things: unity in faith or doctrine, and unity in the life of the Church, i.e., in sacraments and worship. In the first period of the Ecumenical conversation between the East and the West, attention was given mainly to the first aspect, which led to the disappointing discovery that there was a difference indeed, and a difference of such character as to make agreement hardly possible. The *Filioque*, the doctrine of the Eucharist, the invocation of saints, Mariology, prayers for the departed,—on all these points no concession could be made by the Orthodox, although a clear distinction had to be made between a binding doctrine and theological interpretation. This distinction is not easy to make in practice. Unnecessary impediments were sometimes created by intransigeance on either side. Nevertheless, the real difficulty was rooted in the basic fact that the Orthodox East abides by tradition and retains the whole Patristic deposit. The recovery of this Patristic Tradition in the West would have helped the mutual understanding.

In the later period of discussion, the whole ecclesiological problem was brought to the fore. The main issue was: what was the Church Universal? and in what sense do "schisms" belong to the Church? Various answers were given, or often simply taken for granted in advance. Unity of belief does not by itself constitute the corporate reality of the Church, since the Church is a Divine institution. The "Branch-theory" of the Church was obviously unacceptable to the Orthodox. In any case, it minimizes the tragedy of disruption. Again, a schism is not just a human separation: it violates the basic structure of Christian existence. The only alternative available for Orthodox theologians seemed to be this: either separated bodies did not belong to the Church at all, and therefore were, not only historically but also spiritually, outside of it; or they were still, in a certain sense and under special conditions, related to the Church existentially. The latter conception is characteristic of Roman Catholicism, and goes back to St. Augustine; for that very reason many Orthodox would hesitate to accept it. It was, however, held by many Russian theologians, if not quite in the same sense (Philaret; Kireev; Svetlov). Accordingly, the Sacraments were not necessarily reiterated for the non-Orthodox, in the case of conversion, but were understood as having some real charismatic significance even outside of the strict canonical boundaries of the Church. This has been the common practice of the Russian Church in the last centuries. On the other hand, this practice could be interpreted in the light of the theory of *"Economy,"* which is characteristic of modern Greek theology; in this case, the fact of non-reiteration would not imply any recognition of these non-Orthodox ministrations, and should be interpreted simply as a pastoral dispensation. This point of view had already been represented in Russia by Khomiakov, and in recent times was elaborated with daring radicalism by the late Metropolitan Anthony (Khrapovitsky). He had an occasion to express this view in an ecumenical context, when he was invited to participate in the "Conference on Faith and Order," in 1914. The delegation of the Planning Committee in the U.S., appointed in 1914, could not go because of the war but invitations were sent to all Orthodox Churches. In Russia, they were favorably received in high ecclesiastical quarters and some epistolary contacts were established.

Anthony, at that time Archbishop of Kharkov and a permanent Member of the Holy Synod, replied to the invitation with a long letter, in which he frankly stated his point of view. There was no spiritual reality, "no Grace," outside the Orthodox Church. All talks about "validity" are just "talmudist sophistries." What is outside of the Orthodox Church is just "this World, foreign to Christ's redemption and possessed by the Devil." It makes no difference, Anthony argued, whether the non-Orthodox have or do not have "right beliefs." Purity of doctrine would not incorporate them in the Church. What is of importance is only the actual membership in the Orthodox Church, which is not compromised by doctrinal ignorance or moral frailty. "Doctrinal agreement" by itself means little. Membership in the Body is the only thing that counts. But, in spite of this global exclusion of all non-Orthodox from Christendom, Anthony was wholeheartedly in favor of Orthodox participation in the proposed "Conference on Faith and Order." "Indeed, we are not going to con-celebrate there, but shall have to search together for a true teaching on the controversial points of faith." An exchange of letters with Robert Gardiner, the secretary of the organizing commission, followed, in which the whole problem was thoroughly discussed. Another Russian theologian, Hilarion (Troitsky), at that time Professor of the Moscow Theological Academy, and later Archbishop of Krutitzy, published an "open letter" to Robert Gardiner, "The Unity of the Church and the Universal Christian Conference," in which he developed the same radical conception: Separation is infinitely more important than Dissent. This interpretation of unity and schism was by no means commonly accepted, and was exposed to serious objections. In any case, there was no unanimity among Orthodox theologians on this basic problem of "ecumenical theology." The documents just quoted belong to the later period, and, strictly speaking, are outside the scope of the present survey. Yet they summarize authentically the view which has been held and promoted by not a few in the course of XIXth century ecumenical negotiations.[67]

This survey would be incomplete, if we omitted the name of Vladimir Soloviev (1853-1900). Soloviev was never interested in the ecumenical problem, insofar as it concerned the search for unity between the Orthodox and the world of the Reformation. His attitude towards the Reformation and Protestantism always tended to be negative, even if in his later years he would speak occasionally of a "super-confessional" Christianity, and a "Religion of the Holy Spirit." He was openly hostile to the Old Catholic Movement. Nevertheless his contribution to the discussion on Christian unity was momentous. "The broken Unity" of Christendom, "the Great Controversy," i.e., the "Separation of the Churches," were in his opinion the main fact and the main tragedy of Christian existence. The reunion of Christendom was, for him, therefore, not merely one special and particular problem of theology and of Christian action, but precisely *the* problem of Christian life and history. Soloviev was mainly concerned with the question of reconciliation between the East and Rome, and in a sense he was pleading for a very particular kind of "Unia." In fact, he simply did not believe that "Churches" were separated. There was an historical estrangement, an external break, but, in an ultimate sense, there was still One, (mystically) Undivided Catholic Church.

Soloviev's practical plans were utterly utopian. He dreamed of an alliance between a supreme pontiff and an universal emperor, i.e., between Rome and the Russian Empire. He was much less interested in the theological reintegration of the separated traditions. His ecclesiological thought was strongly influenced by Roman theology. He was ready to vindicate the whole doctrinal growth of Roman doctrine, by means of an elaborate doctrine of dogmatic development. His schemes of union were violently criticized by Russian theologians; there was much substance and justice in these criticisms. But critics should not have missed the very point which Soloviev was trying to establish, even if in an unfortunate manner. He was right in his basic vision: the Church is essentially One, and therefore cannot be divided. Either Rome is no Church at all, or Rome and the East are somehow but One Church, and separation exists only on the historical surface. This thesis can be interpreted in a limited sense, i.e., as including only Rome and Eastern Orthodoxy. But it could be re-interpreted in a wider sense, and, in that case, we would have an important and truly ecumenical plea. The merit of Soloviev was precisely that he tried to clarify the presuppositions that underly the Catholic doctrine of the Church. His negative attitude to

Protestantism was to a great extent the result of the limitations of his age: he had in view chiefly the liberal Protestantism of the XIXth century, characterized by an etiolated doctrine and a complete lack of any Church-consciousness. His ultimate "Ecumenical" vision, so vividly presented in his "Story of the Antichrist," included the whole of Christendom, and fullness of Christian tradition: the spiritual insight of the Orthodox East, the authority of Rome, and the intellectual honesty of Protestantism. But this unity transcends history.[85] The true legacy of Soloviev is not his "Romanism," and of course not his utopian, theocratic dream, but his acute sense of Christian unity, of the common history and destiny of Christendom, his firm conviction that Christianity is the Church. It was a true ecumenical vision, as fantastic and dreamy, offensive and repelling, as his union plans and invectives had been. Soloviev's was the challenge. An earnest endeavor at an inclusive Catholic reintegration would be the answer. It would take us beyond all schemes of agreement. The issues which have been discussed time and again in the abortive ecumenical negotiations of the last centuries, and of the preceding ones, are still burning. It is necessary to realize the nature and the scope of those questions which the Orthodox were bound to have asked, and are going to ask again and again, in order to understand and interpret the meaning of the ecumenical encounter between the Orthodox East and the West at large.

IV
NOTES AND REFERENCES

Notes and References

PATRISTIC THEOLOGY AND THE ETHOS
OF THE ORTHODOX CHURCH

[1]F. Kattenbusch, "Kritische Studien zur Symbolik im Anschluss an einige neuere Werke," in *Theologische Studien und Kritiken,* Jg. 51, 1878, ss. 94-121 and 179-253. Kattenbusch deals with Gass in the first part of his article.

[2]F. Kattenbusch, *Lehrbuch der Vergleichenden Confessionskunde.* Erster Band: Prolegomena und Erster Teil: *Die Orthodoxe Anatolische Kirche* (Freiburg i/Br. 1892; the only volume published).

[3]Nicholas N. Glubokovsky, *Orthodoxy in Its Essence,* in "The Constructive Quarterly," June 1913, p. 296-297.

[4]W. Gass, "Zur Symbolik der Griechischen Kirche," in *Zeitschrift für Kirchengeschichte,* Bd. III, 1879, ss. 329-357.

[5]Cf. Ernst Benz, *Die Ostkirche im Lichte der Protestantischen Geschichtsschreibung von der Reformation bis zur Gegenwart* (München, 1952), ss. 195-201, 206-217.

[6]Louis Bouyer, *Le renouveau des études patristiques,* in "La Vie Intellectuelle." Février 1947, p. 18.

[7]Mabillon, in the Preface to Bernard's *Opera,* n. 23, Migne, *P. L.,* CLXXXII, c. 26, quoted recently in the Encyclical of Pope Pius XII, *Doctor Mellifluus* (1953); English translation of the Encyclical in Thomas Merton, *The Last of the Fathers,* N. Y., 1954.

[8]L. Thomassin, *Dogmata theologica,* vol. I, Praefatio, p. XX.

[9]Kabasilas' treatises are reprinted in Migne, *P. G.,* t. CL. Cf. M. Lot-Borodine, *Un maître de la spiritualité byzantine au XIV* siècle: Nicolas*

Cabasilas (Paris, 1958); on the Jesus Prayer see *La Prière de Jésus,* par un moine de l'Église d'Orient (Éditions de Chevetogne, 1951), and also E. Behr-Sigel, "La Prière à Jésus, ou le Mystère de la spiritualité monastique orthodoxe," in *Dieu Vivant,* No. 8 (1947), pp. 69-94.

[10]L. A. Zander, *The Problems of Ecumenism*—Paper prepared for the Study Department of the WCC, not yet published, but distributed in a mimeographed form.

ST. ATHANASIUS' CONCEPT OF CREATION

[1]See, e.g., J. Baudry, *Le Problème de l'Origine et de l'Éternité du Monde dans la Philosophie grecque de Platon à l'ère chrétienne* (Paris 1931), and also Jacques Chevalier, *La Notion du Nécessaire chez Aristote et chez ses prédécesseurs* (Paris 1915). Cf. my article, "The Idea of Creation in Christian Philosophy," in the *Eastern Churches Quarterly* 8, 1949, Supplementary issue: "Nature and Grace."

[2]Etienne Gilson, *God and Philosophy* (Yale University Press 1941), p. 88.

[3]Etienne Gilson, *L'Esprit de la Philosophie Médiévale,* Deuxième édition revue (Paris 1944), p. 82, n. 1.

[4]St. Justin's *Dialogue with Trypho,* c. 5 and 6. See my Ingersoll lecture for 1950-1951, "The Resurrection of Life," in the *Bulletin of Harvard Divinity School;* cf. J. Lebreton, *Histoire du Dogme de la Trinité,* t. II (Paris 1928., p. 635 ff.

[5]G. L. Prestige, *God in Patristic Thought* (S.P.C.K., 1952 [1936]), p. 123.

[6]V. V. Bolotov, *Origen's Doctrine of Holy Trinity* (St. Petersburg, 1879 [in Russian]), p. 380-381. It is still the best exposition of Origen's Trinitarian doctrine, at no point superseded by later research. One may add only H. Crouzel, *Théologie de l'Image de Dieu chez Origène* (Paris 1956).

[7]J. N. D. Kelly, *Early Christian Creeds* (London 1950), p. 137. Cf. also the comments of Antonio Orbe, S. J., *Hacia la primera teologia de la procesión del Verbo* (Rome 1958 [Estudios Valentinianos], vol. I/1), p. 169, n. 14.

[8]Cf. the exposition of Père Jean Daniélou in his recent course at the Institut Catholique in Paris: Le IIIme Siècle: Clément et Origène, Notes prises au Cours par les Élèves, p. 148-154.

[9]Cf. Orbe, p. 77, 176 ss.

[10]Cf. Orbe, p. 165 ss. and especially the summary, p. 185: "Orígenes discurre siempre vinculando la Subiduría personal de Dios al mundo (inteligible, o quizá también sensible). La generación del Verbo, que hubiera en absoluto bastado a explicar el misterio de la prehistoria del mundo, no adquiere autonomía propia. De seguro su coeternidad con el Padre se halla en Orígenes mejor definida que en ninguno de sus contemporáneos; pero las múltiples coordenadas que de diversos puntos traza el Alejandrino para definir igualmente la eternidad del mundo, comprometen las fronteras entre la necesidad de la generación natural del Verbo y la libertad de la generación intencional del mundo en El. Los límites entre la Paternidad y la Omnipotencia na aparecen claros en el Alejandrino." See also P. Aloysius Lieske, *Die Theologie der Logosmystik bei Origenes* (Münster i/W. 1938), p. 162-208, and Endre v. Ivánka, *Hellenisches und*

Christliches im frühbyzantinischen Geistesleben (Wien 1948), p. 24-27 and passim.

[11]Cf. Crouzel, p. 98ss.

[12]See Orbe, p. 674ss., and especially the section: "Orígenes y los Arrianos."

[13]Cf. Crouzel, p. 90ss.

[14]Cf. Ernst Benz, *Marius Victorinus und die Entwicklung der abendländischen Willensmetaphysik* (Stuttgart 1932), p. 329-340.

[15]See the excellent and exhaustive essay of D. A. Lebedev, "St. Alexander of Alexandria and Origen," in the *Trudy Kievskoj Dukhovnoj Akademii* (1915, October/November and December), p. 244-273 and 388-414 [in Russian]; cf. also another article by the same author, "The problem of the Origin of Arianism," in the *Bogoslovskij Vestnik* (1915, May), p. 133-162 (also in Russian).

[16]Only a Syriac version of this important document is preserved. It was published for the first time and retranslated into Greek by Eduard Schwartz, "Zur Geschichte des Athanasius," VI, in *Nachrichten von der Königlichen Gesellschaft der Wissenschaften zu Göttingen* (1905), p. 272-273 (now reprinted in his *Gesammelte Schriften,* Dritter Band (Berlin 1959), pp. 136-143). I am quoting the English translation of Kelly, made from the Greek of Schwartz—*Early Christian Creeds*, p. 209-210. The authenticity of the Antioch Council has been vigorously contested by Harnack and others. The best analysis of all evidence and a convincing defense of the authenticity can be found in a series of articles by D. A. Lebedev: "The Council in Antioch of 324 and its Epistle to Alexander, Bishop of Thessalonike," in *Khristianskoje Chtenije* (1911, July/Aug., 831-858; Sept.), 1008-1023; "On the Problem of the Council in Antioch of 324 and on the Great and Holy Council in Ancyra," in *Trudy Kievskoj Dukhovnoj Akademii* (1914, April, July/August, November; 1915, January); continued in *Bogoslovskij Vestnik* (1915, July/August, p. 482-512). All these articles are in Russian.

[17]See A. Gaudel, *"La théologie du Λόγος chez Saint Athanase,"* in the *Revue des Sciences religieuses* 11, 1931, 1-26; J. B. Berchem, "Le rôle du Verbe dans l'oeuvre de la création et de la sanctification d'après Saint Athanase," in *Angelicum*, 1938, p .201-232 and 515-558; and especially Louis Bouyer, *L'Incarnation et l'Église—Corps du Christ dans la théologie de Saint Athanase* (Paris 1943); cf. also Regis Bernard, *L'Image de Dieu d'après St. Athanase* (Paris 1952).—Professor I. V. Popov, of Moscow Theological Academy, in his book, *The Personality and the Doctrine of Saint Augustine* (1917 [in Russian]), gives an excellent survey of the history of the distinction: essence—energy, from Philo to Pseudo-Dionysius, t. I 2, p. 330-356; see also A. I. Brilliantov, *The Influence of the Eastern Theology on the Western in the Works of J. S. Eriugena* [in Russian] St. Petersburg 1898), p. 221 ss.

[18]Cf. Ernst Benz, *op. cit.,* p. 340-342: "Durch die Scheidung von Substanz und Wirkung des Willens ist die engste substantielle Verbindung von Vater und Sohn und zugleich die Begründung der 'creatio ex nihilo' gegeben." The whole paragraph on St. Athanasius in Benz's book is highly stimulating.

[19]Cf. Orbe, *op. cit.,* p. 465s., 692s., 751.

[20]Louis Bouyer, *op. cit.,* p. 47s.: "Le premier élément nouveau du Contra Arianos—et il est considérable—c'est qu'il nous fait contempler la vie divine en Dieu lui-même avant qu'il nous la communique. Cette contemplation est l'inspiration de tout cet ouvrage, car elle inclut les raisons profondes de la distinction radicale entre Dieu et le créé qui ruine par la base les thèses ariennes. La transcendance divine est vraiment absolue parce que Dieu n'a aucun besoin de ses créatures: il possède la vie en lui-même, et cette vie consiste dans les relations qu'il entretient avec son Verbe."

[21]See F. A. Staudenmeier, *Die Christliche Dogmatik,* Bd. III (Freiburg i/Br. 1848).

[22]Cf. Jacques Liébaert, *La doctrine christologique de Saint Cyrille d'Alexandrie avant la querelle nestorienne* (Lille 1951), p. 19-43; Noël Charlier, "Le Thesaurus de Trinitate de Saint Cyrille d'Alexandrie," in the *Revue d'Histoire Ecclésiastique* 45, 1950, 25-81.

[23]Cf. Th. de Regnon, Études de Théologie Positive sur la Sainte Trinité, Troisième Série: Théories Grecques des Processions Divines, Paris 1898, p. 263ss. "Cette fécondité de Dieu, cette procession par voie d'activité substantielle, telle est l'idée maitresse de la théorie grecque au sujet du Fils" (269).

[24]See, for instance, St. Gregory Palamas, Capita physica, theologica etc., 96, *PG* 150, 1181: εἰ...μηδὲν διαφέρει τῆς θείας οὐσίας ἡ θεία ἐνέργεια, καὶ τὸ ποιεῖν, ὃ τῆς ἐνεργείας ἐστί, κατ' οὐδὲν διοίσει τοῦ γεννᾶν καὶ ἐκπορεύειν, ἃ τῆς οὐσίας ἐστίν... καὶ τὰ ποιήματα κατ' οὐδὲν διοίσει τοῦ γεννήματος καὶ τοῦ προβλήματος. Cf. my article, "St. Gregory Palamas and the Tradition of the Fathers," *The Greek Orthodox Theological Review* 2, 1960, 128-130 and in Volume I of *The Collected Works.* Cf. also Jean Meyendorff, *Introduction à l'étude de Grégoire Palamas,* Paris (1959), especially p. 279ss.

[25]See S. Marci Eugenici Ephesini Capita syllogistica, in W. Gaβ, *Die Mystik des Nikolaus Cabasilas* (Greifswald 1849), Appendix II, p. 217: ἔτι εἰ ταὐτὸν οὐσία καὶ ἐνέργεια, ταύτῃ τε καὶ πάντως ἅμα τῷ εἶναι καὶ ἐνεργεῖν τὸν Θεὸν ἀνάγκη· συναΐδιος ἄρα τῷ Θεῷ ἡ κτίσις ἐξ ἀϊδίου ἐνεργοῦντα κατὰ τοὺς Ἕλληνας.

[26]The latter point of view has been recently ably elaborated by Professor Endre v. Ivánka, "Palamismus und Vätertradition," in *L'Église et les Églises, Études et Travaux offerts à Dom Lambert Beaudouin,* vol. II (Chevetogne 1955), p. 29-46. Ivánka's arguments are not convincing; he seems to miss the crucial point. But it has been the common attitude of Western theology, especially in the Roman Church.

THE PATRISTIC AGE AND ESCHATOLOGY:
AN INTRODUCTION

[1]See e.g. Msgr Joseph Pohle, *Eschatology,* Adapted and edited by Arthur Preuss (Herder Book Co., St. Louis, Mo., & London, 1947), p. 2.

[2]See Kittel's *Theologisches Wörterbuch,* vol. III, p. 451/452, s. v. καινός (Behm).

[3]The question whether this redemptive purpose was the only reason or motive of the Incarnation, so that it would not have taken place if man had not sinned, was never raised by the Fathers, with one single exception. The Christian message was from the very beginning the message of Salvation, and Christ was described precisely as the Saviour or Redeemer of mankind and the world, who had redeemed His people from the bondage of sin and corruption. It was assumed that the very meaning of Salvation was that the intimate union between man and God had been restored, and it was inferred therefrom that the Redeemer Himself had to belong to both sides, i.e. had to be at once both Divine and human, for otherwise the broken communion would not have been recovered. This line of reasoning was taken by St. Irenaeus, later by St. Athanasius, and by all the writers of the IVth century, in their struggle against the Arians. Only in St. Maximus the Confessor we find the suggestion that Incarnation belonged to the original plan of Creation and in this sense was independent of the Fall: *quaest. ad Thalassium,* qu. 60, *PG* XC, c. 621; cf. *Ambigua,* XCI, 1097, 1305, 1308 sq. Cf. the remarks of Fr. Hans Urs von Balthasar, *Liturgie Cosmique, Maxime le Confesseur* (Paris, Aubier, 1947), p. 204-205 (German edition, S. 267-268). See also Aloysius Spindeler, *Cur Verbum caro factum? Das Motiv der Menschwerdung und das Verhältnis der Erlösung zur Menschwerdung Gottes in den christologischen Glaubens-kämpfen des vierten und fünften christlichen Jahrhunderts* (Forschungen zur Christlichen Literatur- und Dogmengeschichte, herausgegeben von Erhard und Kirsch, XVIII. 2), 1938.

[4]On the notion of the circular motion in Aristotle see O. Hamelin, *Le Système d'Aristote* (2 ed., Paris 1831), p. 336ss.; J. Chevalier, *La Notion du Necessaire chez Aristote et chez ses prédecesseurs, particulière-ment chez Platon* (Paris 1915), p. 160ss., 180ss.; R. Mugnier, *La Théorie du Premier Moteur et l'Évolution de la Pensée Aristotelienne* (Paris 1930), p. 24ss.

[5]See Pierre Duhem, *Le Système du Monde, Histoire des Doctrines Cosmologiques de Platon à Copernic* (t. I, Paris 1914), pp. 65ss., 275-296, and especially t. II, Paris 1914, p. 447ss.,—*Les Pères de l'Église et la Grande Année.* Cf. Hans Meyer, *Zur Lehre von der ewigen Wiederkunft aller Dinge,* in Festgabe A. Ehrhard (Bonn 1922), p. 359ff.

[6]See Oepke, s. v. ἀποκατάστασις, in Kittel, I, S. 389: "Vor allem wird

ἀποκατάστασις terminus technicus für die Wiederherstellung des kosmischen Zyklus."

[7]A. Lossev, *Essays in Ancient Symbolism and Mythology* (t. I, Moscow 1930 [in Russian]), p. 643. This book is one of the most valuable contributions to the modern discussion of Platonism, including Christian Platonism. It is utterly rare. The book, and other valuable writings of Lossev in the same field, is obtainable in Fritz Lieb's Library, at the University of Basel.

[8]Cf. my article, "The Idea of Creation in Christian Philosophy," in the *Eastern Churches Quarterly* (Vol. VIII, 1949), 3 Supplementary issue, "Nature and Grace."

[9]See Büchsel, s. v. ἀπολύτρωσις, in Kittel, IV, 355.

[10]Cf. the most interesting remarks of E. Gilson in his Gifford lectures: *L'Esprit de la Philosophie Médièvale* (2nd edition, Paris, 1944), the whole of chapter IX, "L'anthropologie chrétienne," p. 175 ss. Gilson seems to have underestimated the Aristotelian elements in Early Patristics, but he gives an excellent *mis au point* of the whole problem.

[11]R. D. Hicks, in the Introduction to his edition of *De anima*, Cambridge, at the University Press, 1934, p. LVI. Cf. Anton C. Pegis, *Saint Thomas and the Greeks*, The Aquinas Lecture, 1939, 3rd printing (Marquette University Press, Milwaukee, 1951), p. 171. Already E. Rohde, *Psyche, Seelencult und Unsterblichkeitsglaube der Griechen* (3. Aufl. 1903, Bd. II), p. 305, suggested that the whole doctrine of *Nous* was simply a survival of Aristotle's early Platonism. This idea was recently upheld by Werner Jäger, *Aristotle, Fundamentals of the History of his Development*, translation, by Richard Robinson, 2nd edition (Oxford, at the Clarendon Press, 1948), p. 332f.

[12]Hegel, *Vorlesungen über die Asthetik, Sämtliche Werke*, Bd. X. 2, p. 377; cf. the whole section on Sculpture, which was for Hegel a peculiarly "classical art," p. 353f.

[13]Lossev, *Essays in Ancient Symbolism and Mythology*, I, p. 670, 632, 633,—in Russian.

[14]On the Aristotelian background of Athenagoras' conception see Max Pohlenz, in *Zeitschrift für die wissenschaftliche Theologie*, Bd. 47, p. 241ff.; cf. E. Schwarz, *index graecus* to his edition of Athenagoras, in *Texte und Untersuchungen*, IV. 2, 1891, s. v. εἶδος, S. 105. Cf. E. Gilson, *L'Esprit de la Philosophie Médièvale*, p .197. "Lorsqu'on pèse les expressions d'Athénagoras, la profondeur de l'influence exercée par la Bonne Nouvelle sur la pensée philosophique apparait à plein. Crée par Dieu comme une individualité distincte, conservé par un acte de création continuée dans l'être qu'il a reçu de lui, l'homme est desormais le personnage d'un drame qui est celui de sa propre destinée. Comme il ne dependait pas de nous d'exister, il ne depend pas de nous de ne pas exister. Le décret divin nous a condamné à l'être; faits par la création, refraits par la redemption, et à quel prix. Nous n'avons le choix qu'entre une misère ou une béatitude également éternelles. Rien de plus resistant qu'une individualité de ce genre, prévue, voulue, élue par

Dieu, indestructible comme le decret divin lui-même qui l'a fait naître; mais rien aussi qui soit plus étranger à la philosophie de Platon comme à celle d'Aristote. Là encore, à partir du moment où elle visait une pleine justification rationelle de son espérance, la pensée chrétienne se trouvait contrainte à l'originalité."

THE ANTHROPOMORPHITES
IN THE EGYPTIAN DESERT

[1]O. Chadwick, *John Cassian. A Study in Primitive Monasticism* (Cambridge, 1950), p. 16, n. 3; cf. p. 34-35.

[2]A. Lieske, "Die Theologie der Logosmystik bei Origenes," *Münsterische Beiträge zur Theologie* (Heft 22, 1938), p. 45 ff., 133 ff. *"Bei aller Liebe zum gekreuzigten Christus und zum Gottmenschen ... tritt auf dieser höheren Stufe der Glaubenserkenntnis doch das Interesse und die Hochschätzung für das Gottmenschentum Jesu Christi zurück"* (p. 47).

[3]W. Voelker, *Das Vollkommenheitsideal des Origenes* (Tübingen 1931), pp. 109-110. The opposite view is strongly presented by H. De Lubac, *Histoire et Esprit. L'intelligence de l'Écriture d'après Origène* (Paris 1950), and also by F. Bertrand, *Mystique de Jesus chez Origène* (Paris 1951).

[4]Chadwick, p. 149.

[5]See J. Lebreton, *Le désaccord de la foi populaire et de la théologie savante dans l'Église chrétienne du III siècle, Rev. Hist. Eccl.* 19 (1923) and 20 (1924); cf. also his earlier article, "Les Degrés de la connaissance d'après Origène," *Recherches de Science Religieuse* 13 (1922).

[6]A. Struker, *Die Gottebenbildlichkeit des Menschen in der christlichen Literatur der ersten zwei Jahrhunderte* (Münster i. W. 1913), pp. 39-42.

[7]Cf. H. Crouzel, *Théologie de l'Image de Dieu chez Origène* (Paris 1956), p. 153-179, 257ss.

[8]D. Cairns, *The Image of God in Man* (New York 1953), p. 77.

[9]Cf. Struker, s. 76-128; also E. Klebba, *Die Anthropologie des hl. Irenaeus* (Münster i. W. 1894 [=Kirchengeschichtliche Studien, II. 3]), p. 22 ff.; J. Lawson, *The Biblical Theology of Saint Irenaeus* (London 1948), p. 198 ff.; G. Wingren, *Maenniskan och Inkarnationen enligt Irenaeus* (Lund 1947), p. 37-49; Engl. transl.: *Man and the Incarnation. A study in the Biblical Theology of Irenaeus* (Edinburgh-London 1959), pp. 14-26.

THEOPHILUS OF ALEXANDRIA
AND APA APHOU OF PEMDJE

[1]E. Revillout, "La Vie du bienheureux Aphou, Evêque de Pemdje (Oxyrinque)," in *Revue Egyptologique*, III, 1, 27-33.

[2]Francesco Rossi, "Trascrizione di tre manoscritti Copti del Museo Egizio di Torino, con traduzione italiana," in *Memorie della Reale Accademia delle Scienze di Torino*, Serie II, XXXVII, 67-84 (text) and 145-150 (translation). Rossi published in the same *Memorie* several other documents from the Turin collection. There is a separate edition: *I papiri copti del Museo egizio di Torino, trascritti e tradotti*, 2 vols. (Torino, 1887, 1892). Cf. Robert Atkinson, "On Professor Rossi's Publication of South Coptic texts," in the *Proceedings of the Royal Irish Academy*, III (Dublin, 1895-1898), 25-99.—A minor, but rather important, emendation of Rossi's text was suggested by Oscar von Lemm, "Koptische Miscellen," XLVI, in *Bulletin de l'Académie Impériale des Sciences de St. Petersbourg*, VI série, II, 7, 15 Avril 1908, 596-598.

[3]V. Bolotov, "Iz tserkovnoj istorii Egipta: II. Zhitie blazhennago Afu, episkopa Pemdzhskago," in *Khristianskoe Chtenie* (1886, 3/4), 334-377.

[4]E. Drioton, "La discussion d'un moine anthropomorphite audien avec le Patriarche Théophile d'Alexandrie en l'année 399," in *Revue de l'Orient Chrétien*, Deuxième série, X [XX], (1915-1917), 92-100 and 113-128.

[5]"Manoscritti copti esistenti nel Museo Egizio nella Biblioteca Nazionale di Torino, raccolti da Bernardino Drovetti e indicati dal Prof. Francesco Rossi," in *Rivista delle Biblioteche e degli Archivi*, X, 9, Settembre 1899, 114.

[6]*Catalogus Codicum Copticorum manu scriptorum qui in Museo Borgiano Veletris adservantur, auctore Georgio Zoega Dano* (Romae, MDCCCX), p. 169.

[7]See Francesco Rossi, "Trascrizione di un Codice Copto del Museo Egizio di Torino," in *Memorie*, Ser. II, XXXV (1884), 165-167, and also: "Trascrizione di alcuni testi copti tirati dai papiri del Museo Egizio di Torino," in *Memorie*, Ser. II, XXXVI (1885), 89-91.

[8]Amedeo Peyron, "Saggio di studi sopra papiri codici cotti ed un stella trilingue del Reale Museo Egiziano," in *Memorie*, XXIX (1825), 78, and also: *Lexicon Linguae Copticae, studio Amedei Peyron* (Taurini, 1835), pp. XXV-XXVI.

[9]Rossi, in *Memorie*, Serie II, XXXV (1884), 166.

[10]E. Revillout, "Le Concile de Nicée, d'après les textes coptes," in *Journal Asiatique*, VII série, I (1873), 2, 217-222: Revillout gives here a transcription of the dedicatory note; at that time he thought that the whole collection was completed already in the *early years* of St. Cyril. Later on he became more

cautious and spoke of *the end* of St. Cyril's pontificate: *Le Concile de Nicée d'après les textes coptes et les divers collections canoniques* (Paris, 1881), p. 112, note I. In the preface to his publication of the "Life" of Aphou he says simply: *before the schism,—Revue Egyptologique,* III, I, p. 28.

[11]Cf. V. Bolotov, "Iz tserkovnoj istorii Egipta: I. 'Razskasy Dioskora o Khalkidonskom Sobore,'" in *Kristianskoe Chtenie* 1/2 (1885), 89-92.

[12]See Th. Lefort, "'Ισον = *Exemplum, Exemplar,*" in *Le Muséon,* XLVII, 1/2, 58: "vraisemblablement aux environs du VIIe siècle." It is just a casual remark: Lefort gives no reasons for his dating.

[13]Zoëga, *Catalogus,* p. 4.

[14]Bolotov assumed that the Arabic *Synaxarion* of Michael, Bishop of Atrib and Malig (XIII century), was based on the Macarian version. See now Georg Graf, *Geschichte der Christlichen Arabischen Literatur,* II (Città del Vaticano, 1947), 416 ff. The history of the Arabic *Synaxaria,* however, cannot be traced in full.

[15]Bolotov, *Zhitie,* pp. 340-343.

[16]Bolotov, *ibid.,* pp. 343-346.

[17]Drioton, pp. 93-94. Marcel Richard thinks that Drioton had exaggerated a bit the historical value of the "Life": "Les Écrits de Théophile d'Alexandrie," in *Le Muséon,* LII, 1/2 (1937), 36, note 16.

[18]Zoëga, *Catalogus,* pp. 363-370 (Codex. Sahid. CLXXII); E. Amélineau, "Monuments pour servir à l'Histoire de l'Egypte Chrétienne," in *Mémoires publiés par les membres de la Mission Archéologique Française au Caire,* IV, 2 (Paris, 1895), 515-516 (Introduction) and 759-769 (text and translation).

[19]See De Lacy O'Leary, *The Saints of Egypt* (London, 1937), pp. 223-224 and 106-107; Hugh G. Evelyn White, *The Monasteries of the Wadi 'n Natrun,* Part II: The History of the Monasteries of Nitria and Scete (New York, 1932), pp. 158 ff; also in the Arabic *Synaxarium Alexandrinum,* under the 7 Paopi,—*Corpus Scriptorum Christianorum Orientalium, Scriptores Arabici,* Ser. III, t. 18 (Roma, 1922), Latin translation by J. Forget, pp. 58-59.

[20]Amélineau, *Monuments,* p. 516.

[21]The English translation quoted in the text was kindly made for me by Professor Thomas O. Lambdin, of Harvard University, to whom I want to extend my warmest thanks.

[22]See, for instance, the chapter "On Holy Anchorites." The Greek text was published by F. Nau: "Le chapitre περὶ ἀναχωρητῶν ἁγίων et les sources de la Vie de Saint Paul de Thèbes," in *Revue de l'Orient Chrétien,* X (1905), 387-417. Nau contended that it was one of the earliest ascetical writings in Egypt, and was used by St. Jerome: "un des premiers écrits ascétiques de l'Egypte" (387). A certain Anchorite is relating his experiences in the desert: ὁρῶ βουβάλους ἐρχομένους καὶ τὸν δοῦλον τοῦ Θεοῦ γυμνὸν (410); ἦν τις ἀναχωρητὴς βοσκόμενος μετὰ τῶν βουβάλων

(414, note 22). An ancient Latin version of this chapter, by subdeacon John, was published already by Rosweyde, *De vitis Patrum,* liber VI, libellus 3,— reprinted in *ML* LXXIII, 1004-1014: *"vidi bubalos venientes, et illum servum De: venientem cum eis nudum"* (1009); *"vidit... hominem pascentem tanquam bestiam"* (1008). Some fragments of a Coptic translation were published already by Mingarelli, *Aegyptiorum Codicum Reliquiae Venetis in Bibliotheca Naniana asservatae* (Bononiae, 1785), pp. CCCXXXVII-CCCXLIII. A Syriac version is in Anon Isho's *Paradisus Patrum:* published by Bedjan, *Acta Martyrum et Sanctorum,* VII (Paris, 1897), 252-260, and, together with an English translation, by E. W. Budge, *The Book of Paradise* etc., (London, 1904), I, 358-362 (translation). There are several stories told by different people; one of them is attributed to Apa Macarius of Egypt. The same material is used in the "Life and Conversation" of Apa Onouphrius (or Benofer). The Coptic text was published twice: by E. Amélineau, "Voyage d'un moine égyptien dans le désert," in *Recueil de Travaux relatifs à la Philologie et à l'Archéologie Egyptiennes et Assyriennes* V (Paris, 1884), 166-194, and then by E. W. Budge, *Coptic Martyrdoms, etc., in the dialect of Upper Egypt* (London, 1914), pp. 455-473. In fact, it is a description of a journey in the desert by Apa Paphnutius. An ancient Latin translation was also published by Rosweyde,—reprinted in *ML* LXXIII, 211-222.—An interesting pericope on wandering hermits is found among the new *Apophthegmata* in the Greek manuscript in the archives of the Library Company in Philadelphia (Greek Commentary 1141),—see Edwin C. Tappert, "A Greek Hagiological Manuscript in Philadelphia," in *Transactions of the American Philological Association* LXVIII (1937), 264-276. A selection of passages from this manuscript is given in English translation by E. Tappert, "Desert Wisdom: The Sayings of the Anchorites," in *The Lutheran Quarterly* IX (1957), 157-172. "Now men set snares there and caught antelopes, and the monk, too, was caught. And his reasoning said to him, 'Put forth thy hand and release thyself.' But he said to his reasoning, 'If thou art a man, release thyself and go to men. But if thou art an antelope, thou hast no hands.' And he stayed in the snare until morning. When the men came to catch the antelopes and saw the monk ensnared, they were struck with fear. He himself said nothing, and they released him and let him go. And he went off, running behind the antelopes into the wilderness." (p. 168).

[23]W. Bousset, "Das Mönchtum der sketischen Wüste," in *Zeitschrift für Kirchengeschichte* XLII (1923), 31 ff.; cf. Hans Frhr. von Campenhausen, *Die asketische Heimatslösigkeit im altkirchlichen und frühmittelalterlichen Mönchtum* (1930), now reprinted in *Tradition und Leben, Kräfte der Kirchengeschichte, Aufsätze und Vorträge* (Tübingen, 1960), pp. 293-294.

[24]See Arthur Vööbus, *History of Asceticism in the Syrian Orient,* I (Louvain, 1958—*C.S.C.O.,* Subsidia 14), 138 ff., and II (Louvain, 1960—*C.S.C.O.,* Subsidia 17), 19 ff. Professor Vööbus discusses at length the wild and exotic character of the early Syrian anchoritism: "The same wildness also becomes manifest in the way in which these texts draw a comparison between the life in monasticism and the life of animals. A frequently occurring feature in these sources is this, that the monks have become the companions of wild animals. Ephrem invites his readers to make the tour with him to see these monks and adds: 'Behold, they mingle with stags and are leaping with fawns.' Moreover it is stated that a life close to animals and nature

is the prerequisite to that sole sphere in which repentance can be obtained"
(II, p. 27).

²⁵See B. Steidle, O.S.B., "Homo Dei Antonius," in *Antonius Magnus
Eremita* (356-1956); *Studia Anselmiana*, 38 (Roma, 1956), 148-200.

²⁶The word μοναστήριον appears for the first time in Philo, *De Vita
Contemplativa*, M. 475.13: οἴκημα ἱερόν, ὃ καλεῖται σεμνεῖον καὶ
μοναστήριον. It denoted here a private chamber, or a closet, reserved for
solitary meditation and worship (cf. ταμεῖον in Mt. 6:6, 24:26, Lk. 12:3).
This passage of Philo was quoted by Eusebius, *HE*, II, 17, 9. The word does
not occur in any other Greek text till the end of the third century, and at
that time it acquires the meaning of an accommodation for a single monk
or hermit. In this sense the word was used by St. Athanasius, and also in
the *Historia Lausiaca*. See the note of Fred. C. Conybeare, in his edition,
Philo About the Contemplative Life (Oxford, 1895), p. 211. Cf. also *Vita
Epiphanii*, cap. 27: *Epiphanius* visited Hierakas ἐν τῷ μοναστηρίῳ αὐτοῦ.
But by the end of the fourth century the word μοναστήριον came to
mean "monastery."

²⁷Cf. Georg Pfeilschifter, "Oxyrhynchos, Seine Kirchen und Klöster, Auf
Grund der Papyrfunde," in *Festgabe Alois Knöpfler* (Freiburg i/Br., 1917),
pp. 248-264.

²⁸Cf. *Hist. monach.*, V: *ipsi quoque magistratus et principales civitatis et
reliqui cives studiose per singulas portas statuunt qui observent ut sicubi
apparuit peregrinus aut pauper, certatim ad eum qui praeoccupaverit adductus
quae sunt necessaria consequatur.*—This description of Oxyrhynchus refers to
the last decades of the fourth century.

²⁹The Greek spelling of the name is Ἀπφύ.

³⁰*Mystic Treatises by Isaac of Nineveh*, translated from Bedjan's Syriac
text, with an Introduction and Registers, by A.J. Wensinck (Amsterdam,
1923) (=*Verhandelingen der K. Akademie van Wetenschappen*, Afdeeling
Letterkunde, N.R. Deel XXIII), pp. 166-167; cf. the Greek version, ed.
Nicephorus Theotoki (Leipzig, 1770), pp. 500-501.

³¹Drioton, pp. 116-118.—The best up-to-date summary of information
on the Audians is by H.-Ch. Puech, in the *Reallexikon für Antike und Christentum, sub voce*, I (1950), coll. 910-915. Puech warns against the indis-
criminate identification of Audians with the Egyptian Anthropomorphites,
but admits, referring to Drioton's article, a possibility of some Audian
influence in Egypt. The Audian movement, which only gradually developed
into a "sect," originated in Mesopotamia, and then expanded to Syria and
later to Scythia, where Audius was banished.—H. G. Opitz, in his article on
Theophilus, in Pauly-Wissowa-Kroll *Realenzyclopädie*, II R., Hb. 10 (1934),
sp. 2154, reserves his opinion on this point: "es ist nicht leicht zu
entscheiden, ob Aphou wirklich Audianer war"; Agostino Favale, *Teofilo
d'Alessandria* (345-412), *Scritti, Vita e Dottrina* (Torino, 1958), quotes
Drioton, but is not certain about the Audian character of the Anthropomorphite monks (pp. 93-95). Giuseppe Lazzati, *Teofilo d'Alessandria*
(Milano, 1935), does not mention Aphou at all and only briefly mentions
the Anthropomorphite conflict (pp. 31-33).

[32]Cf. Karl Holl, *Enthusiasmus und Bussgewalt beim Griechischen Mönchtum* (Leipzig, 1898), pp. 141 ff., 183 ff.

[33]R. Reitzenstein, "Des Athanasius Werk über das Leben des Antonius," in *Sitzungsberichte der Heidelberger Akademie der Wissenschaften*, Phil.-Hist. Klasse (1914), No. 8, pp. 54 ff.

[34]R. Reitzenstein, *Historia Monachorum und Historia Lausiaca* (Göttingen, 1916), p. 89; cf. the whole chapter 4, "Der Mönch als Apostel."

[35]Cf. *Les Pères du Désert*. Textes choisis et présentés par René Draguet (Paris 1942), p. XXXV: "Dans les documents pachomiens, le cenobitisme strict est communément appelé 'la voie apostolique, la voie supérieure des apôtres.' " See also Louis Bouyer, *La Spiritualité du Nouveau Testament et des Pères* (Paris, 1960), p. 369, and Dom Germain Morin, *L'idéal monastique e، la vie Chrétienne des premiers jours*, Troisième édition (Paris, 1921), pp. 66 ff. In this sense the word "apostolic life" was used still by Rupert of Deutz in his treatise *De vita vere apostolica* (*ML* CLXX, 611-664).

[36]The "Life of Blessed Aphou" was never translated into English. Père Pierre de Bourguet, S.J., of the Musée du Louvre, was kind enough to provide me with a French translation from the original. I wish to express my warmest gratitude for his gracious assistance. The English version given in the text was established on the basis of Père de Bourguet's translation, collated with the earlier translations: Russian by Bolotov and Italian by Rossi. Professor Thomas O. Lambdin checked the translation against the Coptic original, for which I am deeply thankful. My best and cordial thanks to my friend and colleague, Ralph Lazzaro, of Harvard Divinity School, for his generous and devoted help in translation. I have to thank also Père Jean Daniélou, S.J., for introducing me and my query to Père de Bourguet.

[37]This passage was misunderstood by all previous translators: Bolotov, Rossi, and Drioton. They missed the point: τὸ ἴσον is a legal term and denotes the original of a document, which is supposed to be deposited in the archives, as an *exemplum*, as *scriptum authenticum*, as a standard. Aphou wanted to check whether that to which he so firmly objected was *in the original* (ἴσον) or whether it was only in that *particular copy* which was sent to Oxyrhynchus, having crept in there by a *lapsus calami* of the scribe, συγγραφεύς. He wanted to know the *official text*. In fact, the "preaching" to which he objected was not a sermon, but rather the formal Paschal Epistle of the Archbishop, that is, an official document which had to be deposited in the archieves of the Archdiocese. See Bernhard Kübler, ""Ισον und 'Απογραφή" in *Zeitschrift der Savigny-Stiftung für Rechtsgeschichte*, Roman. Abt., LIII (1933), 64-98, and Th. Lefort, ""Ισον=Exemplum, Exemplar," in *Le Muséon*, XLVII, 1/2, 57-60.

[38]Drioton also puts the conversation *before* the intervention of monks, p. 121. On the contrary, Felix Haase suggested that it took place shortly after—*kurz nachher*, which is hardly probable: *Altchristliche Kirchengeschichte nach Orientalischen Quellen* (Leipzig, 1925), p. 201.

[39]Cf. Berthold Altaner, *Patrologie*, 5th edition (München, 1958), p. 282, and Johannes Quasten, *Patrology*, III (1960), pp. 386-388.

[40]Cf. Henri Crouzel, *Théologie de Dieu chez Origène* (Paris, 1956), especially pp. 206-211; a brief summary of the book is given in the article of Crouzel "L'image de Dieu dans la théologie d'Origène," in *Studia Patristica*, II (Berlin, 1957), 194-201. See also Th. Camelot, "La Théologie de l'Image de Dieu," in *Revue des Sciences Philosophiques et Théologiques*, XL (1956), 443-471.

[41]Cf. my essay, "The Concept of Creation in St. Athanasius," in *Studia Patristica*, VI (1962), 36-57. Also in this volume.

[42]Cf. Régis Bernard, *L'image de Dieu d'après St. Athanase* (Paris, 1952), pp. 48-54, 62-79, 131 ff. See also the article of Père Camelot, quoted above, and Julius Gross, *Entstehungsgeschichte des Erbsündendogmas*, I (München-Basel, 1960), pp. 125-132.

[43]Cf. Walter J. Burghardt, S.J., *The Image of God in Man according to Cyril of Alexandria* (Washington, 1957), pp. 141-159.—It should be mentioned here that Saint Cyril continued the struggle against the Anthropomorphites in the monastic circles of Egypt. His treatise *Adversus Anthropomorphitas* is actually a later compilation in which his two epistles addressed to a certain Deacon Tiberius and his associates were fused together; see the critical edition by Philip E. Pusey, *Cyrilli Archiepiscopi Alexandrini in D. Ioannis Evangelium*, III (Oxonii, 1872).

[44]W. Bousset, *Apophthegmata, Studien zur Geschichte des ältesten Mönchtums* (Tübingen, 1923), p. 83.

[45]See my essay, "The Anthropomorphites in the Egyptian Desert," in the *Akten des XI Internationalen Byzantinisten-Kongresses*, 1958 (München, 1960), pp. 154-159. Also in this volume.

[46]Tillemont, *Mémoires pour servir à l'Histoire Ecclésiastique des six premiers siècles*, XI (Paris, 1706), 463.

[47]We find a similar phrase in the Coptic record of conversations of Cyril and Theophilus with the monks, published and translated in German by W. E. Crum: Theophilus says to Apa Horsiesius: "So wie der Herr der Sonne, Christus, als er zu dem Himmel auffuhr, ebenso bist du vor mir heute"—*Der Papyruscodex saec. VI-VII der Phillippsbibliothek in Cheltenham*, herausgegeben und übersetzt von W. E. Crum (Strassburg, 1915) (= Schriften der Wissenschaftlichen Gesellschaft in Strassburg, Heft 15), p. 67; also quoted in Haase, *op. cit.*, p. 201.

[48]They are for the years 401 (= Hieron. ep. 96) and 404 (= ep. 100). See Marcel Richard, the article quoted above, and also R. Delobel & Marcel Richard, under the name of Theophilus, in the *Dictionnaire de Théologie Catholique*, XV, I (1946).

[49]Draguet, *Les Pères du Désert*, p. XV: "Écrivant vingt ou trente ans après son voyage, le pieux journaliste a mis du sien dans son reportage: le mythe de la parfaite objectivité ne pourrait d'ailleurs tromper que les pauvres psychologues que nous sommes. Cassien ne cache pas que c'est à travers sa propre expérience qu'il se remémore celle de ses maîtres égyptiens; ce qu'il savait moins, peut-être, et qui ne l'aurait troublé d'aucune sorte, c'est que,

dans les Conférences, il peignait le rustique asceticisme de Scète avec la palette brillante des Alexandrins plus savants."

[50]D. Salvatore Marsili, O.S.B., *Giovanni Cassiano ed Evagrio Pontico, Dottrina sulla carità e contemplazione* (Romae, 1936) (= Studia Anselmiana, V), p. 161; cf. also Owen Chadwick, *John Cassian, A Study in Primitive Monasticism* (Cambridge, 1950).

[51]See especially R. Draguet, "L'Histoire Lausiaque, une oeuvre écrite dans l'esprit d'Evagre," in *Revue d'Histoire Ecclésiastique* (Louvain, 1946), 321-364, and (1947), 5-49.

WESTERN INFLUENCES IN RUSSIAN THEOLOGY

[1]*Otzyvy eparkhial'nykh arkhiereev po voprosu o cherkovnoi reformy,* II (Petersburg, 1906), pp. 142-143. See the brochure by Tarasii (Kurganskii): *"Perelom v drevnerusskom bogoslovii,"* in the edition containing a "Foreword" by Metropolitan Anthony (Warsaw, 1927).

[2]For the early period see B. Leib, *Rome Kiev et Byzance à la fin du 11 siècle* (Petersburg, 1924). This work contains a good bibliography.

[3]See A. A. Pokrovskii, *Drevnee Pskovsko-Novgorodskoe pis'mennoe nasledie, obozrenie pergamentnykh rukopisei Tipografskoi i Patriashei biblioteki. Trudy 15-go arkheologicheskogo s'ezda v Novgorode* (Moscow, 1916), II; I. P. Popov, *O vozniknovenii Moskovskoi Sinodal'noi (Patriarshei) Biblioteki. Sbornik statei* [in honor of A. S. Orlov] (Leningrad, 1934), pp. 29-38.

[4]See especially the works by I. E. Evseev, *Rukopisnoe predanie Slavianskoi biblioteki, Khristianskoe chtenie* (1911); *Ocherki po istorii Slavianskogo perevoda biblioteki, Khristianskoe chtenie* (1912 and 1913); *Genadievskaia Bibliia 1499 goda. Trudy 15-go arkheologicheskogo s'ezda v Novgorode,* II, 1 (1914); see also I. A. Chistovich, *Ispravlenie teksta Slavianskoi biblii pered izdaniem 1751. goda,* Pravoslavnoe obozrenie, 1860, April and May.

[5]B. N. Beneshevich, *K istorii perevodnoi literatury v Novgorode v 15. stoletii, Sbornik statei v chest' A. I. Sobolevskogo* (1928); "Slovo-Kratko" published by A. D. Grigoriev, *Chteniia v Moskovskom Obschestve Istorii i Drevnostei* (1902); see V. Valdenberg, *Drevne-russkoe uchenie o predelakh tserkovnoi vlasti* (M. 1916); A. D. Sedelenikov, "K izuchen'iu 'Slovo-Kratko' i deiatel'nosti dominikantsa Veniamina," *Izvestiia Otdeleniia Russkogo Iazyka i Slovesnosti Rossiiskoi Akademii Nauk,* XXX (1925); *Ocherki katolicheskogo vliianiia v Novgorode v 15-16 vekakh.* Doklady R. Akademii Nauk, 1929.

[6]N. Andreev, O dele d'iaka Viskovatogo, *Seminarium Kondakovianum,* V (1932); "Rozysk" po delu Viskovatogo iz *Chteniia Moskovskogo Obschestva Istorii i Drevnostii* (1847;—and better, 1858); Buslaev, *Istoricheskie ocherki,* II, and in *Istoriia russkogo iskustva* by I. Grabar', Vol. VI.

[7]P. Pierling, La Russie et le Saint-Siège, I (1896).

[8]See his letter to the *Appendix* to *Tvoreniia Sv. Ottsov,* XVII, 2, p. 190.

[9]The "Apokrisis" was translated into modern Russian and newly published in 1869. See N. Skaballanovich, *Ob Apokrisise Khristofora Filaleta* (Petersburg, 1873); concerning the compiler see J. Tretjak, *Piotr Skarga w dziejach i literaturze unii Brzeskiej* (Krakow, 1913); see also M. Hrusevskii, *Istoriia Ukrainy-Rusi,* VI (1907). On Prince Ostrozhskii see K. V. Lewicki, *Ks. Konstanty Ostrogski a Unia Brzeska 1596* (Lemberg, 1933).

¹⁰Hyp. Pociei, *Kazania i Homilie,* p. 539—quoted from Josef Tretjak, *Piotr Skarga* (Krakow, 1913), p. 222.

¹¹On Peter Mogila see the basic but unfinished work: S. T. Golubev, *Petr Mogila i ego spodvizhniki,* 2 vols. (Kiev, 1833 and 1897); quite important is the book by E. F. Shmurlo, *Rimskaia kuriia na russkom pravoslavnom vostoke v 1609-1654 godakh* (Prague, 1928); "Pravoslavnoe ispovedanie" (Greek) in the collections of E. Kimmel, *Monumenta fidei Ecclesiae Orientalis* (1850), or J. Michalcescu, Θησαυρὸς τῆς Ὀρθοδοξίας (1904), or recently in J. Karmiris, Τὰ δογματικὰ καὶ Συμβολικὰ Μνημεῖα τῆς Ὀρθόδοξου Καθολικῆς Ἐκκλησίας, 1. II, Athens 1952. See also the edition of the Latin text with notes and a foreword by A. Malvy, S.J. and M. Viller, S.J. in *Orientalia Christiana,* X, 39 (1927); on Peter Mogila's *Euchologion* see E. M. Kryzhanovskii, *Povrezhdenie tserkovnoi obriadnosti i religioznykh obychaev v iuzhno-russkoi mitropolii, Rukovodstvo dlia sel'skikh pastyrei* (1860) and *Sobranie Sochinenii,* I (1890). See my *Puti russkogo bogosloviia* [*Ways of Russian Theology*] for the literature on the Kievan Academy.

¹²See, for a precise analysis of *"Kamen' very,"* I. Morevi, *Kamen' very mitr. Stefana Iavorskogo* (Petersburg, 1904); see also the well-known book by Iurii Samarin, *Stefan Iavorskii i Theofan Prokopovich, Sobranie Sochinenii,* V (1880); S. I. Maslov, *Biblioteka Stefana Iavorskogo, Chtenie v obshchestve Nestora Letopistsa,* 24, 2 (1914); Hans Koch, *Die russische Orthodoxie im Petrinischen Zeitalter* (Breslau, 1929).

¹³The basic work is: P. V. Znamenskii, *Dukhovnye shkoly v Rossi do reformy 1808 goda* (Kazan', 1881); S. T. Golubev, *Kievskaia akademiia v pervoi polovine 18-go stoletiia* (Kiev, 1903); N. I. Petrov, *Kievskaia akademiia v kontse 17-go i nachale 18-go stoletiia* (Kiev, 1901); D. Vishnevskii, *Znachenie Kievskoi akademii v razvitii dukhovnoi shkoly v Rossii s ucherezheleniia St. Sinoda,* Trudy *Kievskoi dukhovnoi Akademii* (1904, 4 and 5); *Kievskaia akademiia v getmanstvo K. G. Razumovskogo,* Trudy (1905), 5; *Kievskaia Dukh. Akademiia v tsarstvovanie Imp. Ekateriny* II, Trudy (1906), 7, 8-9, 11; V. Serebrennikov, *Kievskaia akademiia v polovine 18-go veka do preobrazovaniia v 1819 godu* (Kiev, 1897); S. K. Smirnov, *Istoriia Moskovskoi Slaviano-Greko-Latinskoi Akademii* (Moscow, 1855); *Istoriia Troitskoi Lavrskoi seminarii* (Moscow, 1867); see also the works of the history of specific seminaries: the Vladimir Seminary by K. F. Nadezhin (1875) and by N. V. Malitskii (1900); the Suzdal' Seminary by N. V. Malitskii (1900); the Tver' Seminary by V. Kolosov (1889); the Riazan' Seminary by Agntsev (1889).

¹⁴There is a rather comprehensive work on Theophan Prokopovich: Ia. Samarin, *Stefan Iavorskii i Feofan Prokopovich, Sobranie Sochinenii,* V (1880); I. V. Chistovich, *Feofan Prokopovich i ego vremiia* (Petersburg, 1866); on Theophan's "theological system" see the article by Pl. Cherviakovskii, *"Khrist. Chtenie,"* (1876-1878); F. A. Tikhomirov, *Traktaty Feofana Prokopovicha— o Boge edinom po sushchestvu i troichnom v litsakh* (Petersburg, 1884); A. I. Kartashev, *K voprosu pravoslaviia Feofana Prokopovicha, Sbornik statei v chest D. A. Kobeko* (1913); P. V. Verkhovskoi, *Ucherezhdenie Dukhovnoi kollegii i Dukhovnyi Reglament,* I and II (Rostov-on-Don,

1916); Hans Koch, *Die russische Orthodoxie* (Breslau, 1929); see also the interesting essays by R. Stupperich in *ZoG,* V and IX in *Zeitschrift für slavische Philologie,* XII, 332 ff., also in *Kyrios* (1936), 4; also R. Stupperich, *Staatsgedanke und Religionspolitik Peters des Grossen* (Königsberg, 1936); and also the article by V. Titlinov in the *Russkii Biograficheskii Slovar'.*

[15]See Filaret (Gumilevskii), *Obzor russkoi dukhovnoi literatury,* II, 3 (1884); on Metropolitan Platon see I. M. Snegirev, *Zhizn' mitr. Moskovskogo Platona,* 1-2 (Moscow, 1856); F. Nadezhdin, *M. Platon Levshin, kak propovednik* (Kazan', 1882); N. P. Rozanov, *M. M. Platon* (Moscow, 1913); V. P. Vinogradov, *Platon i Filaret, Mitropolity Moskovskie, Sravnitel'niia kharakteristika ikh nravstvennogo oblika* in *Bogoslovskii Vestnik,* 1913 1-2. See also "Iz vospominanii pokoinogo Filareta, mitrop. Moskov.," *Pravoslav. Obozreniia* (1868, August)—("iz zapisok A. V. Gorskogo").

[16]See the entirety of chapter V—"Bor'ba za Bogoslovie"—in my book *Puti Russkogo Bogosloviia* [*Ways of Russian Theology*], pp. 128-233.

[17]Aleksei I. Vvedenskii, "K voprosu o metodologicheskoi reforme pravoslavnoi dogmatiki," *Bogoslovskii Vestnik* (April, 1914); also published separately.

[18]N. Gilarov-Platonov, *Iz perezhitogo. Avtobiograficheskiia vospominaniia* (Moscow, 1886), pp. 279-280.

ORTHODOX ECUMENISM
IN THE NINETEENTH CENTURY

[1]Cf. the whole chapter on this period in my book, *The Ways of Russian Theology* (Paris, 1937) [in Russian], p. 128 ff. References and bibliography, p. 537 f. The act of the Holy Alliance (the French text) in Martens, *Nouveau Recueil de Traités et Conventions conclus par la Russie avec les Puissances étrangères* (St. Petersbourg, II), p. 656-658. On the Holy Alliance itself see: E. Muhlenbeck, *Études sur les Origines de la Sainte Alliance* (Paris, 1888); M. Godlewski, "Cesarz Aleksander I jako mistyk," (Krakow, 1926; originally in *Przegad Powszechny*, v. 166, 1925, and 170, 1926); W. Naf, *Zur Geschichte der Heiligen Allianz* (Bern 1928; *Berner Untersuchungen zur allgemeinen Geschichte*, I); Franz Buchler, *Die geistigen Wuzeln der Heiligen Allianz* (Freiburg i/Br., 1929); Hildegard Schaeder, *Die dritte Koalition und die Heilige Alliaz*, 1934 (*Ost-Europaische Forschungen*, N.F. 16). Important material is to be found in the "notes et commentaires" of Eugene Susini, in his recent publication of the *Lettres Inédites de Franz von Baader*, v. I (Paris, 1942); vols. II & III (Wien, 1951). The memorandum of Baader presented to three monarchs, *Ueber das durch die französische Revolution herbeigeführte Bedürfnis einer neuen und innigeren Verbindung der Religion mit der Politik* (1815; dedicated to Prince Galitzin), in his *Sämtliche Werke*, Bd. VI, and in Baader's *Anthology*, published by J. Sauter, *Herdflamme*, Bd. 14 (Jena, 1925). On Baader see especially E. Benz, "Die abendländische Sendung der östlich-orthodoxen Kirche," in *Akademie der Wissenschaften und der Literatur*. Abhandlungen der Geistes—und Sozialwissenschaftichen Klasse (Jahrgang, 1950, Nr. 8). On Jung Stilling see Benz, "Das Reich Gottes im Osten," in *Evangelium und Osten*, VII. 12 (1934), and VIII. 4 (1935), and "Jung Stilling in Marburg," in *Marburger Vorträge*, 3 (Marburg, 1949). For a wider background see Jakob Baxa, *Einführung in die romantische Staatswissenschaft* (2nd ed., Jena, 1931) (*Die Herdflamme*, Erganzungsband 4). On the Russian Bible Society: A. N. Pypin, *Religious Movements under Alexander I* (2nd ed., Petrograd, 1916), and I. A. Chistovich, *History of the Russian Translation of the Bible* (2nd ed., St. Petersburg, 1899—first published in 1873),—both books in Russian; rich documentation. Some material is available in J. Owen, *The History of the Origin and First Ten Years of the British and Foreign Bible Society* (3 vols., 1816 a. 1820); E. Henderson, *Bible Researches and Travels in Russia* (London, 1826); Robert Pinkerton, *Russia, or Miscellaneous Observations on the Past and Present State of this Country and its Inhabitants* (London, 1833); J. Paterson, *The Book for every Land. Reminiscences of Labour and Adventure in the Work for Bible Circulation in the North of Europe and in Russia* (Edited with a prefatory memoir by W. L. Alexander, 1858). On the Emperor Alexander's links with the Society of Friends see J. Cunningham, *The Quakers* (London, 1868); and especially *Mémoirs of the Life and Gospel Labours of Stephen Grellet*, ed. by Benjamin Seebohm (Philadelphia, 1862),

v. I, p. 293, 313, 315 f., 386-478 Cf. Peter v. Gotze, *Fürst Alexander Nikolajewitsch Galitzin und seine Zeit* (Leipzig, 1882). Further Bibliography in Benz, *Die Sendung*, 846-848. On De Maistre see Georges Goyau, "La Pensee religieuse de Joseph de Maistre," in *Revue des Deux Mondes* (1921), and separately; M. Jugie, *J. de Maistre et l'Église Greco-Russe* (Paris, 1922); Émile Dermenghem, *Joseph de Maistre Mystique*, Nouvella edition, La Colombe (Paris, 1946). Cf. *Quatre chapitres inédits sur la Russie par le comte Joseph de Maistre*, publiés par son fils, le comte Rodolphe de Maistre (Paris, 1859); "Un écrit inédit de J. de Maistre," in *Études*, v. 73 (1897); Wilhelm Schwarz, *Die Heilige Allianz* (Stuttgart, 1935); Robert Triomphe, *Joseph De Maistre* (Geneva, 1968).

²Philaret's *Conversation* was never translated into any Western language. In Russian it has been republished many times, slightly revised by the author himself; in the later editions (after his death), the concluding part of the treatise, dealing with the "ecumenical" question, was usually omitted. In this chapter, the 2nd edition has been used, Moscow, 1833. As early as 1811, Philaret wrote an "Exposition of the differences between the Eastern and Western Churches, concerning the teaching of faith," probably for Empress Elizabeth of Russia. In the original it was published only in 1870, *Readings in the Moscow Imperial Society of Russian History and Antiquities*, 1870, I; but in English translation (from the manuscript supplied by Philaret himself), it had appeared in 1833, in Pinkerton's *Russia* etc., p. 39-54; German translation (extracts) in the review of Pinkerton's book, *Evangelische Kirchenzeitung* (published by Hengstenberg), Bd. XV., 1834, Nrs. 71-73, 77-79 etc. On Philaret, see my *Ways*, p. 166-184 and *passim* (Bibliography). Cf. A. P. Stanley, *Lectures on the History of the Eastern Church* (1861); new edition in Everyman's Library, p. 377: "Philaret, the venerable Metropolitan of Moscow, represents, in some measure at least, the effect of that vast wave of reactionary feeling which we sometimes associate exclusively with England, even with Oxford, and a few well-known names in Oxford, but which really has passed over the whole of Europe... The gentle and saint-like representative in Russia of opinion and practices which in England are too near ourselves to be described more closely." Cf. Stanley's article in *Macmillan's Magazine*, February, 1868. Stanley, "Philaret in 1857": see *The Life and Correspondence of A. P. Stanley*, by Rowland E. Prothero, v. I, New York, 1894, p. 527-530. On Philaret see also: *Memoirs of Stephen Grellet*, I, 395 f., 414, 421 (personal impressions); and *Notes of a visit to the Russian Church in the years 1840, 1841*, by William Palmer, selected and arranged by Cardinal Newman, London, 1882, *passim*. Only some sermons of Philaret are available in English, but probably his sermons were his major theological contribution: *Select Sermons of the late Metropolitan of Moscow Philaret*, translated from the Russian, London, Joseph Masters, 1873 (translated by E. Th. Tyutchev); cf. *Choix de Sermons et Discours de S. Em. Mgr. Philarète*, traduits du Russe par A. Serpinet, 3 vols., Paris, 1866.— Soloviev's critical comments in his *La Russie et L' Église Universelle* (Paris, 1886; English translation, *Russia and the Universal Church*, London, The Centenary Press, 1948, p. 54-55. In this connection, one should mention another interesting attempt to interpret the relation between the Eastern and Western (Roman) Churches: *Considerations sur la doctrine et l'Ésprit de l'Église Orthodoxe*, par Alexandre Stourdza, Stuttgart, Cotta, 1816; German translation by A. von Kotzebue, Leipzig, 1817. Stourdza (1791-1854) was

deeply involved in the mystical movements of the first decades of the century, and his book betrays the influence of Baader etc., although he was a conservative Orthodox. His point of view is close to that of Philaret. It has been recently suggested that unless the "Considerations" of Stourdza had been published, probably the famous book by Joseph De Maistre, *Du Pape*, would not have been written at all; Susini, III, p. 92; cf. Camille Latreille, *Joseph de Maistre et la Papauté*, Paris, Hachette, 1906. On Stourdza see Susini, III, 82 ff., and Benz, *Die Sendung*, p. 785 ff. Stourdza's book is reprinted (in French, as it was written) in his *Oeuvres Posthumes*, t. IV., Paris, 1860.

[3]Moehler's book on Unity was recently re-published by E. J. Vierneisel, Mainz, 1925 (*Deutsche Klassiker der Katholischer Theologie aus Neuerer Zeit*, Matthias Gruenewald Verlag); French translation by Dom A. Lilienfeld, O.S.B., Paris, 1938 (*Unam Sanctam*, Les Éditions du Cerf). On Moehler see the centenary volume: *L'Église est Une, Hommage à Moehler*, ed. by Pierre Chaillet, Bloud & Gay, Paris, 1939 (the same in German); K. Eschweiler, *J. A. Moehlers Kirchenbegriff*, Braunsberg, 1930; G. R. Geiselman, "Geist des Christentums und Katholicismus: J. A. Moehler und die Entwicklung seines Kirchenbegriffs" in the *Theologische Quartalschrift*, Bd. 112, 1931; and especially Geiselmann's later publication, *J. A. Moehler: Die Einheit der Kirche und die Wiedervereinigung der Konfessionen*, Wien, 1940. In English: Serge Bolshakoff, *The Doctrine of the Unity of the Church in the works of Khomyakov and Moehler*, S.P.C.K., London, 1946. On the general background see Georges Goyau, *L' Allemagne Religieuse*, v. II, Paris, 1905, and especially E. Vermeil, *Jean Adam Moehler et l'école catholique de Tubingue*, Paris, 1913. Moehler's *Symbolik* has been translated into English by James Burton Robertson: *Symbolism: or Exposition of the Doctrinal Differences between Catholics and Protestants, as Evidenced by their Symbolical Writings*, 2 vols., London, 1843.

[4]Cf. Yngve Brilioth, *The Anglican Revival*, London, 1925, p. 329. On Moehler's influence in the Tractarian Movement see H. Boehmer, "Die Kirche Englands und der Protestantismus," in the *Neue Kirchliche Zeitschrift*, 1916. Convergence between Moehler and Newman was strongly stressed by Jean Guitton, *La Philosophie de Newman. Essai sur l'idée de development*, Boivin & Co., Paris, 1933, p. 48, 118 n. 3. 129. Newman actually mentions Moehler (and De Maistre) in the Introduction of his treatise on "The Development of Christian Doctrine": New edition, by F. C. Harold, Longmans, 1949, p. 28. It would be interesting to compare Newman's *The Arians of the Fourth Century* (first published in 1833) and Moehler's *Athanasius der Grosse und die Kirche seiner Zeit, besonders im Kampfe mit dem Arianismus* (2 Bde, 1827); cf. Guitton, p. 221. Moehler's influence on Newman and the "British Critic" was censured by some Tractarians as "romanizing": the principle of "development" seemed to contradict the appeal to "antiquity." See W. Palmer (of Worcester College, Oxford), *A Narrative of Events, Connected with the Publication of the Tracts for the Times* (1843); New edition, with an Introduction and Supplement extending to the Present Time, London, 1883, p. 151 f., 166 f.; cf. Palmer's *Treatise on the Church*, 3rd ed., v. II, p. 443 f.

[5]Ks. A. Pawlowski, *Idea Kosciola wujeciu rosyjskiej teologji i historiosofji*, Warszawa, 1935, p. 89 f., 229 f., admits a direct influence, and probably

he is right. It is denied by others: A. Gratieux, *A. S. Khomiakov et le Mouvement Slavophile*, v. II, Paris, 1939, p. 105, n. I; P. Baron, *"Un théologien laïc Russe au XIX-e siècle. A. S. Khomiakov (1804-1860). Son Ecclesiologie: Exposé et Critique,"* Roma, 1940, p. 58-60 (*Orientalia Christiana Analecta*, 127); Bolshakov, p. 216-262. Cf. also S. Tyszkiewicz, S. J., "La théologoie moehlerienne de l'Unité et les théologien pravoslaves," in *L'Église est Une*, p. 270 ff.; P. Yves Congar, "La pensée de Moehler et l'eccléliologie Orthodoxe," in *Irenikon*, 1935.

⁶Dr. Darwell Stone, a man of enormous erudition in all fields of Church History, "was once heard to remark that he did not know of its ancestry." Upon the strong recommendation of Lord Halifax he would not use it himself.—F. L. Cross, *Darwell Stone. Churchman and Counsellor*, Dacre Press, Westminster (1943), p. 55, n. 3. Cf. T. A. Lacey, "The Unity of the Church as treated by English Theologians," London, S.P.C.K., 1898 (*Tracts of the Church Historical Society*, XXXV).

⁷Newman, *Parochial and Plain Sermons*, v. III, "Submission to Church Authority," November 29, 1829; New edition, Rivingtons, London, 1885, p. 191 f.

⁸Newman's "Prefatory Notice" to W. Palmer (of Magdalen College, Oxford), *Notes of a Visit to the Russian Church*, p. v-vii.

⁹Pusey makes the same point in his "Eirenikon." "Suspension of inter-communion" does not estrange the separated Churches from Unity; "The Church of England a Portion of Christ's One Holy Catholic Church, and a Means of Restoring Visible Unity." An Eirenikon, in a Letter to the author of *The Christian Year*; first published in 1865; reprinted, 1866, p. 248 ff. Cf. A. S. Duncan Jones, "The Oecumenical Ideals of the Oxford Movement," in *Northern Catholicism: Centenary Studies in the Oxford and Parallel Movements*, ed. by N. P. Williams and Charles Harris, S.P.C.K., London (1933), p. 446 ff.; H. Brandreth, *The Ecumenical Ideals of the Oxford Movement*, S.P.C.K., London, 1947; P. E. Shaw, *The Early Tractarians and The Eastern Church*, Morehouse, Milwaukee & Mowbray, London, (1830).

¹⁰*The Early Tractarians*, 76; cf. the whole chapter, "The Early Tractarians and Reunion," p. 59 ff.

¹¹Pusey to Rev. R. Harrison, Feb. 21, 1840, in *Life of Edward Bouverie Pusey*, by H. P. Liddon, v. II, London, 1893, p. 148-149.

¹²*The Articles Treated in Tract XC Reconsidered, and Their Interpretation Vindicated, in a Letter to the Rev. R. M. Jelf, D.D.*, Oxford, 1841, p. 184-185.

¹³On the Jerusalem Bishopric see first of all W. H. Hechler, *The Jerusalem Bishopric*, London 1883 (all official documents in the Appendix); cf. Shaw, *The Early Tractarians*, chap. IV, p. 101 ff. See a new presentation of the whole story by Kurt Schmidt-Clausen, *Vorweggenomme Einheit. Die Gründung des Bistums Jerusalem im Jahre 1841* (Berlin and Hamburg, 1965).

¹⁴George Tomlinson, *Report of a Journey to the Levant, Addressed to His Grace the Archbishop of Canterbury, President of the Society for Promoting*

Christian Knowledge, s.d. (1841?); cf. J. Beaven, *On Intercourse between the Church of England and the Churches of the East, and on the ecclesiastical Condition of the English abroad,* London, 1840; see Shaw, 142 ff. and the other book by the same author, *American Contacts with the Eastern Churches. 1820-1870.* Chicago, Ill. (1937), p. 41 ff.

[15]The whole story in Shaw, *American Contacts,* p. 35 ff. The American "Mission" seems to have been originally conceived as a "mission" in a narrow sense, but actually "was operated in support of Tractarian theology" (51), and this attitude involved Southgate in a bitter conflict with the other ("Protestant") missionary agencies in the East, creating a disappointment in certain quarters in The States. It is interesting to compare this Episcopal "mission" with an earlier one, the "Greek Mission" in Athens, instituted in 1830. The missionary, Dr. Hill, was very cautious in his action, but even in the official instruction given by Bishop Griswold it was assumed that the Greek Church somehow "departed from the purity and simplicity of primitive times and scriptural example" (first published in S. D. Denison, *A History of the Foreign Missionary Work of the Protestant Episcopal Church,* v. I, New York, 1871, p. 142-144). Dr. Hill himself was quite emphatic on this point. He wrote in 1839: "The primary object of the Church in its Mission to the Greeks should never be lost sight of, viz., the spiritual renovation of our Mother Church." His purpose was, in his own words (1844), "to impart to the people religious knowledge, the effect of which, when widely disseminated, must be *a reformation of the whole system* within their Churches," (Quoted by Dr. Wallace E. Robbins, in his chapter, "The Mission to Greece," in the *History of The Theological Seminary in Virginia and Its Historical Background,* ed. by the Rev. Wm. A. R. Goodwin, Rochester, N.Y., s.d., 1924, v. II, p. 260. The heroic struggle of the Greeks for their national independence in the early decades of the XIXth century inspired much sympathy in the Anglo-Saxon world, and "Philhellenism" was widespread in those years. But Greece, and the rest of the Levant, were regarded mainly as a "mission field," and missionaries were sent there with the prospect of contributing to the revival and reformation of the Church of the country. This attitude could not fail to provoke resistance on the side of the Church and people, and a strong feeling against the "proselytism," which still colors the Greek reaction to all "ecumenical" ventures. The early decades of the Greek independence were marked by a strong conflict between the "liberal" (Westernizing) and "traditional" trends within the Church of Greece itself. See P. E. Shaw, "American Contacts," and E. R. Hardy, Jr., "The Greek Mission of the Protestant Episcopal Church," 1828-1899, in the *Historical Magazine of the Protestant Episcopal Church,* September, 1941, p. 183-201. Cf. also *Beiträge zur Kenntnis des gegenwärtigen Geistes und Zustandes der Griechischen Kirche in Griechenland und in der Turkei,* gesammelt von J. Wenger, Berlin, 1839 (some documents in translation in the Appendix). For general background J. N. Karmiris, *Orthodoxy and Protestantism* (in Greek), p. 277 ff. (Bibliography) and Chrysostomos Papadopoulos, *History of the Church of Greece* (in Greek), v. I, Athens, 1920.

[16]Pusey, *A Letter to His Grace the Archbishop of Canterbury, on some Circumstances connected with the Present Crisis in the English Church,* Oxford, 1842, p. 118; for background see Liddon, *Life of Pusey,* II, p. 272 ff.

[17]Shaw, *The Early Tractarians,* p. 119 ff.

[18]Palmer's *Notes,* p. 11 f. On Sibthorpe s. R. D. Middleton, *Magdalen Studies,* S.P.C.K., London, 1936. It is interesting to discover that the editors of *The Christian Remembrance* already in 1841 prefaced the sermon of Philaret in Moscow on Christmas day, which they published in translation, with a general note on the Greek Church of the following content. The Greek Church was at once better and worse than the Church of Rome: better as it was not formally committed to any objectionable doctrinal innovations, worse "as being more sunk in superstition and carnality," and therefore offering less hope "that it should be quickened anew unto spirituality." Such was "the general feeling of thoughtful Churchmen," it was stated, and the editors concluded: "we fear, however, that it has too much foundation in truth" (July, 1841, p. 51). E. D. Clarke, a renowned Cambridge scientist and traveller, who brought from the East the famous "Codex Clarkianus" of Plato, simply described ikons as idols: "the myriads of idol painting dispersed throughout the Empire . . . each of them will afford the reader a very accurate idea of a Russian Bogh." A plate appended to the text and representing several ikons was inscribed: "Barbarous idols of the Greek Church in Russia."—*Travels in various countries of Europe, Asia, and Africa. Part the first: Russia, Tartary, and Turkey,* Cambridge, 1810, p. 25 and Plate opposite p. 26.

[19]Letter to Frederick Rogers (Lord Blachford), quoted by Maisie Ward, *Young Mr. Newman,* Sheed & Ward, New York, 1948, p. 379.

[20]See my book, *The Ways...,* ch. V, "The Struggle for Theology," p. 128-233.

[21]Louis Bouyer, *Newman: Sa Vie. Sa Spiritualité.*—Les Éditions du Cerf, Paris, 1952, p. 315: "Vers les années 1845, il faut dire qu'il n'y avait plus de théologie catholique. Le foi du charbonnier, reposant sur des apologetiques delirants ou des systematisations fantaisistes, c'est presque tout ce qu'on peut trouver sous ce nom." Cf. R. Aubert, "Le Pontificat de Pie IX," in *Historie de l'Église,* ed. by Fliche et Jarry, v. XXI, Bloud & Gay, Paris, 1952, ch. VIII, "Les sciences ecclésiastiques jusqu'au Concile de Vatican," p. 184 ff.

[22]J. M. Neale, *Life and Times of Patrick Torry, D.D.,* 1856, p. 224 f.

[23]Palmer's *Notes of a Visit* (already quoted); *An Appeal to the Scottish Bishops and Clergy, and generally to the Church of their Communion,* Edinburgh, 1849 (published without the name of the author; gives the full story of Palmer's negotiations in Russia up to the date of publication); Roundell Palmer, Eari of Selborne, *Memorials,* Part I, Family and Personal, 1766-1865, vols. 1 & 2, London, 1896; Part II, Personal and Political, v. 1, 1898 (by a brother of W. Palmer); *Russia and the English Church, etc.,* ed. by W. J. Birkbeck, London, 1895 (see below); Fr. Basile Fortunatov, "Reminiscences of W. Palmer," in *Doukhovnaia Beseda,* 1867 (in Russian; contains some unpublished letters by Palmer); A. Mouraviev, "Profession de foi de Palmer," in *Question religieuse d'Orient et d'Occident,* v. III, Paris; Frederick Meyrick, *Memories of Life at Oxford, and Experiences in Italy, Greece, Turkey, Germany, Spain and Elsewhere,* New York, 1905, p. 79 f. (M. went with Palmer to Greece); R. D. Middleton, *Magdalen Studies,* S.P.C.K., 1936, chap. on Palmer, p. 99-114; cf. Shaw, *The Early Tractarians,* chap. on the Palmer Episode, p. 150-176 (and Bibliography);

Bolshakov, op. cit., 77 ff. (incomplete); S. Tyszkiewicz, S. J., "Un épisode du mouvement d'Oxford: La mission de William Palmer," in *Études*, v. 136, 1913. It is very probable that a review of Mouravieff's *History of the Church of Russia* (translated by Blackmore, Oxford, 1842) in *The Christian Remembrancee*, October, 1845, p. 241-331, was by Palmer: the Nikon episode singled out and discussed at great length. In any case, it could be written only by a person very well acquainted with the subject.

²⁴First published only in 1864, in Russian, in *Pravoslavnoe Obozrenie* [*The Orthodox Review*], and again in the 2nd volume of Khomiakov's *Works*, Prague, 1867. English translation (by an unknown person), Bruxelles, 1864; another translation by W. J. Birkbeck, in his *Russia and the English Church*, ch. XXIII, p. 192 ff. New edition, S.P.C.K., 1948. Two German translations should be mentioned: by Baroness v. Rahden, Berlin, 1870, and in the anthology, *Oestliches Christentum*, ed. by Hans Ehrenberg and N. v. Bubnoff, v. II, München, 1923.

²⁵See Khomiakoff: *L'Église Latine et Protestantisme au point de vue de l'Église d'Orient*, Lausanne et Vevey, 1872,—several articles, written in French by the author and published originally in various periodicals.

²⁶Khomiakov's letters to Palmer were first published in Russian, in *Pravoslavnoe Obozrenie*, 1896, with notes by Fr. A. M. Ivantzov-Platonov. The full text in English in Birkbeck, *Russia and the English Church*, London, 1895, and in Russian in the *Collected Works* of Khomiakov, v. II, 4th ed. Moscow, 1900. His essay on the Church, "The Church Is One," first published in Russian in *Pravoslavnoe Obozrenie*, 1864, and again in the *Collected Works*, v. II, Prague, 1867. English translation in Birkbeck, ch. XXIII; an earlier translation—by an unknown author—Bruxelles, 1864; there is a new edition of B.'s translation, S.P.C.K., 1948. Two German translations should be mentioned: by Baronesse v. Rahden, Berlin, 1870, and in the anthology, "*Oestliches Christentum*," ed. by Hans Ehrenberg und N. v. Bubnoff, v. II, München, 1923. Khomiakov's articles on the Western Communions, written in French by himself and published in various periodicals, were republished under the title: *L'Église Latine et Protestantisme au point de vue de 'Église d'Orient*, Lausanne et Vevey, 1872. On Khomiakov, see the literature given in n. 24.

²⁷"Letters" of the V. Rev. E. J. Popov on the Religious Movements in England are published by L. Brodsky in *Kristianskoe Chtenie* [*The Christian Lecture*], 1904, April, May, June, and 1905, June, July, September (they cover the period from 1842 to 1862); cf. also "Materials concerning the question of the Anglican Church," consisting of notes and letters of Fr. Popov and Fr. Joseph Vassiliev (Russian Chaplain in Paris), 1863-1865, in the same magazine, 1897, July and August. Fr. Popov was closely associated with J. M. Neale.

²⁸The student was later Russian chaplain in Stuttgart, Fr. J. J. Bazarov; see his "Memoirs," in *Russkaja Starina* [*The Russian Old Age*], 1901, February, p. 300-301.

²⁹The story in the text is told on the basis of Fr. Eugene Popov's letters to the Chief Procurator, Count Pratassov, *Kristianskoe Chtenie*, 1904, May and June. Several "Tracts on Christian Unity" seem to have been published in

1849, up to 1853; see also *Reunion with the Eastern Church: A Few Words in Defence of the Memorial addressed to the Russian Synod*, London, 1851 (private edition; not available to the author).

[30]"The true basis of Re-Union," *Essays on the Reunion of Christendom*, by Members of the Roman Catholic, Orthodox and Anglican Communions, edited by the Rev. F. G. Lee, D.C.L., London, 1867, p. 290-296. "The Editor was assisted by an Orthodox layman and an Eastern Ecclesiastic in preparing this statement for the press."

[31]Liddon, *Life of Pusey*, v. IV, p. 134, n. 3.

[32]See W. R. Churton, "The Rev. George Williams and his part in the Reunion Movement, in *Revue Internationale de Théologie*, 1895, v. III, 3 and 4, p. 538-552 and 690-702. Williams' book appeared in 1868 (see above).

[33]John Octavius Johnson, *Life and Letters of Henry Parry Liddon*, London, 1904, p. 100 f. To W. Bright he wrote about the services: "there was an aroma of the fourth century about the whole." The New Testament was widely circulated among the people. Liddon's interest in *rapprochement* was stimulated by his apprehension in view of an alarming growth of unbelief in Europe. It may be noted that Philaret in his talk with Liddon strongly criticized Newman's essay on "Development."

[34]See Bp. Eden's preface to the English translation of *Romanism in Russia*, by D. Tolstoy, London, 1874, v. I, p. viii-ix; also, R. Eden, *Impressions of a recent Visit to Russia. A Letter . . . on Intercommunion with the Eastern Orthodox Church*, London, 1867.

[35]Dr. J. L. Ver Mehr, Rector of the first formally organized Episcopalian parish at San Francisco, Grace Church (1850-1853), relates in his *Auto-biography* the following conversation with another Anglican minister in the area, the Rev. Flavel S. Mines: " 'The Russo-Greek Church,' said he, 'is perhaps nearer to the true organization of the Catholic Church than any. How would it do to get Episcopacy from them?' . . . 'At any rate,' said I, 'we ought to call a convention of what there are of clergy and responsible laity in California, and *organize*. We then may call a bishop, whether from the East or from the West.' " Quoted in William Stevens Perry, Bishop of Iowa, *The History of the American Episcopal Church 1587-1883*, v. II, Boston, 1885, p. 314, n. 2. As Bishop W. I. Kip, the first bishop in California, stated, "the early founders of the Church on this coast had no idea of uniting with the General Church in the East." They wanted "the Church in California." A convention was held in 1850, and Bishop Horatio Southgate, early missionary in the Levant, was invited to become the bishop. He declined the offer, and not until 1853 was a missionary bishop appointed by the General Convention (to become a regular Diocesan in 1857). Quoted in Perry, 314 and 315. Cf. *An Outline History of The Episcopal Church*, by the Rt. Rev. Frank E. Wilson, D.D., Bishop of Eau Claire, 1929-1944. Revised by the Rev. Edward R. Hardy, Jr., Ph.D.; Morehouse-Gorham Co., New York, 1949, p. 46.

[36]*Journal of the Proceedings of the Bishops, Clergy and Laity of the P.E.C. in the U.S.A.*, 1862, p. 100 f., 161 f.

[37]See "Report of the Russo-Greek Committee" in the *Journal of the Proceedings in 1865* (Boston, 1865), Appendix D, p. 325-342; cf. letters of Popov in *Kristianskoe Chtenie*, August, 1897.

[38]Russian material on this episode: letters of various persons to Philaret, in *Letters of the clerical and lay persons to the Metropolitan Philaret of Moscow, 1812-1867*, ed. by A. N. Lvov, St. Petersbourg, 1908, p. 192 f., 342 f., 349 f., 623 f.; Philaret's Memorandum in the *Collection of Comments and Replies*, v. V, p. 537 ff.; his statement on Anglican Orders in *Pravoslavnoe Obozrenie (The Orthodox Review)*, 1866. See also *Journal of the Proceedings in 1865*, p. 107, 117, 127, 203.

[39]Oxford edition of Pearson, 1797, is quoted in *The Christian Remembrancer*, p. 502: "Exposition of the Creed," Article VIII, note r, v. II, 407. In the Bohn's Library edition it is note I on p. 494 (actually on p. 495). In fact, Pearson felt that both sides in the controversy were guilty of intransigeancy: the addition was unlawful, but the doctrine was not heretical, as the Greeks contended.

[40]Pusey, *Eirenikon*, p. 248 ff. Cf. the unsigned review of *Eirenikon* in *The Christian Remembrancer*, January, 1866. The clause has been "insensibly and unintentionally" circulated in the whole of the Western Church. There is no real heresy in it. The English Church had nothing to do with the Great Schism of the East and West. The clause therefore should not be an impediment or obstacle for the restoration of intercommunion, which is the only real problem.

[41]*Journal*, 1868 (Hartford, 1869), p. 148, 169, 256, 258 f., 276, 421 f., 484 f.

[42]*Journal*, 1871, Report of the Joint Committee, p. 564 ff. Cf. Karmiris, *Orthodoxy etc.*, p. 332 f. (references to the literature in Greek). The late Archbishop Germanos regarded this action as "the first step towards the *rapprochement* of the Churches in a purely Ecclesiastical matter."—"Progress towards the Reunion of the Orthodox and the Anglican Churches," in *The Christian East*, v. X, No. 1, 1929, p. 23.

[43]"Abstract of a Conference" at Ely was appended to the report of the Russo-Greek Committee in 1871, *Journal*, 1871 (Hartford, 1872), p. 577 ff.; cf. p. 571 f. Report of Archbishop Lycurgos in Greek in the *Evangelikos Kyrux*, v. 2 (1870) and with English translation, separately, London, 1876; cf. review in the *Church Quarterly Review*, v. III, p. 64-94; G. Williams, *A Collection of Documents relating chiefly to the Visit of Alexander, Archbishop of Syros and Tenos to England in 1870*, London, 1876; Skene, *Life of Alexander Lycurgos* etc.; D. Balanos, "Archbishop A. Lykourgos," in *Theologia*, v. I, 1923, p. 180-194 (in Greek); cf. Karmiris, p. 337 f.

[44]*Journal*, 1871, p. 197, 350 f., 355; Report of the Committee, p. 565 ff.

[45]*Journal*, 1874, Appendix X, p. 540 ff. Cf. reports of Bishop Bedell on his negotiations with the "Oriental Churches," printed for the Joint Committee, 1875-1879.

[46]Cf. Report of the Joint Committee, *Journal*, 1874, p. 548 ff.

[47]Baader's book reprinted in his *Sämtliche Werke*, ed. by F. Hoffmann, Bd. X, s. 89-259. His other writings related to the same problem are collected in vols. V and X of the same edition. Important material is also scattered in his correspondence, partly in v. XVI of the *Sämtliche Werke*, but especially in the *Lettres inédits*, recently published by E. Susini, v. I, Paris, 1942; vols. II and III, Wien, 1951 (important notes and commentaries). Cf. Benz, *Die abendländische Sendung* (Bibliography); Ernst Gaugler, *Franz von Baaders Kampf gegen die Alleinherrschaft des Papstes in der katholischen Kirche*, in I.K.Z., 1917, No. 3.

[48]Dr. W. Guettée, *Souvenirs d'un prêtre romain devenu prêter orthodoxe*, Paris, 1889; cf. Meyrick, *Memories*, p. 181-182; Vassiliev, *Letters from Paris* (1846-1867), ed. by A. I. Brodsky, Petrograd, 1915 (in Russian); S. Soushkov, Obituary of Guettée, *Tserkovny Vestnik*, *(The Ecclesiastical Messenger)*, 1890, Nr. 22 and 23. Vassiliev's *Open Letter to the Bishop of Nantes* and the following discussion—two pamphlets in French, Paris, 1861; also his Open Letter to Guizot. Cf. A. Kireev, "Der Oberpriester Joseph Wassilieff," in *Revue Internationale de Théologie*, IV, 4, 1896 (also some excerpts from his Correspondence with Bp. Jacqmet and a brief note by Michaud). See also Jean-Remy Palanque, *Catholiques liberaux et Gallicans en France face au Concile du Vatican* (*Aix-en-Provence*, 1962); and Raoul Dederen, *Un reformateur catholique au XIXe siècle, Eugéne Michaud, 1839-1917* (Genève, 1963).

[49]Overbeck's Obituary, by Fr. E. Smirnov, in *Tserkovnye Vedomosti*, 1905, No. 50 (in Russian); some additional biographical data were communicated by Canon Edward Every, Jerusalem, who had at his disposal the unpublished correspondence of Overbeck with various persons. The more important writings of Overbeck (his articles in *The Orthodox Catholic Review* not included) are as follows: *Die Orthodoxe Katholische Anschauung im Gegensatz zum Papstthum und Jesuitismus, sowie zum Protestantismus*, Halle, 1865; *Die Providentielle Stellung des Orthodoxen Russland und sein Beruf zur Wiederherstellung der Rechtgläubigen Katholischen Kirche des Abendlandes*, Halle, 1869; *Die Rechtgläubige Katholische Kirche. Ein Protest gegen die päpstliche Kirche und eine Aufforderung zur Grundung katholischer Nationalkirchen* ,Halle, 1869; *Die einzig sichere Ausweg für die liberalien Mitglieder der Römisch-katholischen Kirche*, Halle, 1870; *Die Wiedervereinigung der Morgenländischen und Abendländischen Kirchen*, Halle, 1873; *Die Bonner Unions-Conferenzen*, Halle, 1876; in English: *Catholic Orthodoxy and Anglo-Catholicism*, A word about Intercommunion between the English and Orthodox Churches, London, 1866; *The Bonn Conference*, 1873 and 1876. Anglican objections—in the report of the Russo-Greek Committee, *Journal*, 1874, p. 553 ff. The text of the Patriarchal prohibition is given in full (in translation, the Greek text in the "Neologos"). The basic biography of Overbeck is by Wilhelm Kahle, *Westliche Orthodoxie. Leben und Ziele Julian Joseph Overbecks* (Leiden-Köln, 1968).

[50]Brief survey and analysis: Dr. Steinwachs, "Die Unionsbestrebungen im Altkatholizismus," in the *International Kirchliche Zeitschrift*, 1911, Hf. 2 and 4. For the early period of the Movement one should consult the minutes ("Verhandlungen") of the Congresses and information in the *Deutscher Merkur. Bericht über die Unions-Konferenzen* 1874 and 1875, ed. by Dr. H.

Reusch, Bonn, 1874, 1875; English translations—*Reunion Conference at Bonn,*
1874, Rivingtons, London, 1874; *Report of the Union Conferences...,*
translated by The Rev. S. Buel, with a Preface by The Rev. R. J. Nevin, New
York, 1876. "Theses" of Bonn repeated in the Appendix to the *Report of*
the Doctrinal Commission (appointed by the Lambeth Conference of 1930),
1930. Cf. (an unsigned article) "The Reunion Conferences at Bonn," in
the *Church Quarterly Review*, v. I, 1875-76, p. 383-407; "The Filioque Controversy and the Easterns," *ibid.*, v. III, 1877-78, p. 421-465 (in connection
with the books by Pusey and Swete). There was a French edition of the
Process-Verbaux of the meetings of the Russian Society of Friends, etc.
("Societé des Amis de I'instruction religieuse"), several issues, Bruxelles,
1872 ff. Important information is to be found in Meyrick's *Memories of*
Life, p. 259 ff. Meyrick was deeply impressed by the Russian delegates at
Bonn: astonishing command of languages and a surprising erudition, equal to
that of Döllinger. Cf. *Correspondence between members of the Anglo-*
Continental Society and (1) Old Catholics, (2) Oriental Churchmen..., ed.
by the Rev. Frederick Meyrick, M.A., Rivingtons, London, 1874. Cf. reports
to the Synod of Athens by Professor Rhossis (1876) and Professor Damalas
(1875)—in Greek. On Pusey's position see Liddon, *Life of Pusey*, v. IV,
p. 292 ff. Pusey contended that *Filioque* could be found in Epiphanius and
St. Cyril of Alexandria; see in the Preface the *Commentary on the Gospel*
according to St. John, by St. Cyril (in the *Library of the Fathers*), edited by
Philip E. Pusey,—a large part of it written by E. B. Pusey (Liddon, p. 432).
Cf. E. Michaud, "L' état de la question du Filioque après la Conference de
Bonn de 1875," in *Revue International*, III, 1, 1895; Kireev and Meyrick, ibid.;
Kireev, "Erklarungen von Professor Ossinin in München und Bonn" (1871
und 1875), *ibid.*, IV, 2, 1896, p. 489-501; J. Ossinin, *An Eastern View of*
the Second Conference at Bonn, English translation, Boston, 1876; "Briefe
von Döllinger, Reinkens, Weber, v. Schulte and General Kirejew," ed. by
D. N. Jakschitsch, in *Internationale Kirchliche Zeitschrift*, XIX, 1 a. 2, 1929.
"Quelques lettres du General Kireev au Professeur Michaud sur l' Ancien-
Catholicisme," 1893 (cf. J. H. Morgan, "Early Orthodox-Old Catholic Relations," General Kireev and Professor Michaud, in *Church Quarterly Review*,
1951). See an interesting open letter by Ivan Aksakov to Döllinger in the
very beginning of the Old Catholic Movement—"Brief an Döllinger von
Einem Laien der Russischen Orthodox Kirche aus Moskau," Berlin, 1872,
p. 39: it is not enough to denounce the Vatican Council, as innovations do not
begin only in 1870—"*Filioque*," Tridentinum; is a Catholic remnant possible,
as an ecclesiological formation?

[51]Brief survey in the article of Steinwachs (see n. 50). One can follow
the course of negotiations and discussions in the articles and chronicle of
the *Revue Internationale* (1893-1910) and *Internationale Kirchliche Zeitschrift*
(since 1911). Summary of Kerensky by Kireev, R.I.Th., III, 1895, 2. Bishop
Sergius, "Qu'est-ce qui nous separé des anciens-catholiques," *ibid.*, XII, 1,
1904, p. 159-190. Extracts from the articles by Svetlov: "Zur Frage der
Wiedervereinigung der Kirchen und zur Lehre von der Kirche," *ibid.*, XIII,
2 a. 3, 1905; cf. his Russian book, *The Christian Doctrine*, v. I, Kiev, 1910,
p. 208 ff. "Theses" of Bolotov (unsigned)—R.I.Th., VI, 4, 1898, p. 681-712
(Russian text—from the manuscript—in *Khristianskoe Chtenie*, 1913,
May; cf. A. I. Brilliantov, "*Bolotov's Works concerning the question of the*
Filioque and Polemics against his 'Theses' in Russian literature," *ibid.*, April.

On Kireev: Olga Novikoff, *Le General Alexandre Kireev et l'ancien-catholicisme*, Bern 1911. "Materials on the History of the Old Catholic problem in Russia" (Letters of Janyshev to Kireev and of Kireev to Archbishop Nicolai—one time in America—with notes by Professor J. P. Sokolov), in *Khristianskoe Chtenie*, 1911, May, June, and November. Bibliographical survey of the literature on Old Catholicism in Russian—in an article by A. Triumphov, in *Strannik* [*The Pilgrim*], 1913, July-August. See an interesting letter of Professor Kyriakos to Michaud, in R.I.Th., XIII, 4, 1905, in which he describes the situation in Greece and states his own point of view: "selon moi, vous n'avez pas besoin d'être reconnus comme Église Orthodoxe par aucune autre Église; vous êtes orthodoxes *ipso facto*." He adds that the same will be true of the Anglican Church, when it repudiates the Articles (p. 720). But the majority were of another opinion, as was Patriarch Joachim III. An earlier Encyclical by Patriarch Anthimos in translation in R.I.Th., IV, 1896; cf. the letter of the Patriarch to Professor Michaud, *ibid.*, IV, 2. Cf. on Janyshev and his participation in the conversations with Old Catholics the article by Professor J. P. Sokolov, in *Khristianskoe Chtenie*, 1911, February.

[52]Resolution and relevant passages from the Lambeth reports collected in *The Christian East*, XI, 2, Summer 1930,—"Previous Lambeth Conferences and the Orthodox East," p. 73-76 (based on *The Six Lambeth Conferences*, London, S.P.C.K.).

[53]The whole story is told by W. J. Birkbeck: *Birkbeck and the Russian Church*, Containing Essays and Articles by the late W. J. Birkbeck, collected and edited by Athelstan Riley, London & New York, 1917, Chapter I; cf. also *Life and Letters of W. J. Birkbeck*, by his wife, with a preface by Viscount Halifax, Longmans, 1922; cf. *The Life of Edward White Benson, sometime Archbishop of Canterbury*, by his son, A. C. Benson of Eton College, v. II, London, 1899, p. 155 ff. (based on information supplied by Mr. Riley).

[54]See *Birkbeck and the Russian Church* for facts. Cf. *Life and Letters of Mandell Creighton*, D.D., Oxon. and Cam., *Sometime Bishop of London*, by his wife, 2 vols. London, 1905. In English: *One Chapter from an Enquiry into the Hierarchy of the Anglican Episcopal Church*, by Sokolov, The Church Printing Co., London; *The Question of Anglican Orders, in respect of the "Vindication" of the Papal Decision*, by A. Bulgakoff, Church Historical Society, S.P.C.K., London, 1899 (translated by Birkbeck).

[55]*Previous Lambeth Conferences*, p. 76-79.

[56]*Life of Bishop John Wordsworth*, by E. W. Watson, Longmans, 1915, p. 217 ff., 339 ff. On his return to England, Bp. Wordsworth delivered a lecture at the summer school of Clergy at Oxford, July 27, 1898, which was then published: "The Church of England and the Eastern Patriarchates," Oxford, Parker, 1898, p. 38.

[57]The Russian Synodal "Epistle" was first published in English translation in *The Guardian*, August 28 and September 2, 1903, and is reprinted in *Birkbeck and the Russian Church*, ch. XX, p. 247-257; Birkbeck's comments in the following chapter, 258 ff.

[58]J. A. Douglas, *The Relations of the Anglican Churches with the Eastern-Orthodox, especially in regard to Anglican Orders,* London, 1921, p. 17.

[59]Douglas, p. 66 f.—The recent summary of the doctrine of "Economy" is by Professor H. S. Alivisators: *Economy according to the Canon Law of the Orthodox Church,* Athens, 1949 (in Greek); some "extracts" from this book in English in *Dispensation in Practice and Theory,* S.P.C.K., 1944, p. 27 ff. More comprehensive is the monograph by Jeronymus I. Kotsonis (one time Archbishop of Athens), *The Problems of "Ecclesiastical Economia"* (Athens, 1957; in Greek; a French translation exists).

[60]Douglas, p. 16-17.

[61]Quoted in *Revue Internationale,* X, 2, 1902; *The Guardian,* November 16, 1904.

[62]*Previous Lambeth Conferences,* p. 79-81.

[63]*The Works of Rt. Rev. Charles C. Grafton,* ed. by B. Talbot Rogers, Longmans, 1914: v. VI, "Fond du Lac Tracts," VI, "The Reunion of Orthodox and Anglican Churches," p. 326 ff.; v. IV, "A Journey Godward" (a kind of autobiography), on Pusey, etc., p. 407 ff.; on the Russian visit, 252 ff; letters to Metropolitan Anthony, 259-270. Cf. B. Talbot Rogers, "Bishop Grafton and the Eastern Orthodox Church," in *Int. Kirchl. Zeitschrift,* 1916, 3, and note by R. K. (Keussen) in the same issue, 350-351.

[64]The "Report" was published in the *Alcuin Club Tracts,* by W. J. Barnes and W. H. Frere, with valuable notes by the latter, Mowbray's, 1917, and once more in *The Orthodox Catholic Review,* v. I, Nr. 6, June, 1927, Brooklyn, N.Y.

[65]A. C. Headlam, *Teaching of the Russian Church,* Rivingtons, London, 1897; "Eastern Church Association," *Annual Reports,* 1893-1910; *Anglican and Eastern-Orthodox Union,* Reports of 1906-1914, Berryman, London; *American Branch,* Reports, 1908-1914, The Kane Press, New York; *Society of the Friends of Reunion between the Eastern-Orthodox and Anglican Churches.* Materials and Reports, 1906-1910, St. Petersburg, 1912 (in Russian). See also Karmiris, 344 ff. On Birkbeck see the Obituary by Professor Glubokovsky, in *The Constructive Review,* V, 3, 1917, p. 568-592. In an earlier issue of the same magazine there was an instructive article by Archbishop Platon, of North America, "Admitting All Impossibilities, Nevertheless Unity is Possible," I, 3, Sept., 1913.

[66]*The Anglican and Eastern Churches. A Historical Record, 1914-1921,* London, S.P.C.K., 1921,—esp. p. 27 ff., including a survey by Dr. S. Runkevitch: "The Russian Church in the years 1915-1918"; Resolution of the Council, p. 43-44. Cf. excerpts from letters by Fr. Puller, in the *Report* of the A.E.O.C.U., American Branch, 1912, p. 63-67. In connection with the conversations at St. Petersburg in 1912, see an article on the Anglican Ordinations by Professor I. P. Sokolov, in *Khristianskoe Chtenie,* February, 1913.

[67]"Correspondence of Archbishop Anthony with their representatives of the Episcopal Church in America," in *Vera i Razum [Faith and Reason],* 1915 and 1916, in Russian translation from the French (Original letters are

not among the papers of Gardiner, kept now in General Theological Seminary, New York). Cf. R. Gardiner, "Les Églises orientales et la *World Conference,*" *Int. Kirchl. Zeitschrift,* 1919, 3, p. 234-253; Archimandrite Hilarion, "The Unity of the Church etc.," in *Bogoslovsky Vestnik [The Theological Messenger]*, January, 1917, p. 3-60. Cf. S. Troitsky, "The World Conference on Faith and Order," in *Tserkovnyie Vedomosti,* 1915, Nr. 14 and 15 (a letter of Gardiner to the author is given here in Russian translation—from French).

⁶⁸Soloviev: *La Russie et l'Église Universelle,* Pt is, A. Savine, 1889; English translation, *Russia and the Universal Church,* London, Centenary Press, 1948; the book was originally written in French. No less important are various writings of Soloviev in the eighties, especially the Preface to *The History and the Future of Theocracy,* dealing with the idea of "Dogmatic development" (In his *Complete Works*—in Russian—vols. III and IV). Cf. *Monarchia Sancti Petri. Die Kirchliche Monarchie des heiligen Petrus als freie und universelle Theokratie im Lichte der Weisheit. Aus den Hauptwerken von Wladimir Solowjew, systematisch gesammelt, übersetzt und erklärt von L. Kobilinski-Ellis,* Mainz-Wiesbaden, 1929; also Bernhard Schultze, *Russische Denker,* Herder, Wien (1950). On Soloviev: D. Stremooukhoff, "Vladimir Soloviev et son Oeuvre Messianique," Paris, 1935 (*Publications de la Faculté des Letteres de l'Université de Strassbourg,* Fasc. 69), with an abundant bibliography; Ludolf Muller, *Solovjev und der Protestantismus,* Herder, Freiburg, 1951, with a "Nachwort" by Dr. Wl. Szylkarski, from a Roman Catholic point of view; cf. Muller's *Offener Brief an Herrn Szylkarski, als Erwiderung auf sein Nachwort zu meinem Buche . . .* (Mimeogramm).